P9-AGU-994
PRESS
Pass Through Police & Fire Lines
DAVID H. KENNERLY
NAME
UNITED PRESS INT'L
EMPLOYER
TO THE
1977 State of the Union
Address
DAVID H. KENNERLY
STAFF PHOTOGRAPHER
(213) 387-7221
PRESS
PASS
POLICE
DEPARTMENT
1968
Form 2.12
SIGNATURE
RIGHT INDEX
Pass through police and fire lines. This
pass is subject to revocation by the
THE WHITE HOUSE
DAVID HUME KENNERLY
Personal Photographer to the President
MR. KENNERLY
KENNERLY
OFFICIAL
PASSPORT
hereby
der of this
ucted tour
ISSUED May 27, 1975
AT WASHINGTON D. C.
SIGNATURE OF HOLDER
If found, drop in nearest mailbox. Postmaster: Return to
Room 825 1800 G Street, N.W., Washington, D. C. 20026
ESIDENTIAL TRIP
144 NIXON-AGNEW
PRESS
LONG BEACH—LOS ANGELES
NOVEMBER 2—NOVEMBER 5, 1968
DAVE KENNERLY
UPI PHOTOGRAPHER
PRESS
DAVE KENNERLY

SHOOTER

To Peg & Reg,
My old friends who tried
(unsuccessfully) to keep me out
of trouble!
Cheers!
Dave Kennerly
Oct. 22, 1979

DAVID HUME KENNERLY

Pulitzer Prize Winner

SHOOTER

Newsweek Books
New York

Printed in the United States of America

First Edition 1979

Library of Congress Cataloging in Publication Data
Kennerly, David Hume, 1947–
Shooter.
1. Photography, Journalistic. 2. Kennerly, David Hume, 1947– 3. Photographers — United States — Biography.
1. Title.
TR820.K44—770'.92'4 [B]—79-2138
ISBN 0-88225-265-8

Excerpted in Playboy Magazine

Title Page: UPI Saigon Bureau, 1971.
Left to right: Nguyen Thanh Ngoc, Jeff Taylor, Willie Vicoy, Nguyen Ngoc Anh, Kennerly.

Book Design: Mary Ann Joulwan

Contents

A lone soldier walks over a devastated hill at Landing Zone Hotlips. This picture is part of the portfolio that won Kennerly a Pulitzer Prize for photography in 1972.

DEDICATION

This book is dedicated to the photographers who lost their lives in action during the war in Southeast Asia.

Robert Capa
Peter Van Thiel
Huynh Thanh My
Bernard Kolenberg
Dicky Chapelle
Charles Chellappah
Don Gallagher
Bob Ellison
Hiromichi Mine
Charlie Eggleston
Ollie Noonan
Dieter Bellendorf*
Gilles Caron*
Sean Flynn*
George Gensluckner*
Akira Kusaka*
Willy Mettler*
Dana Stone*
Roget Colne*
Tomoharu Ishii*
Rene Puissesseau
Kyoichi Sawada
Remik Lekhi
Larry Burrows
Henri Huet
Kent Potter
Keisaburo Shimamoto
Terry Reynolds*
James Gill
Gerard Hebert
Sam Kie Fie
Terry Khoo
Taizo Ichinose*
Michel Laurent

*Missing and presumed dead

"He's a good shooter."

The Young Shooter

"HE'S A GOOD SHOOTER."

The ultimate compliment. All the awards and professional recognition wither by comparison when a photographer you really admire remarks, "He's a good shooter." You've arrived.

That phrase wasn't in my vocabulary in 1959. In fact, there was not much at all in my vocabulary. I was only in the sixth grade, and at that age all sorts of things excite the hell out of you—lizards, birds, buttons—you name it. My major interest was fires and fire trucks, not cameras. That would come later. The seed of my future career was planted in 1959, on the day when the woodshed up the street burned down. I saw the smoke, then heard the sirens. By the time I arrived the old shed was ablaze and local firemen were yelling to each other over the roar of the fire and water hoses. Suddenly I noticed a well-dressed man standing between the police lines and the fire. He was carrying several cameras. He was a photographer for the Roseburg, Oregon newspaper, and he clearly had the best job in the world. He could go to all the fires, and he could cross the police lines and could get as close to the flames as the firemen without getting tired or dirty. And he got to take pictures. That was for me.

One of the great things about being in sixth grade is that you don't know much. For instance, I didn't know that photographing fires could get you tired and dirty—even killed. That notion never crossed my mind, but over the next decade it would occur on many occasions.

When I was a freshman in high school a classmate named Stuart Speedie taught me to develop and print pictures in his parents' kitchen. By then I had been taking pictures for almost two years, using an old Rolliflex twin-lens reflex. I wasn't convinced at this point that photography would amount to more than an enthusiasm—like following fire trucks—but one advantage of taking pictures was already apparent: It was a great way to meet girls. The photos that Stuart and I were taking, developing, and printing were of the school's cheerleaders.

By the following year, I *had* decided on a career. That year, my sophomore year, I determined I wanted to be a sportswriter, but I became a photographer instead. Because the regular school photographer was sick, the school paper's faculty advisor handed me a bulky old four-by-five-inch camera and told me to shoot the baseball game. I did. They ran the picture. I was hooked.

Midway through the next year, 1964, my parents moved from Roseburg to West Linn, Oregon, several hundred miles to the north. It's tough to leave old friends and familiar surroundings, but when I arrived at my new school I quickly convinced them that I knew everything there was to know about photography—at a time when I'd had perhaps fifteen pictures published in the Roseburg school paper—and they promptly put me to work on the staff of the West Linn *Amplifier*.

When my senior year rolled around, I had it made. Not only was I the paper's chief photographer, I took all the shots for the yearbook and helped teach a photo class. And, thanks principally to honor marks in the photography courses I was taking, I even managed to raise my grade point average to a respectable level.

Alan Scheidegger was the student body president; he also played first-string varsity football and basketball. And he was my business partner. We had cards made up that read "Scheidegger and Kennerly, Photos." Al supplied his name, and I shot the pictures. Our first enterprise involved taking pictures of all the steady couples in school and then selling prints to them. We also arranged to photograph the school's athletic events, and sold those prints to Al's teammates. (Al got his free.)

By this time the local papers were buying my pictures as well, and I was working for both papers on weekends. This activity won me a photography scholarship to Portland State College in the fall. It also presented a problem. At the time I didn't own a camera; I'd borrowed the one I was using from my girlfriend's father with the stipulation that I be really careful with it. Then one day a big brush fire erupted near my home and the old enthusiasm was rekindled. This time, of course, I could cross the police lines, and I hardly cared that I was tired and dirty. I was wading through the flames with smoke and ashes blowing all around me when I heard a bellow. "Kennerly, my camera!" I looked around, and there was my girl's father. I hadn't known he was a volunteer fireman.

I decided then and there that was the time to get my own equipment. That summer I took a job in a flour mill to earn enough money to buy some camera gear. It was particularly strenuous for a skinny kid who weighed just slightly more than the 100-pound flour sacks he was loading onto boxcars. I worked a twelve-hour day and a six-day week that summer. Each night when I dropped into bed I thought: "I really have to make it in photography or I'm a dead man."

At the end of the summer I bought my first camera, a Nikon with a 50-mm lens, and headed off to Portland State. By then I was so eager to test my new equipment—and to pursue photography full-time—that I could concentrate on little else. Midway through my freshman year I quit school for good, but not before securing a position on the *Oregon Journal* at age eighteen. To get the slot I went to see the *Journal's* executive editor armed with a portfolio of photographs I'd taken in high school. I wore a new corduroy jacket that I'd bought to bolster my confidence, but it never really occurred to me that I wouldn't get the job. I was eighteen, and I'd never looked for newspaper work before. I'd never put together a portfolio before, either, and as it turned out, I never would again. Because the *Journal* gave me a chance, every other job I got grew directly out of that first one. In retrospect, I recognize that the *Journal's* offer was my biggest break. Had I appreciated at the time how crucial a break it was, I might have needed more than a new jacket to fortify my courage.

To the older photographers at the *Journal* I was a pain in the ass. For one thing, I was so enthusiastic that I'd cheerfully accept any assignment, no matter how dull. Lisa Patterson, the paper's society editor, loved working with me and laughingly said I was the only photographer on the paper who didn't insult her subjects, even though we both agreed that some of them deserved it. In time my spirit even began to rub off on the old shooters. I think several of them actually began to enjoy taking pictures again, if only to show that "they could do it better than the punk."

Every now and then I blew it. On one of my first big jobs I had to cover a game played by the Portland Beavers, a Cleveland Indians' farm club. I shot the game, but without any film in my camera—always a tough one to explain to the picture editor.

Roy Beadle, editorial page editor, wrote a piece about me in those days. It appeared under the headline "Cub Photographer Gives Editor Fast Fire Trip." Roy spent most of his time sitting behind his desk writing editorials. He did not cover fires—except once, with me. "The way to see a fire," he wrote, "is to tag along behind an eager-beaver photographer." And then he told this story:

> Dave Kennerly and I were on our way back from an assignment when a huge column of smoke "somewhere in the city" became visible. From where we were the location was extremely difficult to spot. But Kennerly, who appears to have a nose for the "big story," became instantly alive. "Let's get out there!" he said. A call to the *Journal*'s city desk on our car radio revealed that the fire was somewhere near the University of Portland, and no other photographer was available.
>
> We headed there as fast as the law would allow. Kennerly's press pass got us through the police blockade. (I later discovered that my pass had expired in 1964.) We parked and legged it through somebody's backyard. Kennerly was ahead of me, and from the edge of the bluff we gazed down on a blazing hell—several acres of burning logs, the property of McCormick & Baxter Creosoting Co. "I've never seen anything like it," yelled Kennerly. Few other people had.
>
> No one spot satisfied Kennerly for long. We headed through one backyard after another. Meanwhile, the danger of the fire sweeping up the side of the bluff into the homes became apparent. Kennerly was not satisfied with the bluff vantage point. "We've got to get down below!" Again Kennerly's pass got us through the police lines.

> We started rushing toward the fire. Kennerly was way ahead of me. The heat was more intense. The smoke was thick. My main problem was to keep Kennerly in sight, as he headed through smoke, dust, and sometimes mud. His camera clicked endlessly. I don't know how many pictures he took—it must have been at least fifteen times more than could be used. When it was over I was glad that I didn't have to follow him around very often. I was also glad I'm not a fireman.

The real impact of such disasters on people and other living things hit me for the first time when I stumbled upon a doe that had been badly burned in a forest fire. After I took a few pictures, a forest ranger mercifully put a bullet between her sad and terrified eyes. A shot of the deer ran big on the front page of the *Journal* and inspired one reader to write: "The photograph on page one, 'Fire-Trapped Doe Awaits Death' by David Kennerly, is the most horrible, and yet the most heart-rending I have ever seen. It is pictures such as this one that should be on all fire-prevention posters!" As it happens, that picture *was* used in a fire-prevention campaign. Apparently someone else appreciated that a dying doe can say more than any shot of leaping flames about what a forest fire can do. That burned deer may have made someone think twice before flipping a lit cigarette into a forest.

But beyond mere fire prevention, I began to appreciate that what I was doing as a photographer could affect people's lives.

I photographed more than fires in those days. I covered automobile accidents, baseball games, beauty pageants, check presentation ceremonies, and rodeos. There's no better way to get the feel of the Wild West than to attend a real rodeo, and the Tygh Valley Indian Rodeo, held annually in eastern Oregon, certainly qualifies as real. The participants are all full-blooded Indians, and for the most part they are also amateurs. Some were very amateur. The second guy out of the bronco chute held the reins in one hand and a beer in the other. He lasted less than three seconds before biting the dust.

I chose to shoot the action at Tygh Valley from a spot along the fence *inside* the arena. And from that vantage point I learned something that I hadn't known about the rodeo—the hard way. It seems that when a contestant comes out of the chute on a bucking horse, two "haze riders" follow him, one on either side. Their function is to pick the rider off his horse when he has completed his ride. They circle the perimeter of the arena, a fact I discovered when one of them knocked me on my rear as I focused in on the bucking exhibition. From that day on I've made it a practice to keep a wary eye peeled in all directions while taking pictures.

The arrival of a major personality was always news in Portland, and when Igor Stravinsky came to town the paper sent me to photograph him. When I first encountered the renowned composer at Symphony Hall I found him stern and imposing. He had a towel around his neck, and not one but two sets of glasses on his head. He gave me a look that suggested I wasn't exactly welcome, but I shot a roll of film anyway. The way I figured it, Stravinsky's wrath couldn't possibly be any worse than the city editor's would be if I came back empty-handed.

As I finished, Stravinsky's wife entered the hall and came over to talk to me. She asked if I would mind taking a picture of the two of them, adding—to my utter amazement—that they had never had one taken together before. I agreed to help out, only to discover there was one catch: Stravinsky was not to be told what I was up to. Thereupon Mrs. Stravinsky moved close to her husband without making it immediately obvious what we were up to. I got the shot and gave her a large print the following day. In appreciation she had the Russian-born maestro sign one of the photographs I'd taken of him earlier. I still have the photograph, and a lasting impression of Stravinsky as a man who would brook no nonsense from musicians, wives, or photographers.

Then there was the day in 1966 when President Lyndon B. Johnson *didn't* come to town. I can't remember why the President didn't show, and I'm not sure I even knew at the time. The crisis that kept Johnson from making his scheduled stop in Portland was national in nature and in those days I wasn't really involved with events that occurred more than one hundred miles from home.

In anticipation of Johnson's visit local Democratic party types had made thousands of "Welcome LBJ" signs, and the best picture I took was of the disgruntled man who made them, sitting in the middle of his unused work. The placards that were used that day said "Welcome HHH," for Johnson had sent the Vice-President in his stead. There were other placards in use as well, for no sooner had Hubert Humphrey arrived in Portland than he became the focus of a violent anti-war demonstration, which may help explain LBJ's change of plans.

When Humphrey and his entourage arrived at their hotel, crowds of demonstrators tried to block the driveway. Ron Bennett, a fellow *Journal* photographer, and I had a field day recording the scene. We shot rolls of film of protesters being dragged off like rag dolls by the cops, and I got a picture of an older woman being towed unceremoniously from the scene by her foot. My editors never ran the picture because they thought it exposed a bit more of the woman than the public was interested in seeing.

That same year—1966—Portland experienced its first race riot, and I was the only guy to get any action shots at the scene. As I moved deeper and deeper into the ghetto, my editors grew more and more uneasy. At intervals they barked "Get out of the area!" over the two-way radio I was carrying, and one added that other news media representatives were not going into the area. "Great!" I answered. "We'll get the exclusive." I kept shooting.

The only real problem I had was focusing. I was trying to take a few shots out of the window, but the car was bobbing up and down constantly. I looked in the rearview mirror and understood why: several teenagers were jumping up and down on the trunk. I took off fast, and half-way down the street I noticed something else in the mirror—a pair of shoe tips. I also saw fingers gripping the windows on either side of the car. I slammed on the brakes, and the uninvited hitchhiker bounced across the hood, hit the ground, and ran off into the night.

On days when there were no big stories to cover I did what all unassigned new photographers do: I hung out in the newsroom listening to the police radio. On one such night I heard a call that a man had been kidnapped, beaten, and finally released. He was in a local hospital, the radio reported, but no reporters were allowed anywhere near him. In no time I had put a camera under my shirt, a coat over that, and was sauntering into the back of the hospital.

I found the kidnapping victim stretched out on a table in an operating room. I stood in the doorway, allowed my "shirt" to click once, then quickly covered the camera lens. At exactly that moment two doctors came along and asked what the hell I was doing back there. "Looking for the bathroom," I replied. They informed me in no uncertain terms that the area was off limits and that the bathroom was at the other end of the hall. "Thanks," I shouted over my shoulder as I headed back to the *Journal*, which ran my shirt shot on page one the next day.

Periodically national stories landed on my doorstep. One such time was when Senator Robert Kennedy came to town in 1967. Traveling with Kennedy was *Life* staff photographer Bill Epperidge. In those days a *Life* photographer was the closest thing to God that I could imagine, and I don't know which man impressed me more, the United States Senator or Bill. I expected to be overwhelmed by Kennedy, but I was actually most impressed by Epperidge, without whom I might never have gotten within a hundred yards of the Senator.

The hall where Kennedy was speaking was so jammed with people that I didn't know how I was going to get in, let alone close enough to the dais to photograph my subject. Suddenly a voice in back of me said, "Hang onto my coat, Kennerly." With that, Epperidge plunged into the crowd with me in tow, heading for the podium. I would never have made it without his help, and I never forgot the classy "big shot" from *Life* who'd helped out a green kid he hardly knew.

In 1966 I faced a personal dilemma that most guys my age also confronted that year: the draft. I wasn't afraid of being sent to Vietnam, but the prospect of ending up in Vietnam as a foot soldier didn't appeal to me either—and I was reluctant to abandon my career at such a crucial early stage. To resolve the situation, I joined the National Guard.

I wasn't a model soldier by any means, but the only real problem I had occurred on the firing range. We were learning how to shoot the M-14 rifle, and a bunch of us were zeroing in on the paper targets when a bird landed on mine. As it did so our drill instructor issued the standard command: "Ready on the right. Ready on the left. Ready on the firing line. Commence firing." *Blam*. The bird disappeared in a shower of feathers.

"Cease firing!" the angry instructor shouted. He walked over to me and demanded to know why I'd shot the bird.

"I thought that the purpose of this drill was to learn to kill things," I replied, "and I was just getting an early start." That remark cost me extra KP duty. And I never did get a satisfactory answer as to why I shouldn't have shot the bird.

My six-month tour of active duty with the National Guard gave me time to think in a serious way about my career. My job with the *Journal* had been an important first step, but I was ready now to take the next move. When my tour was up I arranged an interview with the Associated Press in New York City. I flew east wearing a gray suit that had fit me perfectly before I began my basic training. It now hung like a sack on my thinner, trimmer, basic-trained frame. To make matters worse, I had a military haircut that was just beginning to grow out, I hadn't entirely recovered from the psychological beating I had taken while becoming a trooper, and my portfolio was six months out of date. On top of that, New York was an alien city to me at the time; even the huge buildings were intimidating.

My appointment was with the general manager of Associated Press. As I sat across from him I had to keep telling myself that I was in New York and not in the military; he reminded me precisely of my former drill instructor. It wasn't the best of interviews. I was not only ill at ease, I was also overanxious. I remember telling him that I'd work anywhere—I'd even sweep out the place at night if he'd only give me a job. "Don't call me, I'll call you," he said at last, and I headed back to Oregon with my baggy gray suit, my outdated portfolio, and no job. At least my hair was starting to grow back.

When I got back to Portland I discovered that my work for the *Journal* had attracted the attention of the *Oregonian,* the state's largest paper. They put me on staff, and once again it was off to forest fires, this time in a light plane piloted by Lev Richards, the *Oregonian*'s aviation editor. Within a month of my arrival we found ourselves headed for what proved to be the biggest blaze of the year, the Big Lake Airstrip fire in eastern Oregon.

You could see the Big Lake fire from miles away. It was spectacular. I asked Lev to circle behind a mountain so I could use it in the foreground of my picture, and the resulting photo made the mountain look like a volcano, with the plume of smoke rising thousands of feet above it. Lev landed first at a small airstrip that was right in a pocket of fire, but the wall of flames moved close and we had to take off again, barely missing some fir trees at the end of the runway. We landed near the Hoo Doo ski area, the center of the Big Lake inferno, learned that some fire fighters were trapped near the top of the ski lift, and decided to attempt to reach them on foot, something no one else had thought of trying.

"How in the hell did you get here?" was the first question we heard upon gaining the summit. "Along that path," Lev responded, pointing behind him. The "path" he indicated was now a wall of flames. "Join the party," said the fireman.

The next five hours were touch and go. We might have died but for a large bed of lava that lay between us and the flames, preventing them from spreading any closer. The fire surrounded us completely. I shot dozens of pictures as the tall trees "crowned out" with a loud roar. The smoke was so thick it was hard to breathe, and our eyes were burning almost as badly as the trees. Ward Monroe, the fire boss, was in constant radio contact with the base. The only advice they had to offer was to keep the group together until things cooled down. "As if there's any place for us to go," he replied sarcastically.

Meanwhile, back at the bottom of the hill, word had reached other newsmen that a group of people were trapped at the top of the mountain, and representatives of the media gradually gathered at the base camp to await word of the group's fate. More than one newsman noted that the *Oregonian* was unrepresented at the base camp and would surely miss the biggest story of the year: the dramatic rescue of the trapped firemen on the flaming mountaintop. The look on their faces when Lev and I, covered from head to toe in soot, emerged from the smoldering forest with the firemen made the whole trip worthwhile. We smiled and waved, then climbed into our plane for the trip back to Portland with our scoop.

Even at this early stage of my career I was more interested in getting the picture than in protecting my own neck. There's an undeniable element of romance and bravado associated with covering dangerous stories, and the way I handle myself in a dangerous situation stems from that childhood image of photographers as invincible and somehow untouched by the events they cover. Only later, as a war photographer in Vietnam, would I begin to suspect that wasn't true. It's hard to say just how much dash and derring-do a photographer can handle without its becoming a fatal affliction, but in the early days I was more concerned with the dash than the possible crash.

My pictures on the Big Lake fire led to a big break for me—a job with United Press International in Los Angeles. I had just turned twenty. Before departing for L.A. I married Susan Allwardt, whom I'd met while she was modeling clothes at a Portland fashion show I covered for the *Journal*. We set out for Southern California in an old Ford, behind which we were tow-ing a U-Haul trailer. In the middle of a redwood forest, thirty miles south of Monterey, the car's engine blew up. A year later our marriage did the same. The combination of our youth and my professional zeal simply wasn't compatible with a permanent relationship.

A Deadline Every Minute

WORKING FOR A WIRE SERVICE is one of the most exciting and competitive jobs in the world. UPI's motto is "a deadline every minute." The unabashed competition between the two major wire services has overwhelmed many young employees and driven others to drink. But I thrive on competition and welcomed the challenge. UPI's main competitor is the Associated Press. Employees of the two outfits are locked in permanent journalistic combat, and for me that battle, at least in the early days, was a personal war as well: I was determined to prove that the AP general manager in New York had made a mistake.

I arrived in Los Angeles just as the UPI photo bureau moved out of the *Herald Examiner* building because of a strike at that paper. In the next few weeks we were to work out of darkrooms at Los Angeles International Airport and Dodger Stadium before finally moving permanently into a building on Olympic Boulevard. For someone who had just arrived in that sprawling city, finding one's office was enough of a problem. But this was ridiculous. "Where's the office today?" I'd ask when I called in.

I hadn't been working for UPI more than five months when an escaped murderer from San Quentin named Arthur Glenn Jones nearly terminated my brief career. I was on another assignment at the time, cruising the freeways near Venice when the radio station I was listening to reported that Jones was holed up in a nearby Manhattan Beach motel, where he was holding the police at bay. I lived in Manhattan Beach at the time—it was the one section of L.A. I could find without trouble—and by racing down the San Diego freeway at over 100 mph, I arrived on the scene in less than ten minutes. Policemen had already blocked off the streets on either side of the motel, and there were men with drawn guns everywhere, including a number who lay prone behind the median in the middle of the street.

The Rancho Motel was typically Californian, a "U"-shaped one-story affair with a central parking area. From the central court you could periodically see Jones as he peeked out from behind a curtain in the window. A detective was standing flat against the wall alongside the window, trying to talk Jones into surrendering. The other officers strongly advised, but did not insist, that my colleagues and I leave the courtyard. The others retreated, and soon Bill Piggett, a cameraman from CBS, and I were the only two media people with a clear view of the murderer's window. The murderer had a clear view of us as well.

What neither Piggett nor I knew at the time was that Jones had a large amount of dynamite sitting on his bed in the room, and that he had been threatening to blow himself up. We also didn't know that the cops had just decided that, all other efforts having failed, it was time to use tear gas to force Jones from his lair. They began lobbing the gas through a bathroom window at the rear of the building, but Jones picked up the canisters as they dropped inside and tossed them back.

Who fired the first shot I'll never know, but within seconds a full-scale shootout between Jones and the cops erupted. Piggett and I were in the midst of it all, taking pictures, when "Kaboom!"—the dynamite went off and shingles from the motel's roof began raining down on us. "Christ, he's had it!" was all I could say. But Jones wasn't dead. In fact, as the dust settled he started to crawl out of the window. Spotting him just as I did, the cops opened up, and for a few seconds it sounded like Chinatown at New Year's. Jones half rose, clutching his chest, and bullets ripped into him. He fell over into a clump of ivy and crawled across the pavement toward me. He couldn't have been more than twenty feet away. Bullets were hitting him, I was taking pictures, and Piggett's camera was rolling as Jones, his clothes smoking from the blast and the bullets, looked up. His eyes caught mine for a brief second—I'm certain I was the last living thing he saw—and then his head rolled to the side.

A figure dressed in a bulky bomb-disposal suit approached Jones. He lifted the bullet-riddled body with one hand—looking for explosives, probably—then let it drop when he found none. I was shaken and speechless, and the officer who came over to me was no comfort. He had been the one negotiating with Jones through the window when the fireworks began, and he told me Jones's last words. "See those two guys in the courtyard?" Jones had said. "They better not stand there or I'm going to shoot them." Piggett had been wounded in a similar episode a few years back when a crazy woman with a pistol shot him in the leg. Some guys never learn.

Figuring I'd heard—and seen—enough, I found a pay phone to call the office. I tried to tell them what had happened, but I wasn't making much sense. The guys at the other end told me to get back to the office as fast as I could. On the way in I found myself listening to a report of the shooting on the car radio and the whole horrific scene returned to me: Jones's life being violently extinguished, the tear gas, the shots, the explosion—and the fact that I had almost gotten killed in the crossfire. I shook so hard I could scarcely drive.

When I reached the bureau someone took my film off to be developed. Ernie Schwork, a stocky, silver-haired vet who'd seen it all, grabbed the negatives as soon as they came out of the darkroom. He held it up to the light, shrugged his shoulders, and declared, "There's nothing here." My heart sank to my shoes, my life flashed before me . . . then I looked around the office. Everyone was laughing. I had fallen hard for the oldest joke in Schwork's repertoire. All I could think of at the time was that if those pictures *hadn't* come out, after all I'd gone through, I'll quit the profession for good.

The pictures had turned out, and they received tremendous

play around the world. I got a tear sheet from the Chicago *Tribune* with my pictures splashed across the front page. There was a note attached from Gary Haynes, UPI's Chicago bureau chief, that read: "The *Trib* hasn't used this many pix since the Colonel died," referring to the founder of the *Tribune*, Colonel McCormick himself.

Every conceivable kind of assignment and situation came my way in L.A. On one occasion, for instance, an SAS airliner crashed in Santa Monica Harbor. When I arrived at dock-side there was only one boat for hire, a large houseboat. "How much to take me to the crash site?" I asked the owner.

"Seven hundred dollars," he said.

I was trying to negotiate a lower price with him when I heard another car drive up. Inside was an AP photographer.

"Seven hundred dollars it is. Let's go now," I said briskly, stepping aboard.

As we pulled away from the slip I could hear the competition running down the walkway, shouting to us to pick him up. "Don't call me, I'll call you," I thought to myself as the boat pulled away from the pier.

It was in many ways a unique crash. The tail section of the 707 had broken off and sunk, but the rest of the aircraft was still afloat. A light rain was falling and waves were breaking over the flooding fuselage, creating one of the eeriest sights I'd ever seen. For some reason I particularly remember the sound of water sloshing in and out of the broken windows in the cockpit. Although a number of people went down in the tail section, over a hundred were rescued from the rest of the plane. Because of the bad weather my pictures weren't especially good, but they did have the advantage of being virtually the only pictures.

That same year—1968—also provided one of the year's worst rainstorms. Carlos Schiebeck, the bureau chief, asked me to find some celebrities who had been affected by the flood. As it happened, I had photographed Ann-Margret for a story a few weeks earlier, so I gave her a call and asked if her home, located in Benedict Canyon, had suffered any damage. She informed me that the whole front yard was heading down the driveway, and added that I was welcome to come up and have a look. By the time I arrived the entire yard had slid several feet closer to the bottom of the canyon. There was no way for me to get to her house except to wade through the mud. The home had once belonged to Humphrey Bogart; I found myself wondering how he would have felt about what was happening.

Bogie wasn't my immediate concern, however; one of my shoes was. The suction of the foot-deep mud had pulled it off my foot, and I couldn't find it in the muck. By the time I reached the front door, where Ann-Margret and her husband, Roger Smith, were waiting for me, I looked as bad as their yard. I did get some pictures of the two of them surveying their waterlogged domain, including one of the actress clutching a bedraggled little dog in her arms. Between the two of them, the damp dog, the lost yard, and my missing shoe, we were a miserable lot. My expense account for that week included "$32.95 for new pair of shoes; lost one in flood." UPI's penny-pinching accountants eventually conceded that there was no way to replace just one shoe, and they reluctantly agreed to buy me two new ones. They should have been happy that they didn't have to replace Ann-Margret's yard.

Although I lived in Los Angeles, my assignments took me all over the state. And so when large-scale student protests erupted at San Francisco State College I was sent to lend a hand to the UPI photographers there.

S.I. Hayakawa was the man brought in to quell the disturbance at San Francisco State. Hayakawa was not a household word in 1968, but I soon found out who he was. Picture a short, middle-aged man of Japanese extraction wearing a tam-o'-shanter. Next, imagine that this improbable figure is the president of a major California university and a semantics expert. Then visualize him standing atop a truck equipped with loudspeakers, tearing out the speaker wires while groups of outraged student dissidents surge around the truck, and you've got the idea.

What ensued on that academic turf was some of the roughest, bloodiest action I'd ever seen off a battlefield—and I was right in the middle of it. At noon each day the protestors would gather on the college green and march on the administration building. In came members of the San Francisco Tactical Squad, a group of police officers noted for their expertise in crowd control, not their social graces. The twain would meet, rocks would be thrown, and clubs would be liberally applied to dissenting heads. This daily occurrence made for dramatic news pictures, and I can fairly say that my coverage favored neither side. In fact, one day I got hit on the head by a rock thrown by a demonstrator, and the next day was clubbed by a cop.

The dramatic climax of this period of unrest came the day the agitators stormed the administration building and attempted to accost the newly installed President Hayakawa. Policemen were positioned inside Hayakawa's office, guarding the door with drawn pistols. As the group entered the office the cops sprayed them with Mace and drove them back out the door. I closed in to cover the clash and found myself once again staring down the barrel of a loaded revolver. This time the gun did not belong to a murderer, but to a cop. I earnestly hoped I didn't look like a dissident. The news business, I thought, was rapidly losing its glamour.

Later that day, I watched a demonstrator hit a policeman on the shoulder with an iron rod, breaking his collarbone. Another cop, seeing this happen, chased the long-haired marksman down and hit him so hard with his nightstick that the hapless student actually bounced when he hit the pavement. The kayoed student and the wounded cop rode the same ambulance to the hospital. En route to the emergency room the injured policeman received first aid; the student was left facedown in a pool of his own blood.

Covering Robert Kennedy was my first major political assignment with UPI. Having taken his picture during my days with the Oregon *Journal,* I knew that he was a great subject for a photographer. And after weeks of badgering L.A. bureau manager Schiebeck—a good shooter in his own right—I was finally permitted to join Senator Kennedy's campaign for the Democratic presidential nomination. I flew to Albuquerque, New Mexico, and there had my first encounter with a politician's staff. It was not a pleasant experience. They treated me with a kind of supreme indifference—which I interpreted as open hostility—simply because I wasn't one of their group, not one of "the boys from Washington." In addition, I looked eighteen at the time, although I was, in fact, twenty-one. No one took me seriously. I had no choice but to deal with them, however, because they could accredit me to cover the campaign. I at last convinced them that I was, in fact, a UPI photographer on assignment from L.A. to cover Kennedy's campaign, and they grudgingly allowed me to board the campaign plane. I felt like a leper. None of the traveling press, and naturally no one on the Senator's staff, was talking to me.

After the Albuquerque stop, Kennedy came walking down the aisle of the plane. He glanced at me, walked by, then turned around and looked again. "I don't remember you," he said. I introduced myself, and he sat down alongside me and asked, "How's it going?" It's not my nature to be indirect, so I told him. I even mentioned that his staff had tried to keep me off the flight. "I got the impression," I said, "that it was like winning first prize just to be let on this plane." Kennedy, who seemed to be the only one in the whole crowd who cared who I was or how I was doing, was apologetic: "Don't worry," he said, adding, "it won't ever happen again." And it didn't. After the next stop there was a remarkable change in attitude toward me, almost as if I had suddenly become one of "the boys."

I traveled with Kennedy for the next couple of weeks, and although we really never got to be friends I did get to know a good deal about him. It was at this time that one of my friends asked, "Gee Dave, you really know Bobby?" "Sure," I responded. "How well?" I was asked. "Well enough that he calls me Dave, and I call him Senator." I watched the Senator deal with all sorts of people during those weeks, and I observed that he related particularly well to small kids and college students. I was standing near Kennedy one day at Window Rock, an Indian reservation in Arizona, when a little girl came up to him. He looked down at her, smiled, and then silently took her hand. She stayed with him during the rest of the tour he was making. A most natural gesture, not put on for the benefit of the press.

A few weeks later, the night of the California primary, I ran into *Life* photographer Bill Epperidge again. This time it was in Kennedy's private suite at the Ambassador Hotel in Los Angeles. It was going to be a terrific evening. Kennedy was leading in the race for the Democratic presidential nomination, and it seemed certain he was going to carry the state. Everyone was in an exuberant mood, one that Ron Bennett, now working in UPI's Los Angeles bureau, commemorated in a picture of Senator Kennedy and me. The Senator then went to a room where some television cameras had been set up and gave an interview. He returned briefly to his room, then went back downstairs to put in an appearance at the victory celebration being held in the ballroom below. Bennett and I flipped a coin to see who would go to the podium with Kennedy, that position being the best point for photographs. Ron won, and I found a spot in the back of the room where I could get a picture of the whole scene.

Robert and Ethel Kennedy entered the ballroom and the place went wild. It was an important milestone in Kennedy's quest for the presidency. With a huge grin, he gave the "V" for victory sign. After a short speech, he started toward the kitchen, his "escape route" to another rally in the hotel. I'd preceded him into the other reception room, where an overflow crowd waited. Minutes passed, and Kennedy didn't show. I sensed that something had gone wrong, and, pushing my way through the crowd of Kennedy supporters, made it upstairs and tried to get into the kitchen area. The passage was completely blocked. By this time reports were flying that there had been a shooting. Figuring that if someone had been hurt they'd take him out front, I hurried outside and saw Kennedy put into an ambulance. I jumped into my car and followed the ambulance to Central Receiving Hospital, a distance of a few blocks. My car was the last to clear the gates before the police sealed off the hotel. When I entered the hospital I found pandemonium. I photographed Bill Barry, a former FBI agent who was Kennedy's personal bodyguard, as he walked, head bowed, through the emergency room door. He was devastated.

Kennedy wasn't kept at Central Receiving for long. He was soon moved to Good Samaritan Hospital, a larger, better-equipped facility, just down the street. As white-uniformed attendants began to lift the comatose Senator into the ambulance again, his grief-stricken wife, Ethel, climbed into the back. No one was yet seated in the front of the ambulance, so I hopped in, opened the little door that communicates with the back, and snapped one frame of Ethel. If I had to do it all over again, I honestly don't know that I could. I am still haunted by the look on her face.

The next two days were a nightmare. We journalists stood in small groups on the street outside Good Samaritan, waiting for some word on the Senator's condition. When it was finally announced that Kennedy had died, I was too exhausted to feel the impact. The following day Kennedy's body was put on a government jet for the flight to Washington. I pleaded with UPI to let me follow the story eastward, but they refused, which was probably just as well. I was a physical and mental wreck. When I returned home, it finally hit me and the tears finally came.

Late in 1968 UPI transferred me to New York. I arrived with a very distorted view of my importance to the company. I could have sworn, at the time, that a sword had been laid on my shoulder, that I had been welcomed to the circle of privileged courtiers surrounding the corporate throne, a photographer-prince. I was wrong. UPI already had a prince, and his name was Dirck Halstead. At least that's what Charlie McCarty called him. And McCarty should have known, for he was the Assistant Newspictures Manager. I was assigned to Larry DeSantis, who was often referred to by his contemporaries as "The Bald Eagle." He was, in fact, one of the best picture editors in the business. DeSantis did not see me as a prince. As far as he was concerned I wasn't even a knight. To him I was just a raw recruit.

DeSantis began the painful process of changing my attitude and my whole way of seeing. "YOU CALL THESE PICTURES!" the Eagle often screamed, tossing my negatives at me as if they were confetti. "Could have sworn I had it . . ." I'd respond weakly. Sometimes DeSantis actually brought tears to my eyes, but I tried hard and luckily improved—in his estimation, anyhow.

I was assigned to sports, an important job at UPI in New York. At first I worked nights, covering the Yankee and Mets games and events at Madison Square Garden. Sixty-nine was the year of the Mets, and I covered practically all of their home games. Sports history will not soon see anything like that season again. The team was young, but the talent was there. Everytime I walked into the dressing room with my cameras and safari jacket, some of them would jump up and down like monkeys and shout, "Booga, Booga!" and suddenly we were all in the heart of the jungle. As comics, they made fantastic ball players. They went straight through the season and into the play-offs, winning all the way. And when the Mets captured the National League pennant, they celebrated as all champions do, with champagne. Someone tossed a brimming glass of bubbly at first baseman Don Clendenon, and I froze the frothy liquid in midair with an electronic flash just as it hit his face.

Covering a major sporting event such as the World Series is, in many ways, like conducting an orchestra. From my position next to the first base dugout, I had an excellent view of the action. I mounted three cameras with motor drives on a tripod in front of me, and hung a fourth around my neck. Each camera was mounted with a different telephoto lens, so that if there were a close play at second base, for instance, I'd have the necessary 300 mm or even 500 mm lens to catch the action. When things began to happen all over the infield, I had to be faster than the players to record the play. First the hit to right field; next, swing to second for the slide; then train my cameras on the people in the stands for reaction shots.

After the Mets won the World Series, New York City went bonkers. Overjoyed fans tore up the playing field so badly after the game that it reminded me of the first pictures I saw of the face of the moon. After everyone left, Tom Seaver, the man who won the last game, came out of the locker room to survey the mess. He stood quietly on the ravaged pitcher's mound. The stadium was completely silent, in sharp contrast to the emotional uproar an hour earlier. I caught both sides of the Mets' finest hour, and the pictures I took that day won me UPI's monthly in-house award.

Shooting is not always satisfying. I don't get much pleasure out of sports photography, except for the satisfaction of pitting my talents against those of speeding athletes to record the split-second moments of truth in each game. But sports photography is a lot more rewarding than "head-hunting"—pursuing a particular celebrity in the hopes of getting a single headshot for tomorrow's paper. One of the things I liked least about my job at UPI was standing in various New York doorways, waiting for a "personality" to walk out so I could take his or her picture. Particularly someone like Jacqueline Onassis, the prime target of all headhunters. I wonder if she ever steps out of a Manhattan restaurant or into a taxicab *without* encountering a photographer. On more than one occasion while I was working for UPI in New York I had to stake out Jackie's apartment, stand in front of a restaurant where she was dining, or wait in front of a theater until she arrived. Headwaiters and restaurant managers eager for publicity make a regular habit of tipping off certain news agencies whenever Mrs. Onassis enters their establishment—and schools of photographers follow her like pilot fish.

Doing personality features was another thing altogether. I was there because I'd been given their permission to shoot, and with any luck I'd get photographs that shed light on the people involved. I was once asked to photograph Mia Farrow, who was filming *John and Mary* with Dustin Hoffman on location in Central Park. Establishing a good rapport with your subject is critical in such circumstances; the way it developed with Mia was unique.

It was a freezing midwinter day, and when I arrived on the set Mia was sitting in a director's chair, warming her feet over a bucket of coals. Her booted feet were resting on a stick that spanned the bucket. Suddenly, the stick caught fire and flames began to lap around Farrow's legs. Ever the cavalier, I bowed gallantly and said, "Let me save you from the flames." Whereupon I waved the burning stick until the fire was extinguished. We both ended up laughing, and the rest of the day yielded some really fine pictures of Farrow, both on and off the set.

John Dominis, a big, rugged-looking *Life* photographer, was also shooting on the set that day. John was one of my few heroes. I felt he was everything you should expect in a photographer. His famous photo-essay on the big cats in Africa had strongly influenced me in the earliest days of my photographic career. They were singularly powerful, action-packed pictures, and when I met Dominis I couldn't resist telling him how special his pictures were to me. He seemed pleased, but embarrassed, and kept shifting from one foot to the other, looking uncomfortable.

Another of my heroes was *Life* photographer Larry Burrows, but I never got a chance to tell him how I felt about his work because Burrows was killed in Vietnam before I ever met him. I was still in high school when *Life* published a Burrows photo-essay entitled "Yankee Papa 13." It followed the crew of an American helicopter into action and recorded the death of a crew member who made a daring attempt to rescue several downed airmen. This series of photographs included a shot of the helicopter pilot as he broke down and cried. It affected me so deeply that it shaped the whole course of my career. I wanted to take pictures like Burrows. A camera without a man like Burrows behind it is a useless machine, and his premature death was a profound tragedy to the profession.

(Text continues on page 41)

THE YOUNG SHOOTER

RON BENNETT

"To the older photographers, I was a pain in the ass."

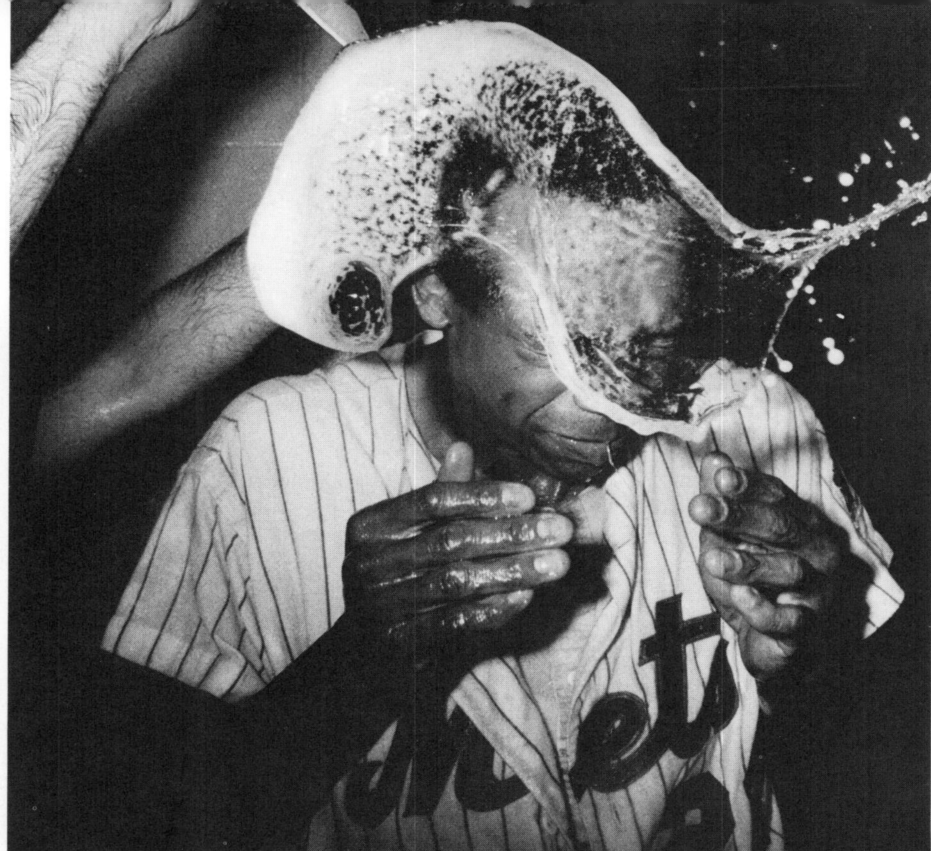

ABOVE: *New York Mets first baseman Don Clendenon gets doused with champagne after his team wins the 1969 National League play-offs.*

LEFT: *Muhammad Ali heads for the canvas after being knocked down by Joe Frazier during their championship bout in Madison Square Garden, 1971.*

OVERLEAF: *A helicopter assists firefighters during a brush fire near Los Angeles, 1968.*

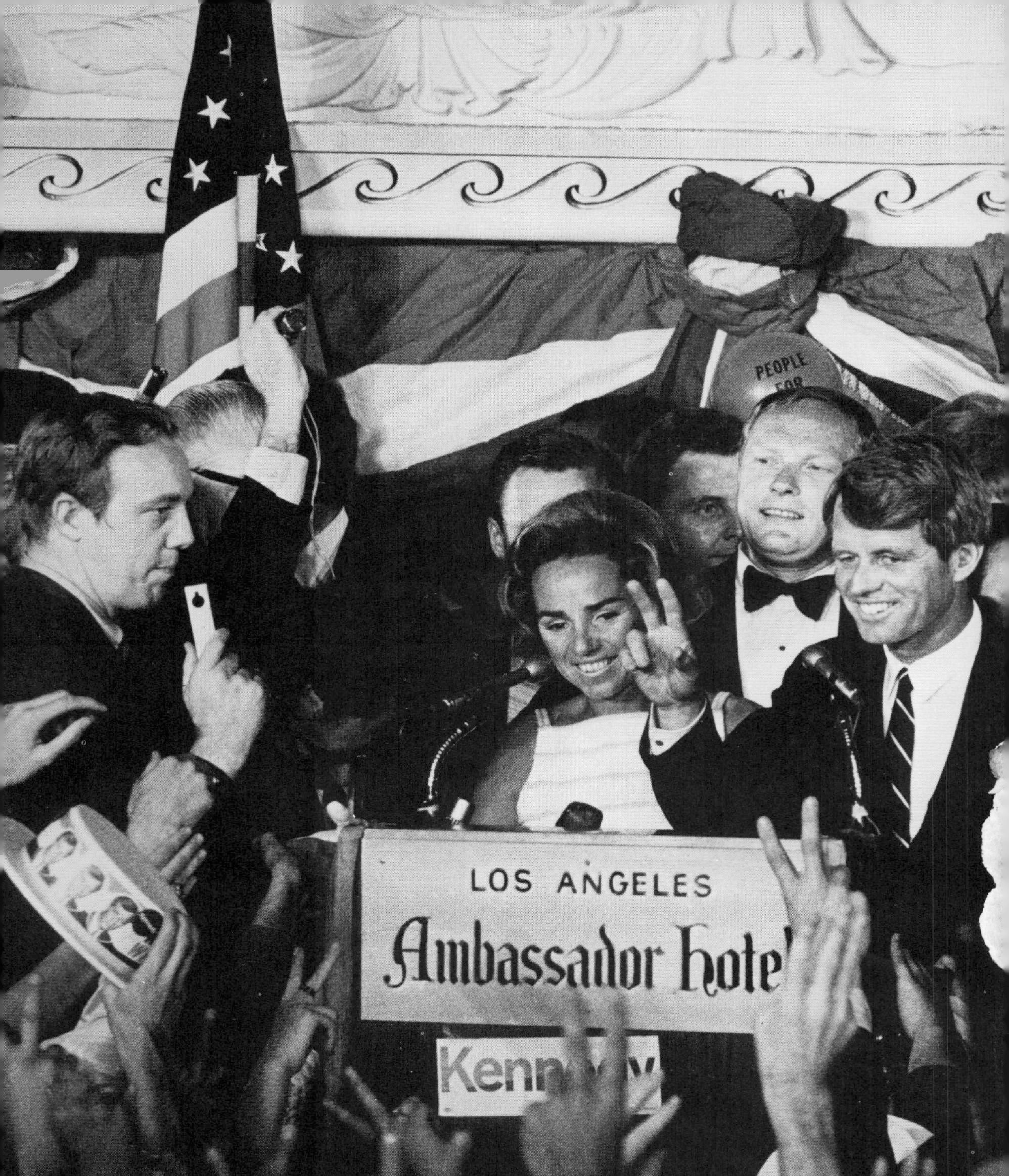

PEOPLE
LOS ANGELES
Ambassador Hote

Robert Kennedy, with wife, Ethel, at his side, flashes "V" sign to his supporters in ballroom of the Ambassador Hotel. Minutes later he lay dying on the floor of a kitchen adjoining the ballroom. Los Angeles, 1968.

Russian-born maestro Igor Stravinsky; Symphony Hall; Portland, Oregon, 1966.

"Send Kennerly"

THE LATE SIXTIES WERE A TUMULTUOUS PERIOD, and because I was both a news photographer and young, I managed to snag many of the decade's most violent assignments. The editors seemed to think that my youth would make it easier for me to identify with what was going on. I suspect the older photographers cheerfully agreed because they didn't want any part of what was going on.

Trouble in Newark: "Send Kennerly." I'd never been to New Jersey, much less to Newark, and I can truthfully say that I have no desire to go back. It was a hot July night, the sort of sultry summer evening when it didn't take much to touch off violence. When I swung around a corner in downtown Newark in my beat-up V.W., I ran square into a large mob of angry blacks, none of them eager to welcome a white face at the moment. There wasn't room to turn around, so I had no choice but to keep going. I accelerated, bearing right down on the crowd. My poor V.W. thumped like the inside of a kettledrum, as rocks and bottles ricocheted off my already battered car. Fortunately none of the windows broke and I made it through the crowd unscathed—but was I scared!

One of the most terrifying aspects of a riot is being caught in the middle of it and not knowing where you are. Which precisely describes what happened to me on that night. After several anxious minutes I did spot a fire station, whose occupants directed me to the nearest police headquarters. Breathing a sigh of relief, I opened the door of the local precinct and once again found myself looking down a gun barrel. This time the gun was a shotgun, but for a couple of seconds I could have sworn it was a howitzer. The nervous cop at the other end of the cannon soon realized that I hadn't come to loot and burn, and he lowered the muzzle. I later discovered that this particular precinct station had been blown up in the last major riot, hence the arsenal.

I also discovered that the Newark cops rated reporters and photographers on a par with the plague and typhoid fever. To say that they were totally uncooperative is as positive a statement as I can make. Having struck out with the police, I turned to the only friendly civilian face in the precinct house, and *he* told me how to get to where the action was. He added that he'd love to take me there himself, but he was tied up at the moment. Only then did I notice that his feet were shackled to a bench. He was a prisoner of the Newark City police.

I departed in the general direction he had indicated, alone and on foot. After some minutes I found myself in the middle of a deserted intersection. Suddenly I heard a voice calling, "Kennerly, Kennerly. Over here." I didn't know anyone in Newark, so I assumed the disembodied voice belonged to a fellow lensman, and peering around I located Mike Evans, then with the *New York Times*. "Get your ass over here!" he shouted. Mike had hidden himself in a darkened doorway. I soon discovered why. A minute later three police cars pulled into the intersection. Three battleships would be a more apt description; sticking out of their windows were more shotguns than I'd seen even on a pheasant hunt back in Oregon. "See what I mean," said Evans. "Yeah," I whispered, "but those are supposed to be the good guys." The cops started shooting wildly into the air and Mike and I discovered, simultaneously, that the pavement behind a parked car was a terrific place to lie low for a few minutes.

When I finally made it back to the office that evening I requested permanent duty in Manhattan. My request was granted, and soon thereafter trouble broke out at City College in New York. "Send Kennerly." Those two words were starting to bore me. Over the next few days I covered a student strike that seemed like a Sunday outing compared to San Francisco State.

One way to get clear of riots, I decided, was to head south—to the nation's capital. There was an opening in the Washington bureau. Although I didn't relish getting involved in the political scene, I knew that the assignments would at least be different, and I took the slot.

The Washington bureau chief at the time was George Gaylin, a distinguished looking, gray-haired man who spent most of his working hours pulling out that hair in sheer frustration. George and I didn't hit it off well at the beginning because of something called the White House rotation system. Five UPI photographers covered the President on a monthly basis. At the end of every fifth month it would be the first guy's turn again. New York headquarters had insisted that I be put on the rotation immediately, overriding George's schedule. Despite the early hostility this caused, George and I eventually became great friends.

I didn't like Washington much in those days, and I particularly didn't like covering the White House. It was, admittedly, glamorous, but only for a while. My first ride with President Nixon on Air Force One was genuinely exciting, and being part of the White House press corps was exhilarating. One gets stars in one's eyes around the President, and members of the press corps are not immune. Like my colleagues, I found myself saying casually, "I'll be out of town with the President next week." It's hard not to get caught up in that scene, especially when you're twenty-three. I did, but not for long.

Being confined by ropes was one of the things I despised about working at the White House. Just before Thanksgiving, for example, the Turkey Growers of America came to present a live bird to the President. Everyone assembled in the Rose Garden for the presentation: the Turkey Growers stood behind their heavily drugged bird while the press lined up behind heavy velvet ropes as the President came into view. The doped-up bird became completely alert as soon as it spotted Nixon. It said "Gobble! Gobble!" spread its huge wings, and whacked the Chief of State right on the nose. He cringed, I shot, and that photo went across the country on UPI wires. The White House staff fumed, insisting it was trick photography. And all because the First Bird had taken a liking to the First Man.

When the White House complained about my turkey shot, I assured them that I'd gladly trade one hundred pictures like it for one good, substantive photograph of the President actually doing something important—working on a speech, conferring with Kissinger, anything—so long as it didn't occur under the glare of television lights and wasn't a situation contrived for the benefit of photographers. Just slip me into the Oval Office for a couple of minutes, I suggested. No dice. I pleaded with Nixon's Press Secretary, Ron Ziegler, and members of his staff on many occasions, but to no avail. Presidents Kennedy and Johnson had had press secretaries who permitted exclusive photo sessions all the time. Nixon, through Ziegler, did not—another instance of Nixon's abiding mistrust of the press.

After a year in Washington, I was ready to hit the road again. "Send me to Vietnam," I suggested to UPI executive Charlie McCarty in 1971. In 1970 UPI had offered me the Vietnam assignment, but I hadn't felt ready for it. Now I did. I wanted to go. The biggest story of the decade was Vietnam, and I didn't want to miss it. My colleagues in the press corps thought I was crazy. Photographers usually go to Vietnam in hopes of getting a plush assignment like the White House when they get back, not the reverse. But I believed then, as I do now, that any photographer who had a chance to go to Vietnam and didn't made a big mistake. The only excuse that made sense to me was fear; some guys said, "You couldn't get me near the place." At least they were honest about it.

As I traded in my pinstripes for fatigues, I began to question the wisdom of my decision. I was so tense and edgy that I could hardly eat, especially after word flashed across the wires that five photographers had been killed when their helicopter was shot down by antiaircraft fire in Laos. Larry Burrows was one of them. The others were Henri Huet of AP, Kent Potter of UPI, and Keisaburo Shimamoto of *Newsweek*. That did it. I couldn't keep anything but bourbon down for a week.

My last assignment in the U.S. was to cover the Ali-Frazier fight at Madison Square Garden on March 8, 1971—the day before my twenty-fourth birthday and the day before I was to leave for Vietnam. As I headed for the Garden I couldn't help but reflect on what had happened to me at the last fight I had covered. To get a clear shot of the action I had done what all photographers do at fights—leaned in under the ropes. I got so caught up in this particular fight that I was only aware of what was happening through my viewfinder. For six rounds I strained for a closer and closer shot, until a fan tapped me from behind and said, "Excuse me, sir, but you should know that your pants are ripped." I felt back where my wallet should be and found nothing but air. Damn, I was embarrassed. Who knows how many thousands of fans found my rear end the prime attraction between rounds. Anyway, I tied a coat around my waist and finished the fight.

The Ali-Frazier affair was billed as the "fight of the century," and for all I know it may have been. The match brought together two undefeated champions, and that was a first in itself. There were at least one hundred professional photographers working the fight—and some non-professionals, too. Directly across from me, Frank Sinatra was shooting for *Life*. Ali had never been knocked down in a pro fight before, and when Frazier blasted him off his feet it was as much of a shock to the fans as it was to Ali. My motor-driven camera with its 24 mm wide-angle lens captured Ali sailing to the mat, and late that night UPI transmitted a sequence of my shots of Ali toppling. One frame froze him in mid-air, a fraction of a second before he hit the canvas. When I picked up the *New York Times* the next morning, that picture was on the front page—a perfect send-off. (I later learned that Joe Frazier had a print of that particular shot blown up wall-size and hung in his home.)

I spent the next day, my birthday, in Chicago with my folks. When we tried to discuss my upcoming trip my mother began to cry. She wondered aloud why I had to go. My father assured me that he understood why I felt compelled to put it all on the line for my profession, and I realized for the first time that he both understood and appreciated what I was doing. As we stood in the local bar drinking straight shots of whiskey it occurred to me that for the first time we were talking not as son to father, but man to man. After six or seven belts I was still stone-cold sober. There was no way of blotting out the immediate future.

As the jet touched down in the stifling humidity at Tan Son Nhut airport in Saigon, my emotions ran the gamut from anxiety to relief, and excitement to dread.

My apprehensions soon vanished. The drive from the airport into downtown Saigon was uneventful. Hundreds of Vietnamese on bicycles, scores of blue and yellow taxis, and thousands of civilians clogged the streets, going about their lives as if there were no war. The only evidence of unrest was the occasional truck filled with troops, or the odd military jeep, speeding by and honking at those who got in its way.

The man who met me at the airport, Nguyen Ngoc Anh, a slight Vietnamese with a big smile and a wispy black beard, also helped to dispel my fears. Mr. Anh proved to be not only a photographer but a driver, chef, entrepreneur, medic, comedian, gourmet, raconteur, and several hundred other less easily named things as well. None of us on the Saigon UPI staff could have mastered the complexities of life in war-time Vietnam without his guidance.

Another character in the Saigon bureau was Nguyen Thanh Ngoc, who printed the film we shot. Mr. Ngoc belonged to a Vietnamese group known as the Hua Haos, a fierce band of people who refused to have anything to do with either the regular government or the Viet Cong. Ngoc was proud of that. He was also proud of his appetite for chicken claws, which even the other Vietnamese had to admit was an acquired taste. Everyone in the bureau used to imitate Ngoc devouring those ugly morsels.

Toshio Sakai, a Japanese photographer who won the Pulitzer Prize for photography in 1968, lived in my apartment building in Saigon. Sakai was a very eccentric type, antisocial and brooding, who didn't get along with most people. We liked each other immediately, and became fast friends. He used to complain to me that he was getting old—he was thirty-one at the time—and I good-naturedly began calling him Father Sakai, which never failed to make him angry. He was a great shooter. Before he left Vietnam he gave me two things. The first was a small good-luck symbol he always carried. "This kept me alive, it will keep you alive," he said, handing me the tiny cardboard chit with Japanese characters painted on it that I carry in my wallet to this day. The other item was a red Japanese doll that is weighted at the bottom so that it will never tip over. It had two large white eyes, one of which Sakai painted black. He said I could paint the other one in when something really great happened to me. "How will I know for sure when to paint it?" I asked. "When *you* win the Pulitzer," he replied.

The time had come for me to face the inevitable: when you come to Vietnam to take action pictures, there's only one place to do it, and that's where men are shooting at one another. Helicopters were the principal means of transportation at the time, ridden as casually as commuter trains in other parts of the world, but my first ride nearly proved to be my last. Our destination was Lang Vei, a camp that had been overrun by North Vietnamese a few weeks earlier but was now back in friendly hands. I was in the company of a group of seasoned photographers who'd been covering Lam Son 719, an operation that had involved sending South Vietnamese troops across the border into Laos. (Burrows and the others had been killed while covering this incursion.) We were witnessing the end of Operation 719.

In the chopper with me were Holger Jensen and Neil Ulevich, both staffers for AP. I was sitting on the floor of the Huey helicopter with my back to the pilot. Seated directly in front of me, and facing forward, was Ulevich. The chopper's nose dipped forward, the normal takeoff position, and the aircraft gained speed as it skimmed over the ground. I was looking at Ulevich when his mouth dropped open and unmistakable panic contorted his features. He grabbed the seat on either side of him. I couldn't see what was going on, but it didn't look very good, judging from Ulevich's expression. As quickly as he had tensed up he relaxed, and then explained that the chopper had lost power and we had headed toward the ground at about 80 mph. From Ulevich's viewpoint, it looked like we were goners. The pilot merely glanced over his shoulder and shrugged.

Our flight to Lang Vei was only about forty minutes, and the pilot made a corkscrew approach into the base, which looked like a big divot taken out of the landscape. (The corkscrew landing got you in quicker, and reduced your chances of being hit by ground fire. It is not recommended for those with queasy stomachs, but then neither is ground fire.) We were just about to touch down when a huge explosion jolted our chopper. The pilot immediately banked sharply to the left and pulled back on the stick to gain altitude. As we read it, the North Vietnamese Army had zeroed in on the landing pad with their artillery, and we were the target. That didn't prove to be the case, however. The explosions were merely unwanted ordnance being blown up by our own engineers, so we landed. It was not yet 8:30 A.M. If every day was going to be like this, I figured I wouldn't last more than a month.

Chopper stories. Everybody had dozens of them. Every now and then the military would assign a helicopter to take the press to big operations, but normally you'd hang out at an airport or air base, give the air controller a few beers, and he'd flag down a passing plane or chopper for you.

One day, UPI correspondent Ken Braddick and I were hitching a ride from Phu Bai up to Quang Tri. Ken is an Australian who hates to fly. That day a Jet Ranger helicopter landed, and after we'd settled into the backseats and tightened our belts, I wanted to get out. The pilot had something written on his helmet that led me to believe nothing was sacred to him. It said, "Fuck Mom." That assessment proved to be correct, because the next twenty minutes provided Ken and me with the wildest ride since Bonnie and Clyde made one of their getaways.

The Jet Ranger was the fastest chopper in use in Vietnam. Because they were highly maneuverable they were normally used for ferrying generals around. And because they were highly maneuverable they tempted pilots to show me, time and again, "what this little baby can do."

Undeterred by Ken's lack of enthusiasm, our pilot started off by chasing a truck up Highway One. The poor bastard driving that rig didn't have any idea we were in back of him until he happened to look in the rear view mirror and discovered that there was a helicopter on his tail. He almost drove off the road. By this time the pilot, who sported a huge, red handlebar mustache, was shrieking with maniacal laughter. He kept looking back at us, wondering how we liked the ride. He didn't seem to be watching where he was going, but Braddick was, and Ken let out a scream when it seemed we were about to slam into a tree head-on. The pilot veered sharply to the right, but not before nicking off a few leaves.

Our close shave did not seem to have any impact on our pilot. His next move was to pull back hard on the stick and before we knew it we were at 10,000 feet. Our stomachs, however, were still following that truck up Highway One. As a result it was two badly shaking correspondents who climbed out of that machine in Quang Tri. We were told that it was dangerous to drive Highway One because of the V.C., but that's precisely how we went back to Phu Bai.

A dead person is scarcely an uncommon sight in a war zone. I spotted my first one as we were driving back to Phu Bai. He lay faceup just off to the side of the road, and I shuddered involuntarily as we drove by. I soon learned that what I'd seen was standard practice where Viet Cong casualties were concerned. It is very important to the Vietnamese that the body be buried so that its spirit won't wander aimlessly for eternity. Leaving a body out was supposed to scare the V.C., but I couldn't see that it did. It didn't bother the two hundred-odd V.C. who attacked a command post in the Central Highlands where I first admitted that I, too, could be killed. Until then, I'd been fairly detached from that possibility. I was bunked in with some Air Force guys who were running a radio beacon for B-52's. When the first flare went up about 3:30 A.M. several black-clad V.C. had nearly made it to the first perimeter.

Incoming mortar rounds were exploding loudly throughout the compound, so the airmen and I crouched behind sandbags in the innermost perimeter. The noise of the shooting was deafening. (I found myself thinking again that the guy who figures out how to photograph sound is going to become a rich man.) "Take this," said one of the airmen as he shoved an M-79 grenade launcher into my hands. "Hey, I'm a noncombatant," I blurted out. "Tell that to the V.C.," he suggested. I never had to use the grenade launcher since the attack subsided almost as suddenly as it had begun, but I couldn't take any pictures either. It was much too dark. "Always try to leave before nightfall," a friend of mine had repeatedly cautioned. Now I knew what he meant. What seemed like years later, the sun finally came up. We could see more than fifty dead V.C., many with live explosives strapped to their bodies.

I was jumpy as hell all that day, and by afternoon I had decided to head to a new locale. As I sat with a couple of other fellows at the edge of a trench near the landing pad, waiting for a chopper, a soldier began to heckle me. "Hey, newby," he said, "they're not going to shoot you." The words hadn't been out of his mouth two seconds when the first 122 mm rocket came in. (Everybody tries to tell you what a 122 mm sounds like. To my ears they sound like bacon sizzling on a frying pan just before they impact. But have no fear—you'd know the sound if you heard it.) The rocket took off the top of the water tower fifty feet away, but I didn't see it hit. I was lying facedown in the trench. The jokester was under a truck.

"It's one hell of a time to change the oil," I shouted at him when he poked his head up.

Saigon, the Glittering Whore

I PLAYED THE PERCENTAGES IN VIETNAM. If I thought there was a better than fifty-fifty chance the chopper I was riding on would take fire going into a landing zone, I wouldn't get on it. Sometimes I would decide not to board a chopper just because it didn't feel right, and sometimes I'd tell a driver to turn around before driving any further up certain roads. Every now and then my hunches would prove out: the chopper I didn't take *would* get shot down, or the next car up the road *would* be ambushed. There's probably not a photographer or correspondent who doesn't have similar tales; it's really a matter of developing a finely honed sense of self-preservation.

One guy who took all the roads and all the helicopters was Dieter Ludwig. Dieter, a big German with long blond hair, didn't seem to know what fear was all about, or if he did he wasn't telling. Firebase Six was where I first became aware of Dieter's contempt for percentages. The firebase had been overrun by the North Vietnamese Army, the NVA, and the South Vietnamese, the ARVN, were determined to take it back. I had a chance to go in with the first wave, but passed it up. Dieter didn't. He was right there with the first group, and as a result he withstood a fierce shelling attack during which the South Vietnamese regulars remained in their bunkers. This irked Dieter. ("How can you take any pictures if they won't stick their heads above ground?" was the way he put it to me later in his heavily accented English.)

To shame the ARVN soldiers into combat, Dieter stood atop the bunker and taunted the NVA. "Shoot me! Shoot me!" he challenged. "See," he yelled to his comrades, "they won't shoot me, and they won't shoot you, so come out of your holes." The ARVN must have thought Dieter a prime candidate for the nut hatch, but a few did poke their heads out.

Dieter had been a movie actor in Germany, but gave it up to come to Vietnam. He looked decidedly shabby at times. His basic wardrobe was old fatigue pants, a T-shirt, and shower shoes. His cameras were so old they could conceivably have been used by Matthew Brady. They hung not from leather straps but from strings around his neck. Half the time he'd have to hold the lens tightly onto the body of his camera with his hand, otherwise his pictures would be fuzzy.

Dieter's appearance caused him all sorts of trouble. On one occasion he and Jeff Taylor, one of my UPI colleagues, were headed for an American firebase near the Demilitarized Zone (DMZ). The base was in the thick of the fighting, and when Dieter and Jeff arrived the U.S. Army wouldn't let Dieter in. Taylor, a tall, thin, blond-haired guy from Hawaii, wasn't sure whether to attribute this to Dieter's generally disheveled appearance or the fact that he was a German citizen. "Don't worry," Dieter told Taylor, "I'll *walk* over to Firebase Fuller," which lay nearby. Now that sounded relatively easy, but Dieter decided to go overland. En route he heard voices and hid in some bush. He had run into a NVA platoon which was getting ready to shell the very place Dieter was heading for. He kept low for a few hours, and when the NVA moved off he made it into the firebase.

Another time Dieter was taking a picture of two South Vietnamese soldiers taking down a V.C. flag from a tree. Either the flag or the tree had been booby-trapped with a hand grenade, which blew up, killing both soldiers. A large piece of shrapnel hit Dieter's camera, which was raised to his eye. It punched a big hole next to the lens, right where his eye would have been. He didn't get a scratch.

Saigon was where I lived and kept an apartment. It was, in those days, as John Saar of *Life* once wrote, "A glittering whore of a city." Many of the old, yellow buildings from Vietnam's French colonial days were still in good shape, and these lined the wide boulevards near the Presidential Palace. My "penthouse" was a one-bedroom apartment above the UPI bureau. It was a penthouse by definition—it was on the topmost floor—but it had none of the glamour one associates with the word. Many foreigners lived in this area off Tudo Street, which was renowned for its bars, restaurants and small shops.

Saigon was desperately overcrowded by 1971, its population swollen by the uncounted thousands of people who had moved to the city from the countryside because of the war. Pedicab drivers wearing conical hats pushed their passengers in near silence through the streets, passing small soup stands set up on sidewalks. In the central market throngs of citizens shouted, bartering for food and whiskey, black-market watches, and radios.

I loved the sights, sounds, and smells of Saigon, and was always happy to return there from the field. One really pleasant evening a bunch of us were having drinks on the balcony of my apartment, which overlooked the Vietnamese navy yard on the Saigon River. I was just saying to a friend how good it was to be back from up country when the nightclub a block away blew up. We dropped our drinks, grabbed our cameras, and ran over. The place was a smoking mess; people trapped inside were screaming for help. Someone had left a satchel full of plastic explosives inside. The final toll: five dead and countless injured.

Besides terrorist attacks from within, we also had to contend with the V.C., who would lob a few rockets into the center of the city every now and then just to let us know they were around. At three o'clock one morning a huge racket jarred me out of a deep sleep. "What was that?" asked a terrified girl friend who was visiting from the States.

"Just the garbagemen, collecting trash," I said in my most reassuring voice. Later that day, we met in my office. "Those weren't garbagemen," I was informed. "It was a rocket! It blew up the apartment building right in back of yours." It had also killed three people.

Soon thereafter the South Vietnamese authorities quelled a student riot that took place in the big intersection opposite my apartment. The police were using liberal amounts of tear gas, which was permeating the air for blocks. I made my way home wearing a gas mask topped by a brown fedora, which I'd picked up in a local market. Still wearing the gas mask and concerned for the safety of my girl friend, I raced up the stairs and knocked on my door. My girl friend opened it and gave a shriek at the apparition standing in the doorway. To her credit, she stayed another couple of weeks in Saigon.

If you weren't out in the field working the chances were you could be found in a Saigon bar. Our two favorite drinking establishments were within falling distance of the office. The one straight across the street was the Xinh-Xinh, and the all-time UPI favorite, the Melody Bar, was right next door.

Each place had a bevy of attractive, young girls on the premises. For 500 piasters, roughly $1.25, you could buy them a "Saigon Tea," a crème de menthe on ice. Purchasing the drink would entitle you to converse with one of the lovelies, but because of their generally poor English the subject might only range from "numbah one GI" to "numbah ten V.C." Not always a satisfying intellectual experience. (For considerably more than 500 P, paid to the mama-san behind the counter, it was possible to have other things besides your intellect tended to.)

There was no real social center in Saigon, no place where everyone went, and newsmen from different outfits usually had their own hangouts. These bars provided a kind of emotional outlet after we'd been in action, and at such times nothing seemed better than having a beer with the boys. We never told war stories to outsiders who drifted into our bars, and even among ourselves the name of the game was to drastically understate any situation. Pity the new man in town who showed up in the bar at night to ask what it was "really like." The general response was to look him in the eye, and say in a deadly quiet tone, "I don't want to talk about it."

CA. Charlie Alpha. To anyone who's ever been to Nam those letters mean combat assault. There are two kinds of CA. The easy kind goes into a cold landing zone, or LZ; the other kind goes into a hot landing zone. Neither has anything to do with temperature. A CA into a hot LZ means the bad guys are shooting at your chopper as it lands. A company-sized CA usually involved four choppers per platoon, six guys to a chopper. To land a full company, sixteen helicopters transport one hundred men in four separate lifts. The advice given me by veteran newsmen was always to go in with the third lift. By that time fifty soldiers were already down, securing the LZ, and another twenty-five would be coming in right in back of you. That sounded pretty terrific, and I decided I'd give it a try.

My first clue as to the kind of LZ we were approaching came when I noticed that the crackle of small arms fire was louder than the rotor blades of the chopper. It was a hot one. I soon found myself running at or half-crawling away from the LZ toward soldiers who were returning the V.C.'s fire. The very idea of being in the middle of a firefight had my heart beating faster than a hummingbird's. My breath was coming in quick, shallow gulps. In other words, I was scared shitless. The area was a twisted mass of mangled tree trunks, upended boulders, and smoking holes left by incoming artillery rounds. I noticed a young private wedged between two rocks. He had been hit in the face and was in a bad way. Everyone else was involved in keeping the enemy at bay, so I took a medical compress from the band of his helmet and tried to stop the bleeding.

The fire slacked off as the V.C. withdrew from the fight. After making sure a medic was available to attend the wounded man, I resumed taking pictures. "What are you doing here, man?" a black G.I. asked. My combat attire, which included a green medical cravat, camouflaged jungle fatigues, the small backpack that all G.I.'s carried, and a brown fedora instead of a helmet, made it clear to him that I was nonmilitary. The clothes, coupled with my beard and cameras, distinctly separated me from the regular foot soldiers. "Just here taking a few snaps," I responded. "Do you have to be here?" he asked incredulously. "Not really," I replied. He looked at me and shook his head. "If I didn't have to, I wouldn't *even* be here."

When I got back to Saigon I told a couple of colleagues about my first firefight, and about the wounded man. One of them asked if I'd taken any pictures of the poor guy. "After I fixed him up," I replied. "You asshole," he said. "Take the picture, *then* put on the compress."

Everytime the G.I.'s paused, even for a smoke on patrol, they gave the spot a name. Landing Zone Lonely, Firebase Gladiator, Marble Mountain, Freedom Hill. They even named their artillery pieces and tanks. One armored personnel carrier I saw had "I love war" written on its side. The air force even got into the act with the ground crews signing their names on 500-pound bombs. (I seriously doubt that any V.C. stuck around long enough to discover who was delivering those deadly parcels.) Names and slogans were everywhere. And some of the best graffiti in the world was written on outhouse walls at the fire-bases. "John Wayne sleeps with a night-light," was a favorite.

LZ Hotlips was where I took more good pictures in two hours than I had in the previous two months. The place had been totally devastated by air strikes, artillery barrages, small arms fire, defoliants, and the elements. The only trees left standing were pathetic sticks, their branches long since blown off. They pointed skyward as if inviting help from above, but all that fell from the heavens was more bombs. The landing zone was silent when I arrived. The temperature exceeded 100 degrees, and the heat was so oppressive that the only refuge was within oneself. Each soldier was lost in his own thoughts.

When there is such a lull in the action the soldiers grow tense, wondering when the barrage will begin again, and from which direction. I glanced up the hill. The men there had started firing a mortar, and from my vantage point they were silhouetted against the destroyed trees and the sky. It was the kind of situation great pictures are made of, and I began shooting. It was an incredibly dramatic scene: the low cloud cover was casting an ominous light over the tableau, and the gloominess matched the mood of the men. The most poignant moment came as a G.I. moved cautiously among some enemy bunkers that had been destroyed earlier. His lone figure was, to me, the single image that best summed up the war.

Next it was Saigon's turn to provide a story. I was at the bureau one day when we got a report that several disabled Cambodian mercenaries who had fought in the South Vietnamese army were threatening to blow themselves up at the Veteran's Administration Building. When I arrived I found a very resolute looking man in a wheelchair facing me. In his hand was a grenade. The pin had been pulled, but he was holding down the spoon. His apparent grievance, and that of his companions, was that they were not getting regular veteran's benefits. They had fought with American Special Forces and encountered a bureaucratic snag, the details of which I never did learn but the result of which was that they hadn't been paid. Suddenly they took up a machete and with a swift stroke one by one cut off a thumb. They placed their severed digits on a plate and sent it to the Director of the Veteran's Administration. This seemed to stimulate the negotiating process, as formerly distant officials fell over each other trying to help the poor veterans. One of the protestors wasn't satisfied, however. He took his wooden leg off and started beating passing cars with it. Tiring of this, he sat down in the middle of the street, wooden leg in front of him, and began reading off a list of demands. A bus went by him, and the shocked looks of the passengers summed up the general feeling. In time it proved possible to part the crippled vet from his live grenade, and life resumed what we in Saigon had come to think of as a normal pace.

"When things get boring, head for the Delta" was another truism of war reporting in Vietnam. The Mekong Delta encompasses some of the richest farmland in the world, and most of Vietnam's rice is grown there. In 1971 it was also the home of the Coconut Monk, so named because that's all he ate and drank. The monk was a truly eccentric man who never spoke or took a bath and who communicated his answers to reporters' questions in writing. The monk's devoted followers lived on a small island, but he himself made his home on a boat anchored along the shore and held audience sitting on a big ceramic dragon whose huge red eyes had blinking lights inside them. Around the wizened little man's head was what looked like a crown but proved to be a pigtail he never cut. Many of his followers sported similarly elaborate hairdos ranging from pompadours to coifs that resembled birds and crosses. The only way to reach the monk's abode was by hiring a boat and cruising downriver. I used to love taking visitors to see him and referred to his sanctuary as Disneyland East.

During a lull in the fighting elsewhere in the country, two of us took off for the U Minh Forest, the so-called Forest of Darkness in the Delta. It isn't really a forest—jungle swamp would be a more accurate description—and it has always been a Viet Cong stronghold. My companion, Matt Franjola, a freelance journalist whom I met in Saigon, spoke fluent Vietnamese, which probably accounts for our having survived. We had heard of a Delta operation that involved a battalion of ARVN troops and a big party of V.C., and we linked up with them. For the next three days we were never out of waist-deep swamp water except to sleep, and we vowed never to return if we managed to make it out.

Protecting your camera gear in such a situation is almost impossible. I always kept two of my cameras, and the film I planned to use, in waterproof containers. The third I'd wear around my neck. That one took considerable abuse whenever the shooting started and I dove for cover, since cover was often a foot or more of brackish water. There was no way to keep dry, and I was constantly soaked to the skin, covered with leeches, and utterly miserable. Good photos were the only reward.

At night the sound of the mosquitos would almost drown out the booming of artillery. They also had no regard for jungle fatigues, which they could bite right through. The only escape was to cover yourself with a rubber poncho, but that meant suffocating in the stifling heat. Either way you lost, and we wanted out. "The chopper will be here tomorrow" we were assured by the major. Fine, we would leave then. But tomorrow came, and it brought no chopper. "Where's the chopper?" Matt asked in Vietnamese. "They said they were coming. I just don't know," was the officer's evasive reply. After twenty-four additional hours of waiting, we began to get genuinely worried. Darkness was approaching, and so were the mosquitos. We had another night of agony to endure.

At dawn the following morning the helicopters arrived, and as we climbed aboard Matt and I looked at each other and grinned with relief. We watched the dark green vegetation slip by as the helicopter raced above the treetops at 90 mph. All I could think of was being in my own apartment in Saigon that night, having a hot shower and then going out for a meal at my favorite French restaurant with one of my lady friends. I closed my eyes and pictured the entire evening in great detail. Suddenly I was jolted back to reality. The chopper had begun a rapid descent, and we were once again landing in the middle of the jungle. This was another combat assault. Like it or not, we were on it. It seemed to us like an instant replay of the past two days, but one hundred times worse in terms of the mental anguish. We were physically and psychologically drained this time around and prepared for Saigon, not the jungle again. We had to get out, and fast.

During a rest break at the new LZ, Matt overheard a conversation among some Vietnamese soldiers. They were laughing about our plight, saying that a chopper was coming for the major but he wasn't going to tell us. Sure enough, a helicopter did land on the other side of a clearing a couple of hours later. We watched the major climb in and without asking anyone's permission we ran across the field and threw ourselves inside. I can never remember enjoying Saigon as much as I did that night.

Covering the War

ALL THE BOMBS IN THE WORLD had nothing on Typhoon Hester, a big wind that hit Da Nang while I was there covering the withdrawal of a brigade of American troops. Although there were warnings that a storm was brewing, none suggested how strong it was likely to be. We soon found out. The first indication we got that a storm of any size was headed our way came at noon when the sky suddenly darkened, and within 30 minutes the gale was full upon us. At one point I was reminded of the tornado scene from the *Wizard of Oz* as cats, dogs and people flew by. There was no yellow brick road for us, however, and for six hours—the storm's peak—roofs were ripped away, buildings disappeared, and five-ton trucks were upended by the 120 mph wind.

I had taken refuge from Hester in a wooden quonset hut and escaped only seconds before the roof collapsed. After crawling to another structure, where a bunch of G.I.'s were huddled, I watched a soldier run a hundred yards in about five seconds, the wind at his back so strong his toes hardly touched the ground. I heard a loud groaning noise and shouted to the guys with me that our building was going. We got out just as the entire back wall of the structure collapsed inward. Across the way a man dashed out of a similar building and looked back just as the whole place dropped in a pile of metal and splintered wood.

We finally found a sturdier shelter. Huge sheets of corrugated tin roofing were flying through the air like the propaganda pamphlets that were dropped on the V.C. (the difference being that these could cut you in half). Although I had my cameras with me, it was almost impossible to shoot. The light was so low and the rain driving so hard that every time I raised my camera it got drenched. After the storm died down I ventured out to take some shots. One from this series that I like is a photo of a sign that read "Chapel on the Hill." Behind the sign was a pile of debris, all that remained of the church.

Hoi An, a town south of Da Nang, was the headquarters of the Republic of Korea (ROK) Marines who fought alongside the ARVN. In the wake of Typhoon Hester, UPI newsman Don Davis and I went to Hoi An to see what the ROK's were up to. It was often said that the Koreans had a platoon of public relations men for every company they fielded, so determined were they to maintain their image as battle-ready warriors. We encountered no P.R. men at Hoi An, but we did meet a rough bunch of fighters. The Koreans were feared by the V.C. for their mercilessness in dealing with captives. It was widely reported that whenever the ROK's took fire from a village or hamlet, they retaliated by destroying the hamlet and everyone in it. Perhaps that is why the Korean area of operation enjoyed relative peace.

Our host at Hoi An was Brigadier General Hur Hung, a tough veteran of the Korean war who arranged for us to join some of his marines in a riverboat assault. These flat-bottomed swamp-boats were powered by rear-mounted airplane propellers. You could hear them coming for miles. Their high-pitched whine, in combination with the ROK battle cries, would scare anyone. I can only assume that the V.C. headed for the next province when they heard us coming, because we saw no sign of them. (I also harbored the sneaking suspicion that the whole thing was staged for our benefit, but neither Davis nor I could prove it.) That evening General Hung invited us to have dinner with him and his officers. It was a typical Korean meal that included kim chee, a form of pickled cabbage laced with hot peppers. Not wanting to offend the general, I downed the hot stuff. "How you like kim chee?" he asked.

"Best ever," I said, picking up more with my chopsticks.

"No," he exclaimed, "too hot," and fanned his mouth.

Later that evening Davis and I discovered that several Korean showgirls, down from Seoul to entertain the troops, were staying in the next room behind a locked door. Davis and I spent some time peeking through the keyhole at them. They giggled and waved. By this time we had consumed large quantities of beer in an effort to put out the fire lit by the kim chee, and the beer had given us great ideas. "Let's pass them a note," Davis said, his face brightening.

We set down a few artful phrases, which a Korean newsman who was sharing a room with us translated, and we passed the message under the door. The occupants of the next room squealed with delight when they read the note and then passed one back to us. At this point Don and I determined that the only way to really get to know the girls well was to open the door. It wouldn't budge. We attacked it with bayonets and fingernails, but to no avail. It wouldn't give. In desperation we sent another note, this one suggesting the girls come around to our side. Five minutes later, there was a soft knock on our front door. "This is it," whispered Davis, who flung open the portal and found himself confronting the biggest Korean we had ever seen. "You no bother girls no more," he stated flatly. We didn't.

Most of the time I covered the war from the land, but one of my assignments took me to sea. To reach the U.S.S. *Newport News*, a heavy cruiser that was one of the biggest vessels in the fleet, I was lowered to the deck by rope from a hovering helicopter. At the time the *Newport News* was patrolling the South China Sea seventy-five miles south of Hai Phong harbor. Seven destroyers escorted the huge cruiser, whose main firepower consisted of nine massive eight-inch guns, enormous cannons that could lob a 57-pound projectile 12.5 miles. Targeted were a surface-to-air missile site and an oil dump near Thanh Hoa harbor. The first foray into the harbor was at night, and there was no way to get any photographs. The next morning was a different story, however. I found myself witnessing one of the few daylight raids ever staged on a North Vietnamese harbor by U.S. warships. The *Newport News* moved at flank speed toward the coastline, and once it reached the mouth of the harbor it turned, slowed down, and began firing its big guns. Over the next hour the cruiser's captain changed course several times, not to escape return fire but to avoid running down some small fishing boats. This struck me as incongruous. They were, after all, here to kill as many North Vietnamese as they could. I decided the captain's motive was simply to avoid killing innocent fishermen.

All of this activity was noticed by the defenders on shore, and they fired back with their artillery.

"Flashes on the beach, 130 degrees . . . flashes on the beach, 135 degrees . . . flashes on the beach, 140 degrees," the radioman said, coolly reporting the location of the enemy artillery as the shells fell all around us. The first round hit off the bow; the second, astern. We held our breath; they had us bracketed. A loud whoosh, and water rained onto the ship. Missed! I suddenly found myself wishing there was a place to dig a hole on the ship.

On our second pass at the harbor, in the words of one sailor, we "really stirred up the hornet's nest." The North Vietnamese were firing with everything they had. They missed, but blew away several of the fishing boats we had taken such pains to avoid. One of these unfortunate vessels bobbed alongside the *Newport News* just as she was preparing to fire. From down below the cruiser must have looked like a great gray mountain. The panicky fishermen who had been swept into our lee made frantic praying motions with their hands. When the huge guns opened up, all you could see of the hapless fishermen were their buttocks sticking out of a hatch in the boat. The noise was deafening, but the fishermen escaped unscathed.

Not a single North Vietnamese shell hit us or any of the destroyer-escorts, but a few sailors did get wet from the spray kicked up by near misses. Even so, not a seaman I talked to afterwards wanted anything more to do with surface-to-air missile sites, oil dumps, or Thanh Hoa harbor.

After more than a year in Vietnam, UPI appointed me bureau chief for photos for Southeast Asia. One of the most fulfilling aspects of my Vietnam experience was the people I worked with and got to know. Our group was truly international and included Jeff Taylor, an American; Willie Vicoy, a Filipino; Anh and Ngoc, both Vietnamese; Shunsuke Akatsuka, a Japanese; and stringers who were German, Canadian, Australian, and French. Dieter Ludwig, whom I've mentioned, was just one in a cast of brave characters who came to cover the war. We had a common bond, not in our diverse backgrounds, but in our desire to photograph accurately what was actually happening on the battlefield, even where doing so meant taking grave risks. It was a very small fraternity, one brought together by the very forces that were tearing Vietnam apart. The photographers came for as different reasons as there were individuals. One came in search of adventure; another, to discover himself. Some came for a lark, and others to document seriously the great tragedy of war. But whatever their motive, all came to take pictures.

Willie Vicoy, the Filipino with the winning smile, was particularly fearless, and on one of his first trips into the field he had an experience that could have been straight out of a John Wayne movie. Vicoy was riding the turret of a tank as it attacked a V.C.

bunker a few feet away. As they closed in, the tank commander tossed some hand grenades and a rush of wind snatched Willie's hat off his head. He retrieved it and discovered that the "wind" had been a bullet from an AK-47 assault rifle. When he showed me the hat in Saigon, Willie poked his finger through the hole.

Taizo Ichinose was another free spirit, a young Japanese photographer who showed up at the bureau one day looking for work. "Send me anywhere," he pleaded through an interpreter. There was a lot of action in the Delta at the time, and the Delta was easy to reach. I asked Taizo if he wanted to go there. He did, and he went. Later that same day he returned to the bureau. "Have good pic-shures," was all he said. In fact, "have good pic-shure" was all he knew how to say in English. When I looked at Ichinose's film, though, I found shots that could not have been done better on a Hollywood set. Taizo had been standing near a truck when it was hit by a mortar round, and his "good pic-shures" showed the truck blowing up and its occupants diving for the ditch. A few months later Taizo went into Cambodia, where he was reportedly captured by the Khmer Rouge as he was riding a bicycle to Angkor Wat. He was never seen again.

One of the bravest and most colorful of the people who showed up mysteriously in Saigon was Gerard Hubert, a fifty-year-old French Canadian. Hubert made the acquaintance of some Vietnamese airborne troops soon after arriving, and he quickly decided that they were the only soldiers he would accompany into battle. Hubert's was a shrewd decision, for the Airborne ARVN were the best troops Vietnam had to offer and were always involved in the biggest and toughest fights. One afternoon in the Central Highlands, Hubert rescued three of "his" soldiers by dragging them back to friendly lines under heavy enemy fire. In the process he was hurled against a tree by an explosion, injuring his leg. ("I get too close to the air strike," he later explained.) The Airborne cited Hubert for his bravery, and three Vietnamese soldiers owe him their lives.

I was at the bureau editing film one afternoon some weeks later when the door burst open and Hubert staggered in. He was

wrapped in bandages. "Jesus Christ, what happened?" I asked.
"The V.C. shot me at An Loc, but here's the film. Now I must go to the hospital," was all he said. It turned out that Hubert had gotten himself into An Loc, which was then totally surrounded by the NVA, but when he tried to get out, the chopper he was riding in was shot down. The chopper that finally rescued Hubert also got shot up, and in the process he took a bullet through one shoulder and a piece of shrapnel from a rocket in the other. Within a few weeks Hubert was itching to get back into action with his favorite airborne and decided to go to Quang Tri, where the fighting was heavy. A couple of days later he was sitting outside a bunker and failed to hear an incoming 130 mm round. They found him dead a few minutes later.

Only later did we discover that Hubert wasn't his real name. Our suspicions were aroused when the body was brought back to Saigon for shipment to relatives and no kin could be located for a Gerard Hubert. It was not until three months later that Art Higbee, the UPI news bureau chief, was able to discover Hubert's real identity. He was, it turned out, an ex-convict from Canada whose mother was living in France. When contacted she informed us that she wanted no part of her dead son. We buried him with the French Airborne in their cemetery in Saigon. If the old saying "he would have wanted it that way" had ever applied, I'm positive it was then.

"This mean you numbah one?"

EVERY NOW AND THEN WE WOULD FEEL A NEED for a break in the action, and on such occasions most of us headed for Hong Kong or Bangkok. Hong Kong is first and foremost a commercial city, and many of us referred to it as the PX of Asia. Every small appliance and electronic device manufactured in Japan could be purchased there, often at a bargain price. You could, it was said, go broke saving money. After months in Saigon, Hong Kong was more than a pleasure; it was a necessity. It offered newsmen a chance to eat in legendary restaurants, associate with old friends at the Foreign Correspondents' Club, carouse in Wanchai, and, most importantly, forget the war for a few precious days.

On one visit to Hong Kong I joined forces with Kate Webb, UPI's bureau chief in Phnom Penh. Kate was a soft-spoken Australian who had once been captured by the Khmer Rouge and, unlike so many others who fell into their hands, had lived to tell about it. She, NBC correspondent Phil Brady, and I spent the evening consuming all the booze in Kate's Hong Kong apartment, after which we decided to go visiting. By then it was 3:00 A.M., but that didn't stop us. We climbed into Brady's small sports car, lowered the top, and careened through the narrow streets of Hong Kong to the apartment of Udo Nesch, a German cameraman who worked for CBS and was a country and western fanatic. Udo also had a taste for wine and kept a well-stocked rack. We pounded on his door, until his sleepy maid finally opened it a crack. "We're friends of Udo's," Phil told the bleary-eyed amah, who reluctantly let us in. Quickly locating the main liquor supply, we proceeded to mix a batch of cocktails.

The sun was coming up over the British Crown Colony when we departed. Udo, asleep in the next room, had never awakened.

That night, Kate and I were sitting at the bar in the Correspondents' Club, nursing Bloody Marys, when Udo walked in. "I've got to stop drinking," he declared.

"Why's that, Udo?" Kate asked.

"This morning when I got up, bottles and cigarette butts were everywhere, and the stereo was playing," he said.

"So what?" Kate asked.

"I could have sworn I'd had no more than a glass of wine before I went to bed, but I must have had a party," sighed Udo.

"Perhaps you should see a doctor," Kate suggested.

Another place I liked to go for rest and recreation was Australia. There everyone spoke my language, and there people seemed genuinely anxious to make me feel right at home. Among them was Pat Burgess, a columnist for one of the big papers in Sydney, who showed me that town. We met for a drink in the Invicta Pub near his office, and during our conversation Burgess said he'd introduce me to some of the local talent. His paper ran daily photographs of beautiful Australian girls in bathing suits, and I wanted to meet one of them. Everything was all set, and I was ecstatic until I returned to my hotel. There I found waiting for me not a beautiful blonde but a cable. Its three words—"Return to Saigon"—ruined my day. The North Vietnamese, it seemed, had begun pouring across the DMZ into Quang Tri Province.

This was the story I'd been gearing up for, and I headed back on the first plane. It was no accident that UPI provided superior coverage of the onslaught. For one thing, I had instituted a new policy when I became bureau chief, which was to pay all photographers the same rates whether they were Asians or Caucasians. This inspired many Asian photographers working for the competition to come over to UPI. In addition, for months I had been buying pictures from stringers, even when we didn't really need their photographs. My policy was put to the test when the North Vietnamese attacked. It worked. The NVA were coming, and we were ready for them. For eight successive days the work of UPI photographers in Vietnam appeared on the front pages of the *New York Times* and in scores of other papers as well.

Virtually every time a shot was fired anywhere in the country we had a staffer or a stringer on the spot with his camera. UPI signed up several new clients on the strength of our coverage of the Easter offensive, and it was clear that we were winning the journalistic war with AP. There was a real sense of excitement and esprit de corps in the Saigon bureau. Photographers would unhesitatingly take assignments from me because they knew I'd been through it. In fact, I was still going through it. I got out into the field to shoot every other week, leaving Jeff Taylor to run the bureau in my absence.

During one of the weeks I was in Saigon, UPI news bureau chief Bert Okuley woke me at 4:00 A.M. "You'd better come down here and have a look at this message," he said. His voice was grave.

"Oh, Christ," I thought. "Something's gone wrong and New York hasn't gotten the pictures from Quang Tri." I'd been up most of the night developing Ennio Iaccobucci's film from that city. He had sensational exclusive photos of the final evacuation, shot mere hours before Quang Tri was overrun by the NVA. I assumed that something had gone wrong with the transmission of the pictures, sent via radio wave to New York, and the main office was bitching.

I ran down the stairs from my apartment and rushed into Okuley's office. "Look at this," he said, handing me a sheet of paper torn from the wire machine. It read: "01170 SAIGON-KENNERLY HAS WON PULITZER FOR FEATURE PHOTOGRAPHY, WHICH BRINGS CONGRATS FROM ALL HERE. NOW NEED EFFORT SOME QUOTES FROM HIM AND PINPOINT HIS LOCATION WHEN ADVISED FOR SIDEBAR STORY, BRANNAN/NX CABLES."

I was dumbfounded. I had won the highest award a photojournalist can receive—and I hadn't even known that I'd been nominated. I thought maybe there had been some kind of mistake. We sent a message to New York, asking for clarification: "02054 EXHSG BRANNAN'S 01170 ARE YOU KIDDING? IF SO IT ISN'T MUCH OF A JOKE. IS THERE A PULITZER AWARDED TO A UNIPRESS PHOTOG AND IS IT KENNERLY? OKULEY." Whereupon the wire machine broke down. For over three hours we were cut off from the world. I hadn't had a cigarette for better than two months, but in those three hours I started again.

Many cigarettes later, the wire machine finally sprang back to life: "01181 OKULEYS 02054 NO KIDDING AND CAN YOU REACH KENNERLY FOR SUDDEN COMMENT NEED TO KNOW WHERE HE WAS WHEN HE GOT THE NEWS. WOOD/NX CABLES."

The Pulitzer Prize is the premier award in the news business, something all photographers and writers dream of winning.

Without my knowledge, Larry DeSantis, the Bald Eagle, had submitted a portfolio of pictures I'd taken in Vietnam, India, and Cambodia to the Pulitzer committee. The citation from the Pulitzer committee read: "For an outstanding example of feature photography, awarded to David Hume Kennerly of United Press International for his dramatic pictures of the Vietnam War in 1971." They also noted that "he specializes in pictures that capture the loneliness and desolation of war." The representative picture the committee selected from my portfolio was the one I'd taken of a G.I., his weapon at the ready, walking over the scarred landscape of a god-forsaken place the G.I.'s comrades had given the improbable name of LZ Hotlips.

The Saigon bureau's reaction was unrestrained, even though two other UPI photographers, Kyoichi Sawada and Toshio Sakai, had previously won Pulitzers for their war pictures. But my favorite comment came from Nguyen Thanh Ngoc, our Vietnamese lab man. Ngoc had no idea who Pulitzer was, but he'd endured the hullabaloo twice before and understood the import. "This means you numbah one now?" he asked.

When things finally simmered down in the office I went upstairs, got the good-luck doll Toshio had given me, and painted in its other eye. For three or four days after that I couldn't sleep. I lay in bed at night, staring at the slowly rotating blades of the ceiling fan while the same question circled in my mind: "What does it mean? What *does* it mean?" I decided it meant I had to go out and take some pictures. My opportunity came the very next day, when Dirck Halstead, one of my closest friends, showed up in Vietnam to cover the offensive for *Time*. Dirck is a tall, urbane New Yorker, well-known among his colleagues as both a gourmet and a wine expert. It was Dirck who had, several years before, convinced the UPI executives in New York that a brash young photographer named Kennerly who was working for them in Los Angeles should be brought to New York for training, and it wasn't long after I'd arrived in Manhattan that I began getting important assignments thanks to Dirck. Halstead had been a star shooter for UPI for years, and I was enormously flattered that he chose to share some of the best jobs with me. He also introduced me to first-class travel, and McCarty once said that Dirck and I were the only two guys in the company whose expense accounts he approved with his eyes shut. (Our expense accounts were nothing compared to the one submitted by an enterprising journalist after the India-Pakistan war. It included this singular item: "Funeral for interpreter: $300.")

"Where's the action?" Dirck asked.

"Highway 13, the road to An Loc," I told him as we jumped aboard an old Ford driven by Tran Van Tam and headed toward Highway 13. With us was Leon Daniel, a UPI newsman who is one of the bravest and most honest correspondents I know, and also one of the best writers. (A former Marine, Leon was shot in the leg during the Korean War and still limps because of his old wound.) We stopped en route to photograph South Vietnamese armored vehicles heading for a tree line. As we stood alongside our car, chatting idly, a bullet glanced off the pavement near Leon's good leg. We all hit the deck.

Two other newsmen, who'd arrived minutes behind us in a white Toyota, decided to depart. A B-40 rocket blew up where their car had stood seconds before. We screamed for Tam to take off in our car, and then we ran toward the ARVN, who were by now returning fire. Mortar rounds were crashing all around us, and it didn't take long to discover we were surrounded.

Intense fire from the NVA kept us pinned down for some time. A score or more ARVN troops were killed, and many were wounded. One soldier lay near me bleeding to death—his genitals had been shot off. Communist troops were so close we could see them running across the road. One South Vietnamese soldier pointed in their direction and started babbling, "Beaucoup V.C., beaucoup V.C." "*Shoot* the sons-of-bitches, don't just *stand* there!" a U.S. advisor shouted at the excited soldier.

We'd been pinned down for better than two hours when the first air strikes came in, directed by an ARVN major. To mark his position he would set off a smoke grenade and then report to the aircraft what color it was so that the pilots wouldn't bomb us by accident. The NVA, who had their radios tuned to our frequency, started lobbing their own smoke grenades. This greatly confused the pilots, who could see nothing but smoke, and didn't know whose smoke was whose. The South Vietnamese major was no idiot, however. Just before one bombing run he announced he'd dropped smoke. The pilot said he saw it. "Good, bomb that smoke. I no drop any!" shouted the gleeful major into his radio. The firing finally died down, and we tried to relax. By this time it was raining and all of us were covered with mud. I crawled over to Halstead and asked if this was what he'd had in mind by way of action. "Not exactly," he said wryly, "but then you never do anything in moderation, Kennerly." Wet and shaken, we were wondering how we were going to get back to Saigon when Tam suddenly appeared driving like the proverbial bat out of hell. We could have kissed him for coming back, but chose instead to celebrate by buying him a few beers when we got back to the bureau.

There were times during my year in Vietnam when I *knew* I was going to die. Like the time I went up Highway 13 with Art Higbee, a UPI correspondent who'd just arrived in the country and wanted a taste of the action, and Bob Wiener, an ABC radio reporter who had been around awhile and who, like me, could take the action or leave it. Preferably leave it.

Shell holes are by definition ugly, but at times they seemed the most beautiful places on earth. Art, Bob, and I developed a particular affection for one such hole just outside a firebase on Highway 13, not far from the spot where Dirck and I had been caught in the firefight the week before. We were walking up the highway when the firebase came under a heavy rocket and mortar attack. It was by then my habit to keep an eye peeled at all times for depressions in the ground—I've yet to see one deep enough—so I'd spotted the crater. All three of us adopted it at the same instant, and for a few minutes we were nothing but a tangle of arms and legs as we clawed for the bottom.

The bad guys were so close you could hear the reports from

their mortar tubes before the rounds landed. The memory of the soldier with no balls left whom I'd seen the week before flashed through my mind. I casually placed my flak jacket over that sensitive area. I would rather have lost my head. I knew I was going to die. One of those rockets was going to land squarely on us, and for one day we'd make news instead of recording it. But it was not to be. Once again a speeding vehicle saved our hides. A jeep had somehow driven right into the middle of the barrage. "Hi," said the U.S. advisor at the wheel. "What're you guys doing out here in the middle of all this shit?"

To fully understand why the highway with the unlucky number proved so much of a problem, you have to appreciate that it went to An Loc. An Loc was a hamlet that had been surrounded since the first day of the 1972 North Vietnamese offensive, and most of its inhabitants were living in bunkers underground. Some American advisors were also trapped there. To cheer them up, Lieutenant Tom Waskow, a Forward Air Control (FAC) pilot, took to circling over the town and reading *Stars and Stripes* on the two-way radio—when he wasn't directing airstrikes.

I tagged along with Waskow one day, trying to get some aerial shots of the besieged town. As we approached An Loc one of the trapped Americans called in. "What's weird Jane up to today?" he asked. The previous day Waskow had read them a story about actress Jane Fonda's statements in support of the very troops then laying siege to An Loc. Waskow supplied an update.

"Hey," I interrupted, "the V.C. are shooting at us!" Tracers were snaking their way toward our slow, twin prop observation plane. As I spoke, Waskow banked over and headed right at them. He fired two smoke rockets, and seconds later an F-4 Phantom jet streaked by and unloaded several 500-pound bombs on the unfortunate gunners. There were two secondary explosions, and the V.C. guns fell silent. An Loc was being systematically destroyed, both by NVA shelling and by our own bombs. *Life* ran a two-page photo of the demolished town with this headline, quoting an American advisor: "It became necessary to destroy An Loc in order to save it."

(Text continues on page 89)

THE ASIAN WARS

WILLIE VICOY

"The only trees left standing were pathetic sticks..."

ABOVE: *Soldiers run from a helicopter during combat assault near the A Shau Valley, Military Region I, Vietnam, 1971.* RIGHT: *Dying Vietnamese soldier in a field alongside Highway 13, 1972.*

Weary soldier near Khe Sahn, Vietnam, 1971.

OVERLEAF, LEFT: *Soldier makes his way through heavy foliage outside Hue, Vietnam, 1971.* RIGHT: *GIs take a break at LZ Hotlips, Military Region I, Vietnam, 1971.*

BELOW: *Wounded South Vietnamese soldier; Central Highlands, 1971.* RIGHT: *A Cambodian mercenary, his wooden leg in front of him, protests unfair treatment by the South Vietnamese government; Saigon, 1971.*

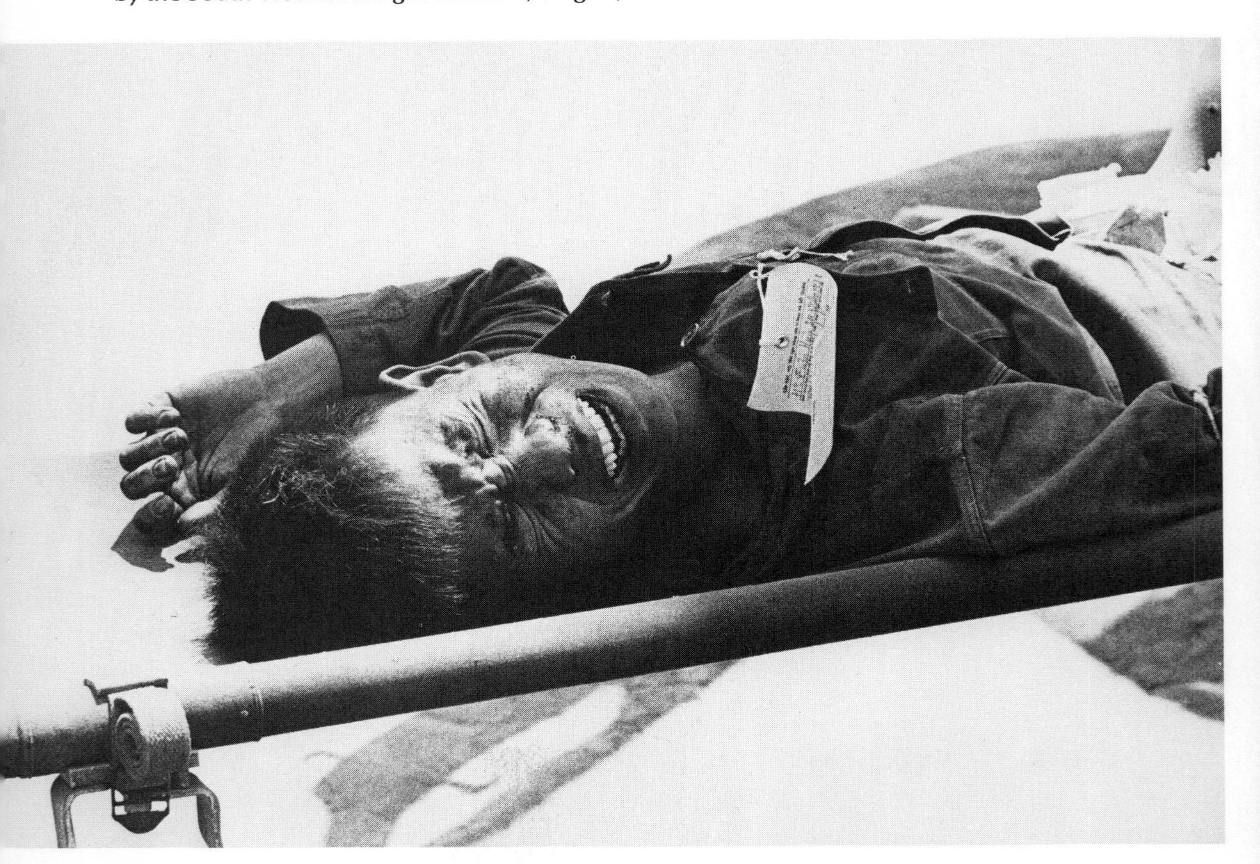

SAiGON
41

ABOVE: *South Vietnamese soldier at Lai Khe, 1972.*
LEFT: *Viet Cong soldier followed by two young boys in their village south of Saigon, 1973.*

BELOW: *American prisoners of war standing at attention in their cell in the "Hanoi Hilton," North Vietnam, 1973.* RIGHT: *POW Agnew waits for his name to be called.*

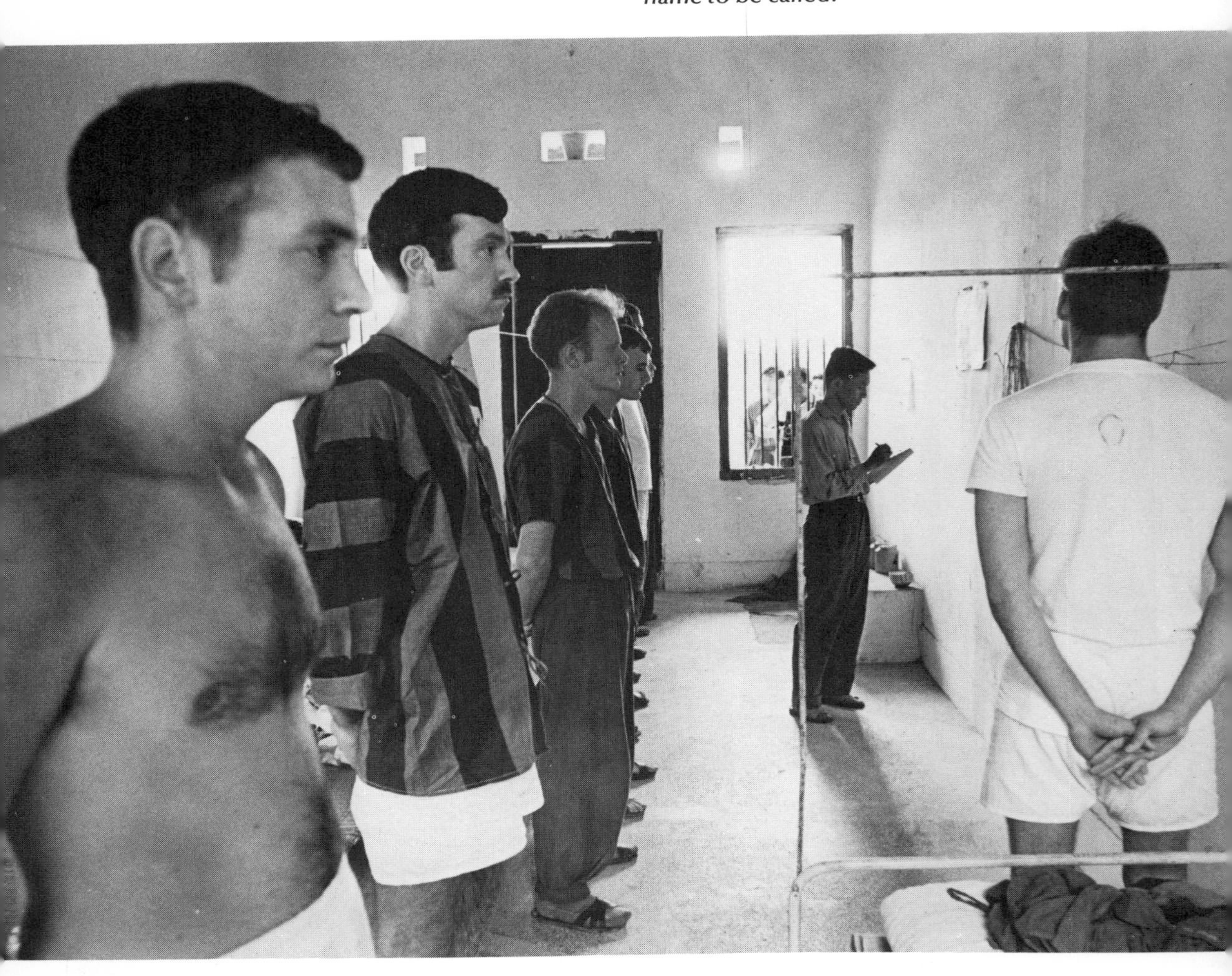

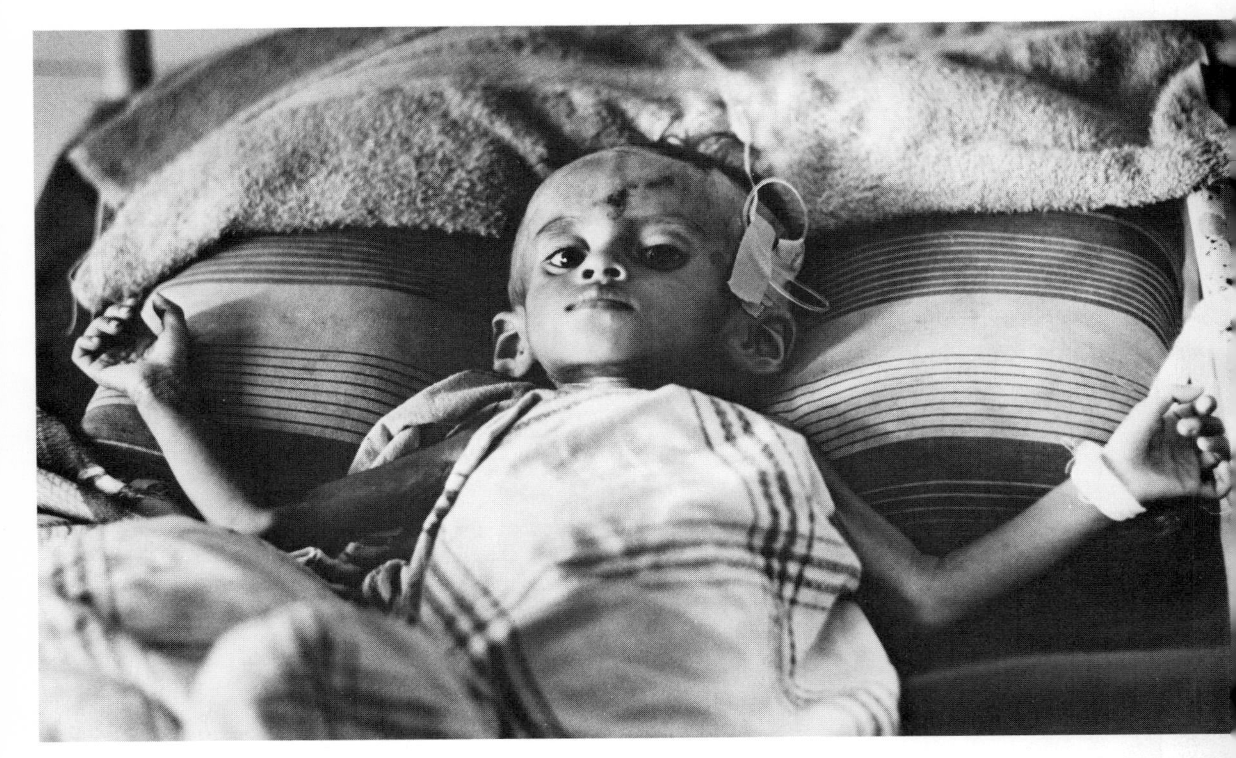

ABOVE: *A Cambodian child dying of malnutrition in Phnom Penh hospital, 1975.* RIGHT: *A Cambodian refugee girl, her eyes vacant of hope; Phnom Penh, 1975.*

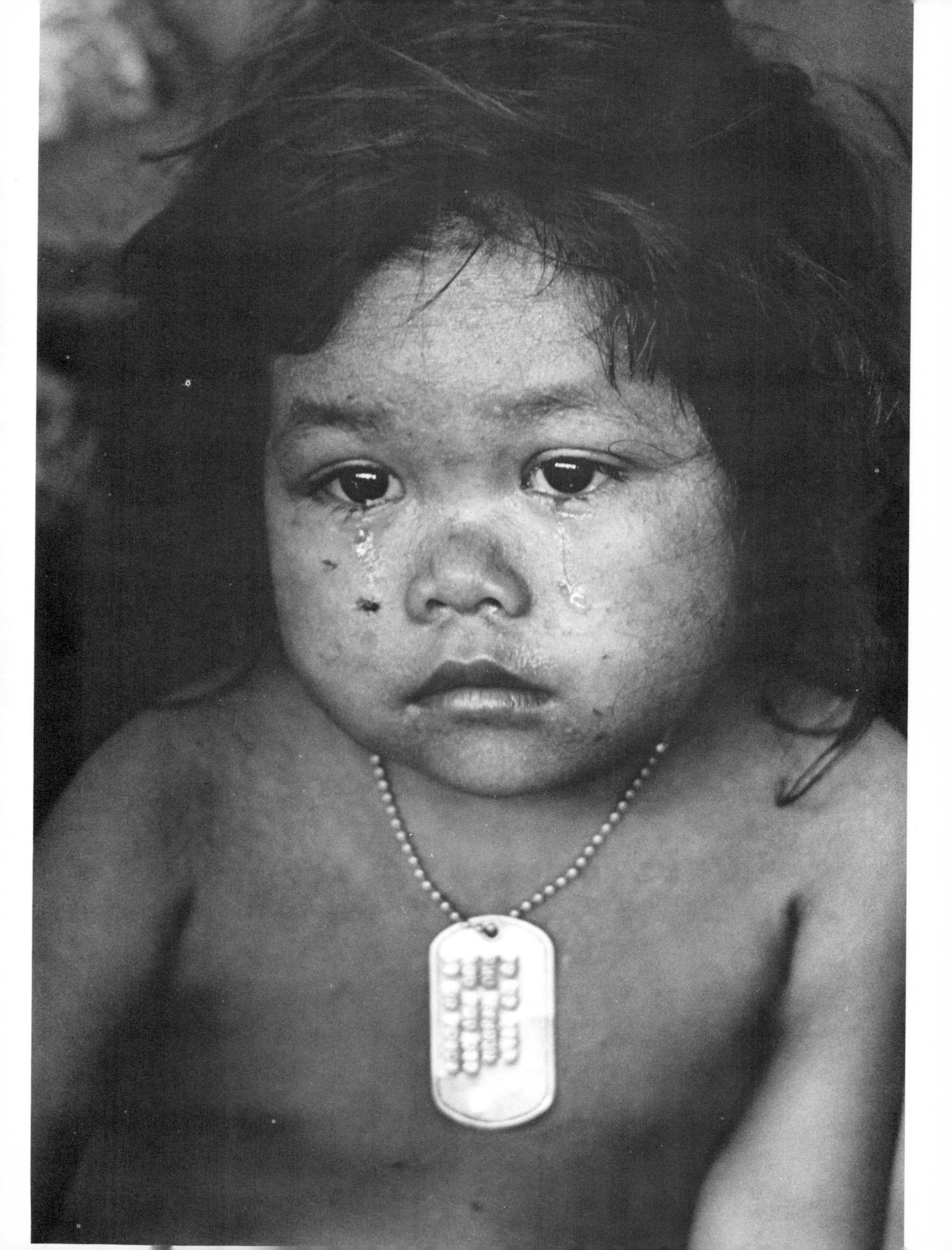

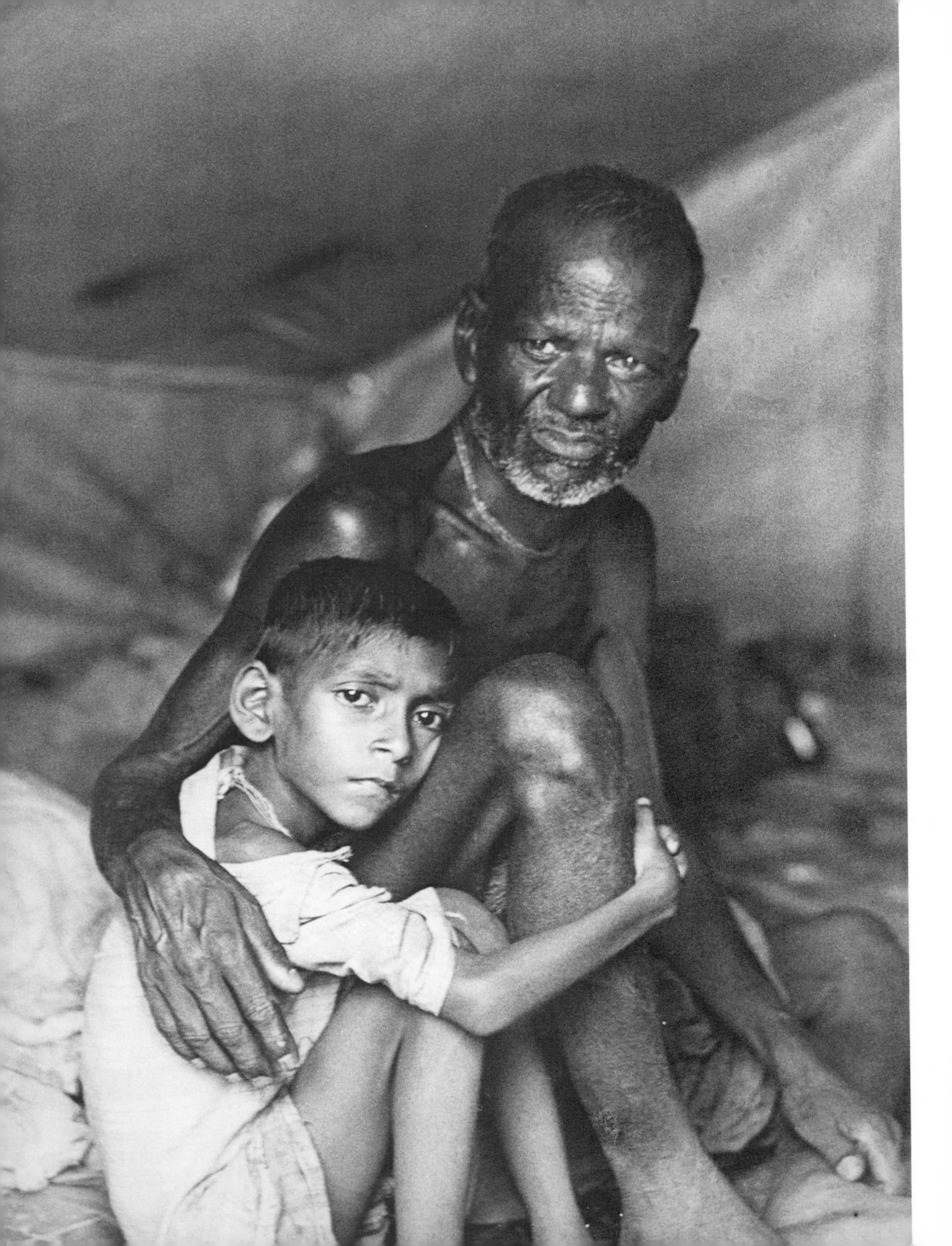

Refugees from East Pakistan in camp outside Calcutta, 1971.

Old Friends, New Duties

IT WAS AUGUST, 1972. I hadn't been back to the States for almost a year and a half, and my younger sister's wedding provided the perfect excuse to return. I felt both exhilarated and a bit silly when I found myself, some days later, driving down a small country road and *not* worrying about being ambushed. I remembered my high school days, when racing down such roads was the only danger.

The wedding ceremony had already started by the time I arrived. I parked the car on a hill overlooking the beautiful park site Chris had chosen for her marriage. I hadn't told anyone I was coming, and didn't want to break up the proceedings. After the ceremony itself was over and guests were kissing the bride, I walked down the small hill toward the group. Jane and Anne, my other two sisters, spotted me first and shrieked. All was bedlam as our family, together for the first time in so long, hugged and kissed. After spending a few days reacquainting myself with family and old friends, I left for New York to look for a new job.

I had reached a plateau at the UPI bureau in Saigon. I had done all I could for their operation and fully explored the job's potential. It was time for a change—for the bureau's sake as well as my own—and so I headed east again, having decided weeks before that it was time to talk to Time-Life about working for them. For as long as I could remember, being a photographer for either *Life* or *Look* had been a specific dream of mine. And now it seemed as if that dream might just come true.

While I was in New York I attended a huge party that Time, Inc. gave on a boat sailing around Manhattan. Despite the lighthearted mood of the party, I found I was melancholy. Dirck Halstead, who was with me, understood my feelings. I found myself thinking, "Look at all these people, laughing and drinking while others are dying in Vietnam." The same thing happened a few days later in Washington, where Ron and Dina Bennett gave a bash in my honor. I spent most of the evening sitting on their front steps, talking about the war with Bill Snead, who had once been UPI pictures manager. It was Snead who articulated what I was feeling: culture shock, amounting almost to fear, at being back in the States, coupled with a sense that nothing was truly significant unless it had to do with the war in Indochina. I cut short my stay and headed back to Asia.

My last UPI assignment was on October 1, 1972. Charlie Smith of UPI, John Roderick of AP, and I were the only Americans permitted to accompany Japanese Prime Minister Tanaka on his historic trip to mainland China. John had covered Mao Tse-tung on the Great March, but this was the first time either Charlie or I had been to the People's Republic. (Charlie, a veteran China watcher, had been reporting second hand on events on the mainland for years.) The border crossing was simple enough—we walked across a covered wooden bridge from Kowloon and entered the People's Republic of China—but the effect was extraordinary. It was like entering another world. Green-clothed soldiers carrying AK-47 rifles were posted at the far end of the bridge. One of them checked Charlie's passport and found it contained a visa for Taiwan. An argument ensued. He wanted Charlie to cut it out. Charlie refused, and was told he couldn't enter the country unless he complied. It was finally agreed that Charlie would cross out the offending visa, and with this last hurdle cleared we proceeded to the train station.

One of the first things that struck me was that most of the train engines were ancient, albeit in immaculate shape. The train we took to Canton was considerably more modern, and the countryside fairly flew past our windows. As the scenery slid by, I observed hundreds upon hundreds of peasants working in the fields. Chinese agricultural methods have changed very little in thousands of years. Planting and harvesting is still done in the traditional manner—by hand—perhaps because the old way works so well in China. The area between the border and Canton was green and lush.

At Canton we switched to an old propeller-driven Soviet Ilyushin for the flight north to Peking. The aircraft itself may have been old and slow, but the service on board more than compensated: "dinner" consisted of a single apple and hot tea. After making six stops over a period of several long hours, we at last arrived in China's capital. We found the streets of Peking thronged with people, most of them dressed in the plain clothes of the revolution. There were buses, trucks, and bicycles by the thousands, but very few private autos. Those belonged to high-ranking Chinese officials.

The Chinese have reason to dislike the Japanese more than the Americans because of the Japanese occupation of China in World War II, and in its own way Tanaka's visit was of greater historic significance than Nixon's. During that war the Japanese army had slaughtered countless Chinese, both military and civilian. This the Chinese were disinclined to forgive or forget.

During his brief stay Tanaka visited all the traditional tourist attractions. So, of course, did I. The Forbidden City, once the preserve of China's sacred emperor, was now overrun by plebians eager to inspect how the nobility had lived before the revolution. The palace was now a museum, but it had lost little of its grandeur, although no place on earth is very forbidding when you're part of an entourage of almost three hundred people. At the Great Wall, whose sloping thirty-foot-high walls snake for 3,500 miles across China's northwest frontier, I found myself unable to put President Nixon's remark out of my mind. Shown the Great Wall by his Chinese hosts during his state visit, Nixon allowed, "Yes, it's truly a great wall." My Chinese escorts must have wondered why I suddenly burst out laughing as I admired their premier tourist attraction.

While I was photographing Tanaka leaving the Ming Tombs, I ran afoul of the authorities for the first time. Unable to get the shots I wanted from what they deemed a proper distance, I closed in. The closer I got, the more nervous they got. I felt a series of sharp tugs on my camera strap, but I kept shooting. The final tug, stronger than the rest, pulled me off balance, and that was the end of the picture taking. I ran on ahead with a smile on my face. I had the pictures I needed.

That night, at the Great Hall of the People, the principal state banquet facility, a similar episode occurred. When Chou En-lai entered the room I was informed that I couldn't take pictures for reasons I was never to find out. "But everyone else is," I protested. "Not you," my escort declared. Thwarted, I immediately switched my attentions to a Chinese general who had just walked in, trying to make it appear that I already knew him. I made motions to my escort intended to suggest that it was okay for me to shoot. The general happened to be nodding his head up and down at that very moment, and my escort, who obviously wanted no trouble with his superiors, gave me the go-ahead. My conversation with the general was no more intimate than "nice weather we're having," but it did allow me to draw nearer to Chou En-lai, a man of formidable presence. Chou's eyes belied his frail physique. They were not unkind, but they had a certain cold resolve.

There are normally two toasts at a state banquet, the first made by the host, the second by his guest. When the Chinese toast, they do so with small glasses of mao tai, a very potent liqueur, and guests follow suit. The Japanese, however, use tiny porcelain cups filled with sake for their salutes. This created an embarrassing situation. After the Chinese leader's speech he raised his glass, and the prime minister raised his cup. Chou Enlai did not drink, but kept pointing to the small glass of mao tai at Tanaka's place. The latter eventually realized his mistake, and switched glasses. He choked audibly on the powerful liquid, and this only added to his embarrassment. A small thing, but to the protocol-conscious Japanese leader, it was a painful blunder.

My great wish was to photograph Mao Tse-tung. It wasn't granted. No foreign photographer had taken his picture for more than a decade and I was not to be the first. The Chinese controlled access to their leader so completely that only visiting heads of state were able to see him, and the pictures that were released of those meetings were carefully doctored so that Mao looked healthy. This led to idle conjecture among the press corps that Mao had been dead for several years, and that dignitaries were being greeted by a Mao look-alike. Even so I was bitterly disappointed that I never got to photograph Mao.

One aspect of the trip that wasn't planned, and that had nothing to do with Tanaka's state visit, was the appearance of three U.S. prisoners of war passing through Peking after their release by the North Vietnamese. When word got out that they would be coming through Peking airport, foreign newsmen rushed out there. This greatly dismayed the Chinese, but we were so determined to cover the event we managed to dodge them and make it to the air terminal in time. These were the first Americans to be released by the Vietnamese—a singularly newsworthy event.

Shanghai was the second stop on Tanaka's itinerary, and John Roderick was especially excited about visiting the old port city. He'd lived there in the 1950's as a correspondent for the AP, and during our stopover we visited the building he'd lived in, the tallest in Shanghai. As far as the eye could see, red flags waved from the tops of the buildings in honor of the Japanese prime minister's visit.

Charlie Smith, our traveling companion, was originally from Alabama. He spoke in a high-pitched voice that audio people in New York had long ago told him could never be used for radio reporting. Suddenly they wanted his reports very badly, and Charlie wasn't at all sure he was going to cooperate. "For ten years those sons-of-bitches wouldn't use me, and now they're calling every five minutes for a radio feed," he chortled. He did supply the broadcasts, and loved every minute of it.

Tanaka's last night in China provided the occasion for yet another banquet. I was seated with a group of Chinese cameramen and photographers who obviously enjoyed their drink. Each time a speaker would say something that prompted applause, we would all raise our glasses and throw back another mao tai. (Mao tai is over 100 proof and has a smell similar to formaldehyde.) The gentleman seated across from me decided to turn the event into a full-scale drinking contest, and in between the regular toasts he would stand, raise his glass to me, and propose a greeting to my president, my country, my parents, my employers. Tradition dictated that I say "Gambay" afterwards. Tradition also dictated that I follow each of his toasts with one of my own, drain my glass, and place it upside down on the table. Between the official salutes at the head table and the unofficial ones at our own, I was rapidly getting loaded. My friend across the table became two friends across the table, but I was determined not to quit. At the end of the meal, he arose, staggered over to my chair, put a hand on my shoulder, looked at me through glazed-over eyes, and then just shook his head. The last I saw of him, he was weaving his way toward the door. "Gambay" I said, raising my glass for the last time.

Tanaka returned to Japan, but Charlie and I stayed on through the Communist Chinese National Day, October 1. To celebrate, the authorities had scheduled several activities, including a huge rally held in People's Park in the middle of Shanghai. A play was performed on the vast stage of an outdoor theater. Its high point was the bayonetting of an "American imperialist soldier" by a victorious Chinese trooper. As the "American" fell I looked around me. The multitudes were clapping and laughing with gusto. Charlie and I decided to split.

This single incident aside, our treatment by the Chinese people during this visit couldn't have been more cordial. Little children approached me on the street, pointed, and laughed. They had seen very few Americans and fewer bearded ones, so I was a great novelty. As Charlie and I strode down the streets that had been blocked off for the festivities, scores of people trailed along behind us. When we'd gathered several hundred followers, we would wheel around and walk in the other direction. This created mass confusion as people stumbled over each other in their haste to change course and avoid colliding with us. We knew what the Pied Piper must have felt like.

Before I left the Chinese mainland I telephoned my eighty-year-old grandmother in Roseburg, Oregon. When the call finally went through, I greeted her and immediately told her where I was. "Shanghai!" she exclaimed. "Have you been kidnapped?"

My feelings about leaving UPI were mixed. The experience—the years in Los Angeles, New York, and, finally, Saigon—had been invaluable, and nearly all the people I'd worked with had encouraged my development as a photographer. But *Life* was where I had wanted to be for nearly as long as I had wanted to be a photographer, and I could hardly refuse their job offer. At 11 A.M. on October 5, 1972, my plane touched down in Saigon, and I stepped out into familiar surroundings but a new life.

My first assignment for the magazine was to cover Lieutenant Tom Waskow's last observation mission. After flying more than 900 hours of combat over Vietnam and Cambodia, Tom was due to be transferred home. His final flight was to be over An Loc, familiar territory to both of us. Some of Tom's associates back at Tan Son Nhut airbase suggested I carry a pistol with me, just in case, but I refused. "What are you going to do if you have to bail out in Indian country?" one of them asked. "If we can't stop them with a B-52 strike, I don't think this .38 is going to do me much good," I replied. Besides, I was adamantly opposed to newsmen carrying weapons at any time.

Once we reached An Loc, which was still under siege, we flew low over several NVA tanks that had been destroyed by American bombs. One had had its turret blown completely off. Waskow directed the air strike, and in the process raised a NVA officer, whom he called the "Red Colonel," on his radio. "Hi, Red Colonel," he said cheerily. "Why don't you let me know where you are so I can drop a few bombs on you?"

"No way," replied the North Vietnamese officer on his captured American radio. The conversation might have gone on in this way for some time except that we began to take ground fire. The NVA had a nasty habit of shooting a plane right after it pulled out of a rocket run. It was the only time the pilot couldn't see the enemy firing and call in an air strike on their position.

"If we get hit and have to bail out," Waskow said to me, "I'll count to three and you better be out that door." The door on my side happened to be the only means of exit for either of us.

"What if I'm not out of here by three?" I asked.

"Then there'll be boot prints on your lap," Tom responded.

To celebrate the completion of his last mission, Lt. Waskow

did a couple of barrel rolls over Tan Son Nhut. And when he arrived back at the hangar, the other pilots and their crews were waiting with champagne. Nearby was a trailer filled with water, also traditionally reserved for pilots completing their last flight. Waskow's comrades picked him up and unceremoniously dunked him in the water, flight suit and all. They then uncorked the champagne and the lieutenant took a big swig. He'd made it through the war.

John Saar, a onetime British Marine, was a writer for *Life* when I met him. He and I collaborated on one of the most ambitious projects the magazine ever attempted in Southeast Asia—a journey by automobile from the southern tip of Vietnam to the DMZ to photograph "Vietnam for *Life*." It was hardly the same thing as driving from Key Biscayne to Atlanta, although the distances are roughly the same. In the States the only potential problems are mechanical failure and local speed traps. In Vietnam, on the other hand, the difficulties included being shot at by the V.C., being shot accidentally by the ARVN, hitting a mine, finding that a road had disappeared overnight, drowning in a sudden storm, having your cameras and money stolen by thieves, and being flattened by a speeding tank.

Saar and I started from the hamlet of Cau Mau, which is about as far south as you can get in Vietnam without falling into the South China Sea. As we started north we found some areas inaccessible, generally due to the fact that the roads had been cut. But for the most part we were able to drive along our predetermined route. We'd decided to use local transportation instead of one car, feeling this would be safer. By using only vehicles normally seen on those roads we hoped to avoid detection by the V.C.

If I had a single overwhelming impression about our odyssey it was that you really don't see a place unless you can drive through it in a somewhat leisurely fashion. I have often suspected that if some of the pilots who bombed Vietnam with such apparent detachment had taken a closer look at the country, they might have had second thoughts. It once was an undeniably beautiful place.

From the rice paddies of the Delta we swung into teeming Saigon and up through the mountains to Da Lat. Da Lat is where most of the country's vegetables are grown. Its mean temperature is lower than that of the rest of the country. There we interviewed and photographed peasants working in the cabbage fields, and dined at one of the best restaurants in all of Asia, La Vie, run by French nuns who sang ballads during the meal. La Vie was a European oasis in the middle of the war zone.

From Da Lat we traveled toward the coast, passing makeshift villages set up by Montagnards, tribesmen who had lived for centuries in the Highlands. The war had forced them to flee their ancestral homeland.

We passed sugarcane fields, more rice paddies, and a beautiful Catholic church on a hill near Qui Nhon. It was there that things began to get uncomfortable. The road to Qui Nhon was closed at dusk, and I was not anxious to spend the night this side of the city. Driving through this area in the daytime was bad enough, but now nobody was around and I had the queasy feeling that we were being watched from the deepening shadows. Normally, Qui Nhon isn't a welcome sight. After years of use as a stockpile for war material it looked more like a huge junkyard than a human settlement, but we were glad to pull in there nonetheless. The very next day we headed for our final destination, Quang Tri.

There were hardly two bricks left together in that northern provincial capital, where saturation bombings and shellings had left the town a smoking rubble heap. As it happened I had driven through the same area in a white civilian jeep some weeks before. Our destination then had been a Marine command post. NVA spotters had picked out our movement and began shelling us with their long-range 130 mm guns. The first round exploded near the back of our jeep, and a red-hot piece of shrapnel punched through the back, passed between the driver and me, and blew a big hole in the windshield. As we ran toward a nearby bunker, another round hit so close that my ears rang for several hours. We encountered no hostile fire this time around, and I got the pictures I wanted, which topped off the assignment.

I was pleased with our story, and the editors back in New York were ecstatic, saying they planned to run at least twelve pages in color. They felt—and I agreed—that I deserved a few days off, so I took off for Hong Kong. Three days later, at seven-thirty in the morning, my phone rang. Bob Schnitzlein, then UPI's picture manager in Asia, was on the other end.

"What're you going to do for a job now?" he asked.

"I don't know what you're talking about," I answered sleepily.

"Now that *Life* folded," he said.

"It's too early for jokes, Bob," I mumbled angrily.

"No joke," he responded. "Look at this morning's paper." Sure enough, there it was. I'd been with *Life* a little over a month, and—poof!—the dream had vanished. Fortunately, my contract was split between *Life* and *Time,* which meant that I would go on working for the smaller-format publication. The story that Saar and I had worked on for so many weeks never ran. It was a final casualty when the magazine went under.

"If V.C. no kill you, maybe we will."

THE CEASE-FIRE IN VIETNAM produced more fighting than I'd ever seen. Both the NVA and the South Vietnamese government were trying desperately to grab as much territory as possible before—and immediately after—the cease-fire was officially announced. To mark their terrain the V.C. ran up red and blue flags, which must have seemed like a good idea at the time but made excellent targets for South Vietnamese bombers. The flags promptly came down.

A few weeks before the cease-fire was announced I covered some fierce action near a small village twenty-five miles south of

Saigon. ARVN officers had told me at the time that the area was almost solid V.C. I decided then that if a cease-fire was arranged I'd come back to get the first pictures of the Viet Cong in their own villages.

Joe Kamalick, a Westinghouse radio correspondent, drove back with me to that particular village the day after the cease-fire was announced. Viet Cong flags were flapping from the treetops only a few hundred yards from the road. Even for someone who had been in Vietnam for more than two years, this was a rare and exciting spectacle.

We turned off the highway towards the village and were immediately stopped by government soldiers. An arrogant young lieutenant announced, "You no go any further. V.C. chop you up, kill you." Joe and I insisted we weren't worried about the V.C. "If V.C. no kill you, maybe we will when you come out," said the officer with a menacing smile. I didn't like the odds and neither did Joe, who was pulling nervously at his mustache. We decided there might be some wisdom in what the lieutenant was saying and returned to Saigon empty-handed.

The following day Ngoc Anh, the senior Vietnamese staffer in UPI's Saigon bureau, drove Jeff Taylor and me back to the V.C. village. With us was Mr. Tam, our interpreter. This time we found plenty of V.C. flags and no ARVN troops. Anh dropped us off. Taylor, Tam, and I ran like hell toward a small hut with a South Vietnamese flag painted on the door. We waited a few minutes to make sure we hadn't been spotted by ARVN, and then headed inland. The next building we came to had nothing painted on it, and we figured that this was the line between government and Communist-held land. We were right.

While Jeff and I waited, Tam went off to find us a V.C. guide. He was taking a terrible risk by guiding us to the V.C.; if government soldiers had caught him, they might well have thrown him in jail, and there would have been nothing we could do about it. A few minutes later, Tam showed up with an old, bearded man dressed in white and wearing a pith helmet. Tam said anxiously, "Hurry. This man will take us where you want to go."

With considerable apprehension Jeff and I set off after Tam and the elderly man. "Do you see what I see?" I asked Jeff, who nodded. The tree line contained several sets of eyes, all focused on us. "V.C.," we whispered to each other. (We later agreed that terror and exhilaration had gripped us simultaneously at that moment.) Our walk across the open rice paddy and toward the trees seemed to take hours, although it couldn't have lasted more than a few minutes.

Two young men appeared out of the dense undergrowth and motioned for us to follow them. We were led to another hut and invited to come inside. Tam translated: Would we care for tea? There were several people in the dark room, none of them smiling. Tam looked edgy as we sat sipping tea. The V.C. made no effort at communication, and Jeff and I had no notion of how to open the conversation. For an hour Jeff and I became adept at exchanging nervous glances. Suddenly a small child ran into our hut, and all at once our hosts started talking to each other. "Something's about to happen," Tam advised. Several men materialized out of the jungle, all carrying weapons. This was the real thing. The leader, a man in his thirties who wore a blue tunic, approached us. At his waist was the Chinese-made pistol worn only by Viet Cong officers. As he walked toward us, our grim-faced hosts surrounded us, and the recently arrived V.C. troopers with the rifles fanned out around the area.

"Holy shit, we've had it," I whispered to Jeff out of the side of my mouth. The man in the blue tunic looked me right in the eye, smiled, and grabbed one of my hands with both of his. As if on cue, everyone else began smiling and laughing. The officer, Lieutenant Tu Phung, insisted on posing for a picture between Jeff and me, holding one of our hands in each of his while Tam took the photo. Lieutenant Phung then beckoned us to follow him and his men. We left the clearing and slipped onto a jungle path. Their village was less than a mile away. Not only were V.C. flags painted on their thatched-roof houses, they flew overhead as well. It had somehow never occurred to me that the V.C. lived in regular villages and had wives and children.

We spent several hours touring that and several neighboring hamlets. Each place was immaculate and children were everywhere. At one of our stops I noticed several teenage girls carrying weapons. Only later did I learn that they were regular Viet Cong soldiers. We watched training exercises in which young soldiers ran around with AK-47 rifles and B-40 rocket launchers. (A few of them carried captured American M-16s. It was the first time I'd been on the receiving end of those particular weapons.) Political cadres carrying flags led groups of children around; speeches were made in a small square.

"What country do you come from?" I was asked. Jeff and I both decided we couldn't duck the question, and I replied, "America." "You are welcome here," my questioner said. "Why haven't you come before?" I tried to explain that differences between the government in Saigon and that in Hanoi had proved a remarkably effective deterrent, but discovered there was no animosity toward us. Lieutenant Phung mentioned in passing that there was always the danger of a jet swooping out of the clouds and dropping napalm, and for the first time I appreciated what it must have been like to live under the constant threat of attack.

It was about that time that I started glancing at my watch, because we had to get back to Saigon with our photos. The lieutenant asked us to stay, and I wanted to. To spend even a few days photographing the "enemy" would have been a unique opportunity, and Jeff and I bade him a reluctant farewell.

We walked back across the rice paddy to the road, and there discussed our next problem—how to get the film back to Saigon without being caught by the ARVN. There was something very bizarre about the whole situation; here we were, plotting how to elude our own side. Tam was genuinely worried about being arrested by government soldiers, but our meeting with the V.C. hadn't seemed to bother him at all—which led me to suspect he had good connections with them. But then most of the Vietnamese I knew had friends or relatives on the other side. Anh was waiting where we had left him, nervously checking his watch. (We'd told him to pick us up at an appointed hour, and to report us captured if we were late.) Stuffing the exposed film into our socks and drawers, we climbed into the car and started back toward Saigon.

In retrospect I don't know which made me the more nervous, walking across that paddy toward the V.C. or driving back to Saigon with the film. Ironically, *Time* never used any of my pictures—an occupational hazard in this business. Only a week before they had obtained photos of the Viet Cong from a source closer to the other side.

A couple of days later, Tam came to see me with tears rolling down his cheeks. "My sister and her children are at Tay Ninh, in the hospital, and there's much trouble there," he sobbed.

"What can I do to help?" I asked.

"Go with me to get them," he said when he could speak.

Tay Ninh is a place I'd decided *not* to visit that week, and for good reason. The road from Saigon to Tay Ninh had been cut and the V.C. had surrounded the town. "When do you want to leave?" I asked.

"Now."

"Okay," I sighed. "Let's go." I gathered up my cameras, helmet and flak jacket, and then called Joe Kamalick and Willie Vicoy to ask if they wanted to go along. It was usually good to have friends along on such an expedition. "Seems like a good day for a drive in the country," Joe replied.

We found traffic backed up at a roadblock outside Tay Ninh where a policeman was stopping all cars and notifying the occupants that there was fighting a half mile farther up the road. "We have to get to Tay Ninh," Tam insisted, and the Vietnamese cop let us proceed at our own risk. Tam swung his car around the barrier, and with Joe, Willie and me hunched under our helmets, gunned through the roadblock. We must have been doing 80 mph when the first shots rang out. I tried to get my whole body inside my helmet. The rounds cracked directly over the speeding car, but none hit us.

When we arrived safely in Tay Ninh, Tam headed for the hospital and I went to take pictures at a refugee camp in a Cao Dai temple. The Cao Dai were a sect that worshiped Martin Luther, among others, and in better times their extravagant temple had been a tourist attraction. Now it was filled with refugees from the countryside. Children were everywhere, many of them shouting "hoa bien," which means "peace." The sound of their young voices was periodically drowned out by the noise of bombs blowing up and shelling nearby.

Tam finally managed to locate his sister in the hospital, but she was too seriously hurt to be moved. Her house had taken a direct hit from a South Vietnamese bomb, two of her children had been killed outright, and she had been severely wounded. The other two youngsters were all right, so we took them back to Saigon in the car with us. I cradled her six-month-old baby in my lap on the return trip, and as we again approached the V.C. ambush point I wrapped the child in my flak jacket and put my helmet over her exposed head. Once again Tam stepped on the gas and we skittered through the hostile area. Again the shots were high, so our precious cargo was delivered intact to Saigon.

Later that same week I flew to Vientiane, Laos, in an attempt to get into Hanoi for the release of American P.O.W.'s. Walter Cronkite was staying at the same hotel for the same reason. He was none too pleased to see me, having thought he was going to get an exclusive on the P.O.W. release.

For a time it looked as though no one would get a story, let alone an exclusive. I spent three days hanging around in Vientiane before approval finally came through from the North Vietnamese for the flight to Hanoi.

Aboard the chartered aircraft were representatives of the three networks, several newspapers, the wire services, Roy Rowan, who was *Time's* Hong Kong bureau chief at the time, and me. Roy was an old Asia hand who had been one of the last Americans expelled from China during the Great Cultural Revolution of 1967. I had established a close rapport with Roy when we first met in Hong Kong.

North Vietnam, like mainland China, was an enigma to most foreigners, particularly those who had been covering the war in the south. "Beaucoup V.C.," dryly noted Joe Fried, the *New York Daily News* correspondent, when we stepped off the plane at Hanoi's Gia Lam airport. We were herded onto a bus for the drive downtown. Throughout that drive, on either side of the road leading into the heart of Hanoi, were signs of the American bombings. A railroad repair yard near the airport had been hit recently; one big train engine still stood on end. As far as we could tell, precision bombing had taken out only military targets; the downtown section of the former French colonial city was untouched. The North Vietnamese weren't immune to curiosity, however. As we rolled into the center of Hanoi a citizen on a bicycle became so enthralled with the busload of "round eyes"—Westerners—so that he ran into the back of a truck that was inching through the crowded streets.

The North Vietnamese dropped us at a hotel that once had been called the Metropole. We were ushered inside for a lunch of beer and bananas. Then our Communist hosts drove us to the infamous "Hanoi Hilton," the tropical-style prison where the American POW's were being held. Thousands of civilians were crowded around the entrance, apparently to witness the departure of the last prisoners.

The main building was in good repair, and the cells we were shown appeared adequate. I assumed—and POW reports later confirmed—that what we had seen was a showcase and by no means reflected the actual accommodations. One jailer was taking roll call in a cell block as we passed by, so I shot a few frames through an open window. As I did so a downed American airman whispered to me, "Got any cigarettes?"

I nodded. "What are they?" he asked, and when I said Winstons he responded: "Sweet Jesus. Do you mind if I have one? I haven't smoked an American cigarette in years." I shoved the pack through the bars and was immediately spotted by a North Vietnamese officer, who started yelling at me. While the incensed jailer was reading me the riot act—in Vietnamese—the

American prisoner deftly hid the cigarette pack under his mattress. I looked straight at the guard, gave him my biggest, most disarming smile and told him—in English—to go screw himself. Fortunately, that was the end of the incident.

One of the most moving moments of the day occurred when one prisoner, tears streaming down his face, said he didn't believe he was really going to be released until he saw Walter Cronkite. Only then did he know it was true. Cronkite and I were at the airport that afternoon to witness a final bit of psychological torture, North Vietnamese-style. As the names of prisoners were read off, they crossed over to where American officers were waiting to receive them, saluted, and boarded a waiting U.S. Air Force transport plane. But the cadence was one name every sixty seconds—until they reached the last name. For five minutes he stood there alone, his hands clenched at his side and his eyes squeezed shut. Finally the loudspeaker blared out his name: "Agnew!" Only the Vietnamese laughed.

All of Asia was my beat. After more than two years in Saigon I felt it was time to move to a calmer, more centrally located place. I chose Bangkok, the capital of Thailand, for many reasons, among them the fact that it is the geographical hub of Southeast Asia. From Bangkok it is a convenient plane ride to India, Malaysia, Indonesia, Burma, and Borneo. It was to the island of Borneo—or, more properly, to Sabah, West Malaysia—that I soon went in pursuit of a story on gunrunning. Working with me was an American writer who was new to Asia. We managed to discover that guns were indeed being shipped from somewhere in Sabah to Communist rebels in Mindanao Province in the Philippines, but there was no way to do the story. Nobody wanted to talk to us, and one contact, who knew the scene intimately, said we'd surely be killed if we pursued the story further. Rather than write off the whole trip, we looked for something else to do and ended up jouncing several hundred miles in a Land Rover over a bumpy, dusty road from Kota Kinabalu to Sandakan. The trip took over ten hours and practically shook us to death.

At our destination on the Sulu Sea, a man told us about a government-sponsored rehabilitation center for orangutans in a nearby jungle. And what, we wondered, was a rehabilitation center for orangutans? "It's where orangs that have been kept in captivity are gradually reacclimated to life in the wild," the man informed us. Almost as interesting, in its way, as gunrunning—or so we thought. We got back in the Rover and headed into the interior. Twenty-five miles from nowhere we found the center.

The orangutans were in fact free, but they seemed content to remain in the area, where an attendant fed them daily. There were plenty of primates around. The large, red-haired animals swung from the branches of the taller trees and looked down at us from above. Suddenly one particularly curious female, her baby in tow, swung down for a closer look. The writer, who was a tall blonde woman, tried to get close enough to mother and child for a picture. The keeper had warned us that female orangs with babies sometimes get jealous of other females, even the human variety, but my companion had forgotten his remark.

The lady orang, however, had not. Without any warning she reached out with an arm as strong as steel and grabbed the reporter by the leg. As she toppled to the ground, screaming, the orang bit her leg.

At this point I dropped my cameras and tried to pull the beast off her. With the keeper's help we finally got her free, but she was in shock. "All I could think of as it bit me," she said later, "was that my toes [protected only by flimsy sandals] looked like little bananas." Luckily, the wound on her leg wasn't serious, and she was more frightened than hurt. The incident did leave her with a bite-shaped scar, however. "What a great story this will make at New York cocktail parties," she said when she'd recovered. "When someone asks me what happened to my leg I'll just tell them I was attacked by a wild orangutan in the middle of the jungle in Borneo."

Bangkok, often referred to as the Los Angeles of the Orient, is a sprawling, dirty, noisy city. The drivers are maniacs, but the food is good and there are great sights to see, including some magnificent temples. One of the prime attractions for males visiting Bangkok—an attraction not listed in any English-language guide book—is the city's red-light district. Walk into one of its many massage parlors and you will be greeted by dozens of pretty girls, all dressed in white, all wearing numbers, and all seated in small rooms behind one-way mirrors. You pick a number, and she is yours for an hour. A massage, as you might guess, is only the most basic of the services offered, with each additional request carrying a supplemental tariff.

My apartment was about three miles from the center of town. Out my back window was a rice paddy where farmers labored daily. All in all, quite a change from the hustle of the city.

At the time, April of 1973, I was heavily involved with a red-haired Parisian model to whom Roy Rowan had introduced me in Hong Kong, where she was modeling for a month in a hotel fashion show. We had spent the next few weeks roaming the British Crown Colony, riding the ferry one day to the Portuguese island colony of Macao. We gambled in the casinos, then climbed the hills of Hong Kong, and finally flew to my newly acquired apartment in Bangkok. Then something happened. She departed. Disconsolate and not caring what happened to me, I flew to Phnom Penh, the capital of Cambodia, determined to get myself into the thick of the war there.

Cambodia at the time was an extremely dangerous place. More newsmen had been killed or had disappeared on assignment there than anywhere else in Southeast Asia; the barbarity of the Khmer Rouge was legendary. One of their pastimes, it was rumored, was eating the heart and liver of a slain enemy.

In Cambodia it was possible to go to the action by chauffeured Mercedes. The problem was that no one was quite sure where the action was—and many of those who did manage to find it never came back.

Fighting was raging all around Phnom Penh when I arrived, even across the river from the presidential palace, formerly Prince Sihanouk's residence. You could actually sit on your hotel verandah, sip a drink, and watch the bombing.

The day after I arrived I hired a Mercedes and headed down the highway. Cambodian drivers, great believers in fate, would take you anywhere, convinced that they would survive if they were meant to survive. We hadn't gone ten miles when I tapped the driver and motioned for him to turn around. Something was wrong, and I had just figured out what it was: I didn't want to get killed for a love affair gone bad. And killed was what newsmen got by driving heedlessly down those roads. The fever had broken; I felt much better.

When I returned to my hotel I joined several correspondents sitting around the swimming pool. One mentioned Bob Sullivan, a UPI writer who had worked out of Cambodia for several months. Sully had gone off one day to buy some money on the black market. (In those days it was almost impossible to get it legally.) Inflation was so bad at the time that what he brought back was a big paper bag filled with Cambodian riels, which he dumped on the table before him. After stacking the money in a big pile he said, eyes gleaming, "These *are* the good old days."

The more I thought about it the more I appreciated that two things had died on that lonely road outside Phnom Penh—my infatuation for a certain model and my enthusiasm for war reporting in general. It was time for a change of venue. When I got back to Bangkok I requested a transfer to Paris, which *Time* granted. I soon settled temporarily into an apartment on the Avenue President Wilson, enjoying the view it afforded of the Eiffel Tower and preparing to investigate a new city when a message arrived from *Time* in New York: "Cover conflict in Mozambique." Reluctantly, I agreed to go. War was becoming a habit. "Will it never end?" I mumbled to myself on the way to the airport. "*Je ne comprend pas anglais,*" said the cabby.

Mozambique is a physically striking country that contains some of the best game preserves in Africa. Its scenery is so breathtaking that it is a favorite of film crews, who do location work there. One of these was being filmed in the lower part of the country while I was there. Up north was a war that wasn't a Hollywood production.

Because Mozambique was a Portuguese colony, the clashes involved regular Portuguese army troops and local insurgents. The action, like guerrilla action everywhere, was hit-and-run attacks on trains, convoys, and isolated villages. There were never any full-scale battles, so I had to dig up stories where I could. I traveled north alone, taking a train from Nampula to Vila Cabral, a distance of some hundred miles. This particular train had been blown up at least once a month and was attacked by small bands of insurgents more frequently than that. Flatcars were hitched in front of the engine so that they, and not the locomotive itself, would blow up if the train hit a mine.

I had two choices: to ride in the caboose or crouch on a flatcar with the Portuguese soldiers. I figured that if I rode in the caboose and nothing happened, I'd get no pictures at all. On the other hand, if I rode on the flatcar and it blew up, I wouldn't get any pictures either, but then it wouldn't matter. I chose to ride in front of the engine.

I didn't know any Portuguese, and the soldiers on the flatcar didn't speak English. Every few miles the train stopped in a small village and the soldiers changed shifts, some getting on, others off. The men who got off would point at me and say something, whereupon the new soldiers would laugh and shake their heads. I wasn't sure I liked being the butt of their private joke, but their laughter was somehow reassuring.

The train was a genuine local. Anyone walking along the track could flag it down. Day turned into night as we jolted along, and the soldiers began to get nervous. The next time the guard changed, the men who got on were neither smiling nor joking. Something was clearly going on, but I had no idea what it was. The soldiers were traveling with their guns at the ready, and I was crouched down with them, wishing there was some way I could communicate with someone. After a few minutes a black Portuguese soldier broke into a huge smile and gave the thumbs-up signal. We had apparently made it through the danger zone, although I never found out what the danger was.

The elite Portuguese commandos provided excitement of

another kind. I joined three of them for an inspection tour in an open jeep that took us from one camp to another. This time one of my companions spoke English, and he kept me amused with tales of ambushes that had taken place along our route. The road was so dusty I wore goggles, and when I took them off I looked like a racoon in reverse. Our ultimate destination was a commando training camp, one of the most spartan and vigorous I had ever seen.

I got a taste of what the recruits had to put up with when I unwittingly stepped into the midst of a convoy of army ants. These are not garden-variety insects. They're big and mean and they travel in groups so large that it was sometimes possible to hear them coming by the clicking of their powerful mandibles. This time I didn't *hear* the ants, but I certainly *felt* them.

I screamed and began slapping at my pants legs. The ants were soon all over me, and blood was running down my legs in rivulets. There were millions of them. Afterwards I had a recurrent nightmare in which I was sleeping on the ground in my bedroll and awoke to find that army ants were carrying me off. It was clearly time to go home.

Exit Agnew, Enter Ford

HOME, IN AUGUST OF 1973, meant turmoil of another kind. By late summer political life had become tumultuous both for Richard Nixon, attempting to suppress the larger implications of the Watergate break-in, and for Spiro Agnew, by then implicated in a kickback scandal that had nothing to do with Nixon's problems.

John Durniak, *Time*'s photo editor, assigned me to cover Agnew at a time when the media were reporting all sorts of allegations about fiscal misconduct on the part of the Vice-President. I had nothing against Agnew personally. In fact, he'd done me a favor shortly after the 1968 Republican convention. Nixon, Agnew, and their entourages had flown to Mission Bay, just outside San Diego, to plan campaign strategy. Dirck Halstead was covering Nixon for UPI in those days, and I had come down from Los Angeles to give him a hand. It was customary for candidates to go to church, whether they did so as noncandidates or not, and I was assigned to cover Agnew on Sunday morning. When I arrived at his residence I discovered that I was the only press person present and that there was no car provided for the motorcade. For security reasons Agnew's bodyguards weren't saying which church he was going to, and it looked like I was going to miss the boat. When Agnew walked out to his car he noticed the distraught-looking photographer waving furiously at him. "What's up?" he asked.

"There's no car for me to cover you going to church," I said.

"That's no problem, ride with me," he said, and to the chagrin of his Secret Service escorts, I climbed into his car.

After the service he spoke to a small group of worshipers of his geniune awe at being selected Nixon's running mate. "I'm just absolutely flabbergasted," he told them.

Five years had passed since that encounter, and things had changed. There would be no more invitations to share a car, I knew, for Agnew was now doing everything to avoid the press. I was the only photographer covering him daily, and to his dismay I was there every time Agnew turned around.

There's a difference between dogging a a political figure who doesn't want to cooperate and tailing someone like Jackie O. when she doesn't want her picture taken. The chief distinction is that the taxpayers don't pay Mrs. Onassis out of their own pockets. She's a private citizen and not accountable to the public. Agnew was the Vice-President of the United States in 1973, and he was accountable. It was our right to know what he was up to.

This is not to say that I particularly enjoyed trailing Agnew, but I thought it was right and proper, so I did it. Once I discovered, for instance, that Agnew was going with some old buddies to a golf match in Ocean City, Maryland, and I drove there. My presence at that club was greeted with something less than wholehearted enthusiasm, and although I did get some pictures of Agnew whizzing by in his golf cart, I never got much closer.

Shortly thereafter Agnew flew to Chicago to make a speech. Normally the Vice-President takes press representatives along on his plane, if there is space available. This time there was space, but my request was turned down, so I flew out to Chicago on a commercial plane. I was determined that he wasn't going to shake me. Whenever he attended a state dinner at the White House or spoke to a civic group, I was there to take his picture. When I heard he was leaving for Frank Sinatra's place in Palm Springs, I headed west as well. Sinatra's place proved harder to get into than Fort Knox. A fence surrounded the property, and just inside the fence was a dense hedge that effectively shielded those inside from view. With no way of gaining entrance I settled down outside with one of my favorite gadgets, a small radio turned to a Secret Service frequency, which is how I learned when and where Agnew was going to play golf. It should have come as no surprise to him then that when he got there, I stepped out of the bushes and took a couple of snaps. But I think it ruined his day.

Agnew next went to Los Angeles to address a group of rabidly loyal Republican women. They detested the press so completely that one reporter actually had to be rescued after he'd been cornered and attacked with purses and umbrellas. But they loved Agnew, and when he uttered his famous words—"I will not resign if indicted!"—they stood on tops of the tables, cheering and screaming. Eleven days later, Agnew resigned. When he appeared in public the following day I took a picture of him in the back of a limousine, looking somber and staring straight ahead. That was the last time I took his picture. Agnew was a private citizen now, and my assignment was to cover the Vice-President of the United States, whoever he might be.

There was much speculation about who would be appointed by Nixon to replace Agnew, but the choice remained a tightly held secret. Durniak, his assistant Rita Quinn, Dirck Halstead, and I went over the list of possible nominees, hoping to photograph them in advance of the announcement for the cover of *Time*. The *Time* correspondent covering the White House was positive that the choice would be Linwood Holton, the governor of Virginia, but Halstead didn't believe it. His own sources there said it definitely wouldn't be Holton, but they didn't say who it was going to be.

Dirck had noticed some peculiar comings and goings at the White House. Hugh Scott, the Senate minority leader, and Gerald Ford, the House minority leader, had been there and had gone, but Dirck had seen Ford come back a second time. "I've got a hunch it's Ford," Dirck told Annie Callahan, *Time*'s Washington picture researcher. He then called Durniak and told him of his hunch. "Better have Kennerly go up and do some portraits," John told Dirck.

That was Thursday night. On Friday morning, the day of the announcement, I secured an appointment with Ford. The pictures had to be in New York that afternoon in order to make the magazine's deadline *before* the decision was disclosed.

I'd never met Gerald R. Ford, but that morning the House minority leader granted me a few minutes to take his picture in his Capitol Hill office. "You're wasting your time," he joshed.

"At least you'll have a portrait to hang on your wall," I said.

I spent only five minutes with Ford, posing him near the window where the light was good, and departed for the office.

After shipping the film to New York, I waited anxiously for the announcement. President Nixon's choice, he informed the dignitaries in the East Room of the White House, was Minority Leader Ford. Ford was wrong—I hadn't been wasting my time. And I had my first *Time* cover.

The next chance I had to talk to Ford was on a plane heading for the West Coast. "Looks like we both made it," I said with a smile. "It's my first time on the cover too," he pointed out, and I found myself struck by how unlike Agnew this man was. Here I was, actually sitting with the Vice-President-designate on his Air

Force jet. I no longer had to jump out of bushes to get my pictures. Ford would be a relief—for me and for the country.

One of the stops on Ford's previously scheduled West Coast itinerary was my home state of Oregon. It was going to be great fun for me, returning home in such style, but I was worried about Ford. He kept referring to the State as "Oragawn," just as virtually everyone born east of the Great Divide does. And if there is anything Oregonians hate more than Californians, it is people who mispronounce the name of their state. "If you want to score points with the locals, say 'Orygun,'" I told him.

Later, when Ford reached the point in his speech where he said "It's good to be here in . . ." he shot me a sly and mischievous glance—"Orygun."

"Did I get it right, Kennerly?" he asked with a grin as we reboarded his plane.

"Spoken like a true native," I assured him.

In addition to me, a hard-core handful of media people were assigned to watch Ford's every move. They were Maggie Hunter of the *New York Times,* Tom DeFrank of *Newsweek,* Phil Jones of CBS, Ron Nessen of NBC, and Bill Zimmerman of ABC. In the weeks preceding the 1974 Congressional elections it seemed to the six of us that Ford tried to campaign for every Republican who was running for office. He was the true party loyalist, and his loyalty took us out of town at least twice a week, sometimes more often. He always opted to return to Washington the same day rather than spend the night in a strange bed. This made our itineraries especially tight.

As Vice-President, Ford rejected the flashier jets preferred by his predecessor and we sometimes ended up on pretty strange aircraft. The plane he used most often for shorter trips was a twin-engine, propeller-driven Convair. The old aircraft was in immaculate shape; the plane's crew had as much pride in their aircraft as did the crew of Air Force One. For longer journeys Ford took a bigger jet from the Presidential fleet, one dubbed the "Flying Tube" because it had no windows. The only real disaster was an ancient, unpressurized Navy DC-4, employed to get us from New Orleans to Baton Rouge. All the seats in the plane faced the back, and the temperature inside seemed twenty degrees higher than the one hundred-degree temperature outside. We found ourselves on board the DC-4 because the Vice-President had gone to New Orleans to dedicate a new dock and needed to get to Baton Rouge for another event. Taking orders from the Vice-President's office about avoiding pretentious aircraft a bit too literally, local authorities had come up with the rickety special. As portly Tom DeFrank boarded he cast a glance around the cabin and then told one of the airmen what he thought of the plane. "You should have seen it before we cleaned it up," the airman replied.

At regular intervals on these jaunts Ford would tell the story of his selection as Vice President. It came to be known among the traveling press as the "telephone story," and went something like this:

> I was at home that afternoon when the phone rang. It was President Nixon. "Jerry, I've got some good news for you, but why don't you put Betty on the phone so she can hear too." Susan was talking on the other line upstairs, which was the only number with an extension. I tried to explain this to the President, and finally suggested, "Mr. President, would you mind hanging up and calling back on the other line?"

Now that was a pretty funny story—the first time. It was even rather funny the second, and probably the third. After that, it wasn't funny; some of us had heard it two dozen times, with no end in sight. On one such occasion I said, "This is the twelfth time we've heard this story, and some of us are beginning to wish the President hadn't called back . . ." "Kennerly!" the voice from the back of the aircraft boomed. Several nights later all the reporters synchronized their tape recorders when the Vice-President got on the plane and played the telephone story all at once as he walked through. He laughed, and we knew he'd gotten the point. The next night he told his audience the telephone story.

I covered many stories other than the Vice-Presidency, including the "Saturday Night Massacre," when Special Watergate Prosecutor Archibald Cox was fired by President Nixon. Besides Cox, Deputy Attorney General William Ruckelshaus got the axe and Attorney General Elliott Richardson resigned. I was forty miles outside Washington that particular Saturday evening, having dinner with old friends, when I got the word. Speeding back to town to cover the story, I was spotted by a police cruiser and confronted a minor crisis: if I stopped, I would almost certainly miss the story. Figuring that my Mercedes could easily outrun his Chevy, I stepped on the gas. It worked.

My first stop was the Special Prosecutor's office, which had already been sealed off by the FBI so that nothing could be removed from the premises. I was told nobody could go in, but I gave it a shot anyhow and got two pictures before I was tossed out by angry G-men. (The second shows a Federal agent with his hand stretched toward my lens. This is the photo *Time* chose to print.) Unable to reach Cox, I tried tracking down the other principals in the story.

My primary assignment in those days was not Justice but the Fords. The magazine wanted an extensive layout of the family that could be run when he was sworn in as Vice-President. Without Betty Ford's help I would never have been able to complete my job. There are some people in this world that you like right off the bat, and Mrs. Ford is one of them. I strongly suspect the reason is that she likes people; her affection is infectious. For instance, one of our first encounters occurred on a Sunday morning. I was supposed to arrive at their home early to take some pictures for the spread *Time* was planning. Instead I called to say I'd be a bit late (too much partying the night before). Although I didn't say so, my voice must have sounded like it, for when I finally arrived Mrs. Ford was standing at the door, waiting for me. In her hand was a cold beer. "Drink this. You'll feel better," she said. She then invited me to share their Sunday breakfast.

Sunday was the only day I could get the two senior Fords together for the picture we'd planned to be shot on the grounds of their church, which was only a few blocks from their home. It was autumn, and the trees were turning brilliant colors. The Fords were dressed casually, and as they walked quietly down the street their affection for one another was as obvious as their enjoyment of that moment of serenity.

Within the next week I flew around the country to photograph all four of the Fords' children. Jack, who was twenty-one at the time and seriously committed to forestry and the outdoors, was staying at a friend's home in Idaho, where he was hunting pheasants and skiing. Mike, the eldest of the four, was a seminary student in Massachusetts. A tall, handsome twenty-four-year-old with sandy blond hair, he was the most studious of the children and the most determined to avoid the limelight of his father's position. His wife, Gayle, went so far as to take a job under an assumed name to avoid the attention paid to the Ford family. Steve, the youngest boy, was a student at T.C. Williams High School in Alexandria; and Susan, the Fords' youngest, was a student at Holton Arms, a private girls' school.

The Ford family rarely assembled in one place, except on Christmas, when they traditionally went skiing at Vail, Colorado. Mr. Ford believed in taking that vacation, and after he was sworn in as Vice-President he maintained the old tradition. That meant that I went to Colorado as well. I'd never been skiing before, so when we got to Vail I gazed up at the snow-covered slopes with great trepidation. It was clear to me that I couldn't really do my job properly if the Vice-President went up the mountain and I stayed below, so I was determined to take a crash course in skiing. Crash is exactly what it turned out to be, and I was plenty sore after the first couple of days. As the Vice-President was overheard to say, "Kennerly skis with 10 percent talent and 90 percent intestinal fortitude."

I never did get to the point where I could ski backwards and shoot pictures, but I was able to negotiate the slopes without serious injury, which for me was a major accomplishment. To repay the Fords for their hospitality, I threw a dinner party at a Japanese restaurant for them while we were in Vail. There were fourteen of us at the table, and after dinner the management sent over a huge tray of fortune cookies. Everyone took one, including Mr. Ford. He opened his, studied it a moment, and slapped it down on the table, covering it with his hand. Mrs. Stan Parris, wife of a congressman and friend of the Fords, was sitting next to the Vice-President. It was she who read the message aloud to the gathering: "You will undergo a change of residence in the near future." It was the first time in my memory that a fortune cookie had ever been truly prophetic.

The next dinner of mine that the Fords attended was of my own making. It was a small gathering at my house in Georgetown to celebrate my twenty-seventh birthday. When Vice-President and Mrs. Ford showed up, Mr. Ford had a huge package wrapped in gold tucked under his arm. Inside was a case of Coors beer, the first I'd seen since Vail. Having the Vice-President of the United States over to dinner is a memorable event, particularly if you're a bachelor living alone. I had done the cooking myself, with a great deal of able support from my mother, who was one of the guests. I had two big pans of beef Stroganoff simmering in the small kitchen, and the other two burners were also in use. The already hectic situation wasn't helped any by the Secret Service agent watching the proceedings. He wasn't there to make certain I didn't poison the Veep—he was watching the rear entrance of my house—but the effect was the same. Every now and then I'd offer him a taste of the food just to get another opinion, and he agreed it wasn't a bad effort. I somehow managed to serve the whole dinner without dropping anything into anyone's lap, and my mother received a great many compliments on the food. No one would believe I'd had anything to do with it.

When Dirck Halstead wasn't in town, *Time* assigned me to cover the White House. Things at the Executive Mansion had gotten worse for photographers since my return from overseas. If the story itself hadn't been so good, I don't think I could have put up with it. On one occasion the metallic drone of the loudspeaker in the press room announced a "photo opportunity" in the Oval Office: Energy Chief William Simon was conferring with the President.

I hadn't seen Nixon in over a month, and I was shocked at his appearance. He looked tired and haggard. After taking the obligatory shot of the two men across the desk from one another, I took seven tight frames of Nixon's face with a small telephoto lens. The following week, *Time* ran one of the close-ups of the embattled President. One of his dark-ringed eyes drooped and the right side of his face appeared to sag. The White House reacted violently to my photo, labeling it "unfair," and the UPI vice-president for newspictures even suggested in a letter to all UPI clients that my photo was "out of context."

Now my integrity was at stake. These incidents were serious, and I felt obliged to defend not only my taking of the picture but *Time's* excellent use of the image. In a private cable to John Durniak, I pointed out that the light in the office was exactly the same as every other time I had been there, and that there was nothing unusual about the expression on Nixon's face, or anything that would cause any distortion. In short, the picture was a true representation of how Nixon looked at that moment.

In the UPI executive's letter he'd said, "If any one of our photographers makes thirty different views of the President, and one of those views makes him look significantly different than the twenty-nine, the rule of thumb is not to use it." The implication was that I'd gotten one shot that made Nixon look unusually bad; the truth was that the other frames made him look *worse*.

The letter also said that the UPI executive had "examined more than a hundred UPI pictures taken over the past two months, and they show no discernible change in his appearance." This led Dirck Halstead to comment, in a separate note to Durniak, that "it can only be interpreted as an indictment of the lack of perception either of UPI's photographers or editors." Halstead went on to say that UPI photographers have to get their shots of such a meeting in the less than sixty seconds afforded photographers in the Oval Office, and they don't have the luxury of being able to concentrate on Nixon the Man. A year later I was told by General Alexander Haig, who had been Nixon's chief-of-staff at the time—and one of the few who knew the true story—that the day I took the picture, Nixon hadn't slept well for three days. He'd been reviewing the White House tapes containing the infamous eighteen-minute gap.

That very week six professional sound-recording and electronics experts had been playing the tape containing the mysterious gap in court. *Time* wanted a picture of all six guys together, which was no easy matter because one is forbidden by law to shoot photographs in a U.S. courtroom. I therefore went into the courtroom and passed one of the men a note reading: "Please ask your five colleagues if they will pose outside for a picture for *Time*." They all said they'd do it.

I arranged to meet the six on the side of the courthouse opposite the spot where the rest of the photographers gathered during the recesses. And when the men walked out I hurriedly assembled them for a group shot. Not ten seconds had passed when I heard the other photographers. I shot a couple of frames very quickly and then, trying to preserve my exclusive, shooed the tape experts back inside.

As it turned out, my pictures weren't very good, and the six, feeling guilty about the other photogs, later came out and posed for everyone. The last laugh was on me: *Time* used a UPI picture.

Scoops and Scandal

IT WAS MARCH 30, 1974, and nuptial rumors were dropping like incoming shells. Will Kissinger get married, or won't he? *Time*'s sage State Department correspondent declared: "Absolutely not. I'll stake my reputation on it." And *Time*'s dependable White House correspondent concurred: "No way." So I called up Durniak and told him that I'd better get down to

Acapulco, where Kissinger was scheduled for a brief vacation the next day. Everyone was saying he wouldn't get married, but I had a powerful hunch it was going to happen. "Take off," Durniak said. "And if Kissinger doesn't get hitched, have a good vacation," he added facetiously.

I was changing planes at the Dallas-Fort Worth airport when a frantic page came over the loudspeaker. It was Durniak, in New York, with a message. "He just got married." "Well, John," I said, "if you'll just let me catch the plane to Acapulco, we'll be way ahead of the opposition." That was time enough, but Kissinger and his new wife were flying in a private jet, and they landed just ahead of my commercial flight. I was met by a representative of the airlines who tried to get me through customs as fast as possible, but even so I was literally hopping from one foot to the other as the customs official went slowly through my bag. I ran out of the terminal and across to the private jet area just in time to see a black limousine pull away from the small plane. I missed them and the deadline was that night. I was really depressed. A clean scoop had been pulled out from under me. By the next day Acapulco would be swarming with photographers and newsmen.

My next problem was trying to figure out where the Kissingers were staying. I hired a driver—who later proved a great asset—and we took off for the hillside resort known as Las Brisas, where we assumed they would be. After going to several large homes in that exclusive area, I finally spotted a couple of Secret Service agents driving by. We followed at a discreet distance, and noted where they turned in. I'd found the honeymooners all right, but they might as well have been in Rio for all the good it was going to do us. A pink stucco house was at the end of a long driveway, and it was guarded by a couple of German shepherds and three or four *Federales* who had no time for photographers. As I'd predicted, the world's press soon began pouring into the area, along with several dozen local photographers. They all hung out in small groups in front of the house's massive wooden doors, which by now were protected by even more dogs and *Federales*.

My principal advantage was the radio that monitored the Secret Service frequencies. Any time Kissinger and his new wife got ready to go out, I heard about it first. The problem was that when the doors opened and the car bearing the Kissingers came out, a caravan of jeeps, trucks, and cars loaded with photographers would follow. The Secret Service presently invented an ingenious plan for beating this situation. The area was filled with winding, narrow roads, barely wide enough for the cars to pass, and as soon as the caravan of newsmen started after the Kissingers, a car full of Secret Service men would stop, blocking the road. Nobody knew where the Kissingers were going—except me. I'd heard their destination on my radio, and I asked my driver if there was another way. *"Si, senor,"* he said, and off we went, tires screeching as we took the corners. We reached the main roadway just as Kissinger's motorcade shot out from a side street; my driver swung in behind them. At last I had my chance to get the first pictures of the newlyweds. Wrong again. Whoever it was Kissinger had come to visit had *Federales* of his own, as well as massive wooden doors and a shepherd under every palm tree. The Kissingers drove through the doors, they closed, and that was that.

Again through the miracle of modern electronics, I found out that the happy couple was going to take a ride in a sailboat. I even found out where, and I hired a motor boat and had it waiting under the Kissingers' departure point. As it turned out, they were already at sea, and after about two hours of speeding vainly about we finally spotted them. They were leisurely cruising along. A couple of high-powered launches were trailing behind, filled with gun-toting *Federales* and Secret Servicemen. We began a casual drift in their direction. "Get away! Go back!" the agents shouted. I started taking pictures, although I couldn't tell who was who on the boat. For the next hour we made repeated runs at their boat, at a fairly safe distance so as not to get shot, and tried for some decent snaps. No luck. They made it back to the villa unphotographed.

I was beginning to get desperate. At this stage I was willing to try anything. I even inquired about renting a hang glider, thinking I might sail over the blissful couple and snap them as they sipped daiquiris on their verandah overlooking the bay. Finally, Kissinger decided he'd had enough of the Keystone Kops routine everytime he left his house, and it was announced that the honeymooning pair would appear for photos at a friend's home if everyone would leave them alone afterward.

The next day the world's paparazzi assembled for the great event. Henry and Nancy came walking out to greet the madly clicking mass of photographers, and then both sat down to answer a few questions. In five minutes it was all over, and 99 percent of the reporters left satisfied. I was the one percent that wasn't. Everyone had gotten essentially the same shot. After all I'd been through, that just didn't seem fair.

The film was shipped off to New York, and by agreement everyone, including me, left the couple alone for several days. Then I got a call from Durniak, who wasn't happy. Nancy Kissinger had been wearing huge sunglasses, and you could hardly tell who she was. "Isn't it possible to get anything else?" Durniak asked. I called Jerry Bremer, one of Kissinger's aides. "Jerry, Nancy looks like hell in the pictures we took and *Time* is planning a color page. Unless I get something different, that's what they'll have to use." Five minutes later the phone rang. "Be at the villa at 4:00 P.M."

At three forty-five sharp I was outside the wooden doors. This time the dogs weren't barking, and the *Federales* were smiling. The villa itself was extremely pleasant. It overlooked Acapulco Bay from a point halfway up the hill and I found myself wondering how my hang glider picture might have turned out. Peering over the steep cliff, I decided I could only have gotten killed.

Secretary Kissinger greeted me. I told him that I had to hurry, as the last plane was leaving soon for the States and I was right up against my deadline. A few minutes later, Nancy came out wearing a fuchsia-colored pantsuit.

Kissinger, playing the shy, newly married husband, insisted I take pictures only of her. Nancy and I had to coax him to let me photograph the two of them together. The photos were great, exclusive, and exactly what I needed.

My problems were not yet over, however, for I pulled up in front of the airport terminal just in time to see the day's last plane for the States take off. I frantically contacted all the other airlines to see if there were connections to the U.S. from anywhere else. The next plane wouldn't leave until tomorrow, and the earliest I could get to New York would be late the following afternoon—past the deadline.

Suicide was not an unreasonable alternative at this stage, and I was giving it serious thought when I noticed a Pan Am 707 on the field. "Whose plane is that?" I inquired. "Oh, that belongs to an IBM charter group," I was told. "Where is it going?" "To Kansas City, but unless you are part of the group, there is no way to get on it." "Bullshit," I thought. If that plane is going, I'm going with it, even if I have to strap myself to the landing gear. I located the guy who was in charge of the group, explained my plight, and found him very sympathetic. The only problem was seats. He didn't think that there were any left, and without one, I couldn't go. However, he would check for me. Eventually he came back to report that there was the possibility of a seat, but he really couldn't authorize me to go. However, if I were simply to get in line and get on the plane . . . .

"Occupied." That's what the sign on the airplane's restroom read. At least that's what it read until the plane took off because it *was*—by me.

After I was certain that there was no chance I would get thrown off the flight, I nonchalantly walked down the aisle and found the last empty seat. "Hi," I said somewhat nervously to the suntanned pair next to me. They asked how I had enjoyed myself in Acapulco. "Fine," I replied. "We didn't notice you during our stay." "I just try to keep a low profile," I told them.

I arrived in the Kansas City airport at 12:30 A.M., where my next surprise awaited: No flights *anywhere* until 6:00 A.M., and that one to Chicago. Jesus, will it never end, I thought. After an uncomfortable night on an airport bench, I caught the flight to

Chicago and a connecting one to New York. The cab driver at La Guardia didn't seem surprised that a guy carrying a couple of cameras and wearing only a dirty bush jacket in the freezing rain was beating him over the head and shouting at him to go even faster to the Time-Life Building. When I got there, the film was rushed to the lab. It was already 11:00 A.M. and if the pictures weren't shown to the editors before they went to lunch, it was "*adios*" to my exclusive.

It was already past deadline, but as soon as the pictures came out of the processor, photographer Ted Thai and I ran upstairs with them. I edited the transparencies that Ted handed me as I rushed down the hall, leaving a trail of bad exposures on the floor behind me. When I arrived in the conference room the editors were just getting ready to leave. Durniak practically jumped up and down. "Here he is! Here he is!" he shouted. The first slide went into the projector, a stunning solo portrait of Nancy Kissinger. It was followed by photos of the two of them together and shots of the house.

A few weeks later I ran into Secretary Kissinger and he complimented me on the photos of Nancy, but added, "That cover picture last week made me look too fat."

"There's only so much a camera can do, Mr. Secretary," I replied, smiling.

By July of 1974 the Watergate Scandal was entering its final phase. In public, at any rate, Vice-President Ford was one of Richard Nixon's last defenders, saying time and again that he didn't believe the President was guilty of an impeachable offense. A meeting with Alexander Haig on August 1 changed his mind. On that date Haig informed Ford of the contents of the Watergate tape of June 23, 1972, which was a week after the Watergate break-in. In it Nixon suggested that his staff throw the FBI investigation off the track by saying they'd be interfering with an ongoing CIA operation. That "smoking gun" tape linked Nixon directly to the cover-up. In Haig's meeting with Ford he indicated that the tape's contents, once publicly revealed, would be "devastating and catastrophic." Haig then asked Ford if he was "able and ready to assume the Presidency."

As far as I know, Vice-President Ford had never really faced that possibility head-on. He certainly hadn't discussed it with any of us. I felt he was so conscious of the fact that people would take any reference to Nixon's possible resignation as proof he was trying to elbow Nixon aside that he simply wouldn't talk about it. Consequently, he made no effort secretly to plan a transition. The only move in that direction was mounted without his knowledge by his lawyer, Phil Buchen, who outlined areas that would immediately concern a new President, such as appointing a press secretary and new legal counsel.

Ford maintained his normal schedule throughout this period, and one of the things on his agenda was a dinner with me. The night after his meeting with Haig, which none of us had known about, the Fords came to my house for a drink. We then drove out into the country to the Old Angler's Inn for dinner. Mr. Ford certainly had a lot on his mind, but he enjoyed the respite. And it may well have been the only dinner in Washington that evening where the name Richard Nixon was not mentioned.

The next day we left for Mississippi and Louisiana, for yet another round of campaign appearances on behalf of Republican congressional candidates. Even as Ford spoke, Nixon's resignation speech was being drafted at Camp David. On August 5 we returned to Washington. The damaging tapes had been made public that afternoon, and as soon as Ford had departed from Andrews Air Force Base his press secretary handed out a statement saying the Vice-President would have no comment on the situation until "facts are more fully available." He did not have to wait long: on August 8 Nixon announced his resignation. And on August 9, at noon, Gerald R. Ford became President.

Before he took the Oath of Office, Vice-President Ford and his wife escorted the Nixons to the south lawn of the White House. I followed with my camera. Nixon ran up the steps of the waiting helicopter, precisely the way he had done so many times before, turned, and waved. His lips were pursed as he made this one last public gesture as President of the United States. Several hours later, high above the nation's heartland, the clock struck twelve aboard Air Force One and Richard M. Nixon became a private citizen once more.

"The Photo Empire"

"OUR LONG NATIONAL NIGHTMARE IS OVER." With those words, President Gerald R. Ford announced the start of a new era, one with which I would be intimately associated.

After the swearing-in ceremony, Mrs. Ford invited me to their home in Alexandria. They were having a small dinner for some of their personal friends that night, and I knew there would be dozens of my colleagues outside the Fords' home when I arrived. I didn't want them to know I was going to be taking pictures—they would have objected to the show of favoritism—so I got one of Ford's Navy stewards to help me out. He met me in the parking lot of a school near the Fords' home and we put all my cameras in a cardboard box. Then *he* walked by the assembled press with the carton, which I'm sure they thought was more food. And I entered without my cameras, just like any other invited guest.

I got some pictures of the toasts being made to the new President and made one of my own with a glass of champagne. During the buffet supper the President asked me if I would mind staying after the other guests left. When, in time, they did, President and Mrs. Ford and I sat down together in their living room. We spent some time discussing the day's events and then he asked me what I'd like to do if I were to go to work for him. Until that moment we'd never talked about that possibility, and, to be quite frank, I found the whole idea of Ford's wanting to discuss a job for me on the same day that he became President of the United States, almost surreal. I seized the opportunity, however, and told Ford that to produce a true photographic document of his Presidency, I would have to have unlimited access to his meetings. He allowed as how the idea had merit and then suggested we go into the den to watch the eleven o'clock news, which would have coverage of his swearing-in ceremony. The television in that room wasn't working, so we went upstairs to their bedroom to watch. Mrs. Ford sat in a chair; he, on the edge of the bed. Susan came in and lay down near her father.

I could have pinched myself. Not only was I sitting with the man whose image was being relayed around the world as he was sworn in as President, but that same man had discussed a job for me on terms that satisfied both of us. "Dave," he said to me as the broadcast ended and I was preparing to leave, "if you come to work for me, won't it be taken badly by your colleagues? I mean, after what's happened the last few years and all."

"Mr. President, if you're the kind of President I know you're going to be, my friends in the business will be proud to have me work for you," I responded.

Before I departed we shook hands, and Ford held mine with both of his. "I just want you to know," he added, "that you're a really good friend."

What are the next few years going to hold for this man? I thought—or for me.

The following morning I photographed the new President leaving his Alexandria home, headed for his first full day at the White House, and then went to *Time*'s offices. I was still in the mailroom with my feet on a desk, talking to my best friend, Dave Burnett, and marveling at the events of the last week, when the phone rang. The switchboard operator said in a quavering voice, "It's the President for you, Dave. He's actually on the line and I just talked to him." Hugh Sidey, *Time*'s Washington bureau chief and writer of a regular column on the Presidency, was walking by the desk at the very moment that I answered. "Hello,

Mr. President." Burnett later told me the look on Sidey's face was worth a million bucks.

"How'd you like to come to work?" Ford asked.

"When do you want me to start?" was all I could think to say.

"Get over here right away," he responded. "We can't have you wasting the taxpayers' money by working only half a day." Slamming the phone down after Ford had hung up, I jumped up and yelled to Burnett, "I got it!" And, blue jeans and all, I charged across Lafayette Park to the White House. After I showed my press pass, someone from the photo office came to take me to the press room to look over my new digs.

At 4:05 that afternoon I got an urgent call from Nell Yates, the President's receptionist. I was expected in the Oval Office immediately. In fact, the President had been expecting me at 4:00 P.M. sharp, but nobody had bothered to tell me of the appointment. "Off to a great start: late for my first meeting," I thought as I ran up the stairs from my basement office. But as it turned out the President just wanted to say hello, and after taking a few pictures, I left.

He chose not to make any formal announcement about my appointment at the time because Ollie Atkins, President Nixon's official photographer, was still on the staff. He'd gone to San Clemente on Air Force One with Nixon, and President Ford wanted to make sure Atkins knew of my appointment before he went public with it. As things worked out, Ollie stayed on for a few months to help me with the administrative details. His work was now complete; mine was just beginning.

I had to get a "top secret" security clearance, which meant the FBI thoroughly investigated my background. For a while I was getting phone calls almost daily from old teachers and school buddies who thought I was in some kind of trouble. "Hey, Dave, what'd you do? The Feds were here asking about ya." After the clearance came through there were no restrictions on what I did. In fact, I was the only nonmember who was allowed into National Security Council (NSC) meetings. For the first couple of days I kept notes about everything going on around me, but I soon stopped. I was only recording my impressions of my subjects, but my scribblings were making my subjects rather nervous. The fact that I took pictures of what was happening didn't bother anyone, but writing down what was happening did.

The President's first few weeks in office were bizarre even by presidential standards, for he was commuting from nearby Alexandria to 1600 Pennsylvania Avenue. Early every morning he'd walk out in his bathrobe and collect the newspaper from the front steps. A crowd of cameramen and reporters would gleefully record this mundane event. Then, after breakfast, he'd pick up his briefcase, kiss his wife and head out the door. Just as he did every other morning, he waved at the neighbors and climbed into his chauffeured car. That, however, is where real life ended. The car was bulletproof and it was driven by a Secret Service agent. Following Ford's limo was a station wagon filled with G-men, and behind *that* were cars filled with staff and press. When he finally reached his office the President would be greeted by more cameramen and reporters. This ritual continued for a week until the Fords moved into the White House.

Ford's initial meeting with his Cabinet took place in the Roosevelt Room, which is opposite the Oval Office. When he entered, the small, elite group stood and applauded. Thereafter people came and went at a fantastic rate, for the President wanted to see as many congressional, labor, business, and foreign representatives as he could. Things were so hectic during the changeover that I even got a picture of Henry Kissinger struggling into the Oval Office carrying his own charts—an unprecedented event.

Every time a new appointment entered the Oval Office the President insisted on introducing me to them. It wasn't easy to take pictures with one hand while shaking someone's hand with the other, so I finally persuaded the President he had no obligation to introduce me to his guests. I wouldn't feel at all slighted, I said, and he'd be doing me a favor by forgetting my presence.

A few members of the White House staff, particularly the Nixon people, greeted me with raised eyebrows. But they soon noticed that the President wasn't paying any attention to me and quickly got over their suspicions. The advantage of having unlimited access was that it enabled me to accurately record the Presidency in all its moods and colorations.

I was the third civilian to hold the job of personal photographer to the President. Each Chief Executive determined how he wanted his photographer to function, and each wanted something different. The only other newsman who had similar access to a President was Yoichi Okamoto, Lyndon Johnson's official photographer and the first civilian to hold that position. Before Okamoto, photographing the President had been handled by military cameramen. Okie, as he was known, told *Popular Photography* magazine, "There wasn't the close personal relationship between us [Johnson and Okamoto] that there is between Ford and Kennerly. I was always LBJ's subordinate. Everybody was a flunky—including McNamara and Rusk." Okie, then, was the man who paved the way in documenting the Presidency, but he had problems. Among them was a Washington commentator's report that Okie had shot over 11,000 negatives at a time when Johnson was talking about saving money. Johnson, embarrassed, sent Okie back to his old job at the U.S. Information Agency. Fortunately for photographic history, he later brought Okie back, and Okamoto's pictures are among the most powerful ever taken of a President.

The next civilian to hold the office was Ollie Atkins, who came to the Nixon White House from the *Saturday Evening Post*. Ollie faced a totally different situation, as he told *Popular Photography*: "I never had any real understanding with Nixon about the importance and role of photography in his Administration. Picture sessions were usually formal and stiff. Ron Zeigler, who understood nothing about photography, controlled the whole White House photo office and stood in the way of ever getting through to Nixon. I never got to discuss anything with the President, not even the weather." Even so, the night before Nixon resigned Atkins took some remarkable photographs of the beleaguered President hugging his daughter Julie.

After Ollie, who always wore pin-striped suits and neat white shirts, I appeared on the scene with my full beard and blue jeans. As writer Perry Deane Young put it in an article on the Ford Administrtion, "The only beards inside the White House in recent years were on the portraits of long-dead Presidents." No question about it, things *were* different under Gerald Ford, right across the board.

There were times when the action would slacken for a few minutes. On one such occasion I walked into the Oval Office and found the President sitting behind his desk, the same one Nixon had used. The President, rummaging through it, pulled out a little round plastic strip—a dictaphone belt—and laughingly said, "I wonder if this is one of those tapes?" As we talked he paced around the Oval Office, his hands in his pockets. Gazing up at the engraved Presidential Seal on the ceiling, he mused, "You know, Dave, all I ever wanted to be was Speaker of the House, and that never happened. I never wanted to be President, and here I am." With which he walked wearily back to his desk, where the papers were already starting to pile up.

After Ollie Atkins left the White House, I started to make some changes. My office was in the basement of the West Wing. Other staffers with offices there referred to it as the "ground floor," but it was clearly the basement. Directly across from my office was the barber shop, where Milton Pitts trimmed everyone's hair, from the President's to mine (although neither of us had that much left to cut). Around the corner was a room full of vending machines, and a few steps from my door was the Secret Service command post known as W-16. They always say about White House office assignments that proximity to the Oval Office means power. If that is indeed true, then the vending machines were as powerful as I.

Over the next few weeks I had the walls to an adjoining office knocked down and enlarged the available staff space to three times its original size. In doing so we acquired—and I took over—a nice wood-paneled office that had once been the White

House vault. Scouting around for furniture in the attic of the Old Executive Office building across the street, I found a rocking chair that White House historians told me had once belonged to President Kennedy. I temporarily took it over too. Then, instead of a regular rectangular desk, I chose a round table. I added table lamps and a striped couch, got rid of the more formal straightback chairs and suddenly the place looked like home. A good thing, too, for I was spending more time there than in my Georgetown house.

My new telephone had a silver handle that read, "Robert Haldeman," given to me by someone who had worked for him. It also had several buttons connecting me to the White House operator and to various other staffers. I felt I was flying a jet whenever a bunch of calls came in at once. On my walls hung signed photos and other memorabilia. In back of me on a table was a tank full of fish, a gift from Jack Ford. My favorite was an ugly Oscar named Zarkov, who ate only live goldfish. It never occurred to me that his eating habits would create trouble, since big fish eat little ones every day. But when someone from the *National Enquirer* did a very descriptive piece about the poor little goldfish that were being torn to bits and devoured by big, mean Zarkov, I started getting mail from goldfish lovers around the country. One was addressed to: "David Kennerly, Barbarian, The White House." They went downhill from there.

On top of my book cabinet was a small box known as a "family locator." Secretary of State Kissinger, Vice-President Rockefeller, and all members of the Ford family were hooked into this system, and every time one of them changed locations the locator beeped and their new destination appeared in orange letters on a tiny screen. The device was devised by the Secret Service to keep track of everyone's whereabouts, but it was also immensely useful to me. My sanctum was fifty paces from the front door of the Oval Office, and there was a direct line between the two. If an unscheduled guest showed up to see the President or if Ford wanted a photograph, Nell would pick up the hot line that rang directly from her desk to my office. Then I or one of the other photographers would bound up to the Oval Office in less than fifteen seconds.

I was finally moved in by now and had launched what some of my colleagues dubbed "the photo empire." Kathy Tindle, my secretary and personal assistant, sat outside my door. Sandra Eisert, the picture editor I hired away from the Louisville *Courier-Journal*, where she had won the National Press Photographers Association's Picture Editor of the Year award, sat in an adjoining room. When not busy with other tasks Sandra would sometimes stand on a chair in the middle of the room with a spoon in her ear. When asked why she did this she replied emphatically, "I used to do it *all the time* in Louisville."

One time, after I'd complained to her about the dearth of hate mail—only four or five truly nasty letters in eight months—she sent me the following memo, headed HATE, Inc:

> It has come to our attention that you are concerned about the lack of hate mail coming into our office. Since we know that you are a person particularly deserving of this attention, we are as appalled as you are at the neglect. Our services include a full range of hate mail, threats, and blackmail for your selection. Bad publicity can also be provided upon request.

Bill Fitz-Patrick and Karl Schumaker, also on the staff, had both been hired by Ollie Atkins during the Nixon Administration. It was Fitz who made up the famous sign, affixed to the side of my briefcase, that read "His Photoship." The name stuck, at least with the office staff. Karl Schumaker dealt principally with Mrs. Ford's photo needs. My fondest remembrance of Karl is of him standing, a bewildered look on his face, on a road on the island of Corregidor (in the Philippines) as our motorcade sped past. He had leapt out of his car thinking the President was going to stop at that location, but all he did was slow down.

Jack Kightlinger had been a photographer for Lyndon Johnson, and he remained on through the Nixon Administration. A former Army photographer with dark, curly hair and a pencil-thin moustache, "Kite," as we called him, supplemented his income by playing gin rummy with me. He was otherwise assigned to photograph Vice-President Rockefeller and stayed with him throughout the Ford Administration. I also hired Ricardo Thomas, who had done work for both UPI and *Time*, and he usually worked with me covering the President. (Thomas was also the first black photographer ever to work in the White House.) Mary Beckman, my staff researcher, had been at the White House since Eisenhower and knew every facet of the operation.

And finally, there was Billie Shaddix, our office manager. He ran the photo lab for me, and ran much more as well. I trusted him implicitly, valued his judgment, and used him as a sounding board for both personal and professional problems. I have always felt that it was a tribute to the talents of my staff that most of them, except for those who chose to leave, were kept on by the Carter Administration.

A Fly on the Wall

DURING THE WHITE HOUSE YEARS I shot principally in black and white (generally Tri-X at 800 ASA). Many people wondered why I never shot color. There were several good reasons. In most situations I found myself in weak light. And because I was to be a "fly on the wall" during these gatherings, my presence had to go unnoticed. This meant I couldn't use a flash and my cameras had to be quiet. When working in the Oval Office and the Cabinet Room I most often used a Leica M-4, a range-finder camera that is the least noisy on the market, as well as my Nikons.

By shooting at 800 ASA, one f-stop above the normal film ratings, I was able to take pictures in available light, which creates a more natural, more accurate picture. Black and white film also retains an image longer; color tends to fade over several years.

And black and white helps you focus on what's happening in the picture; you're not distracted by the problems of composing color. Finally, and perhaps most important of all, black and white photography lends itself best of all to dramatic documentary presentation.

My first photos released from the White House showed the activity of those early days—people rushing in and out, various meetings, and general political retooling. But above all else they showed a relaxed new President taking over after the horrible events of the past year. One picture that suggested this with particular force showed Ford in the Oval Office, his feet up on the desk, empty shelves in the background, reading a document. In that unposed situation, in this new but seemingly natural environment, the transition was completely evoked.

The President had a little buzzer that he could sound when he wanted his assistant, Terry O'Donnell, to come into the office. Next to that buzzer was a panic button, which summoned the Secret Service if something untoward happened in the Oval Office. During the first week the President was in office he accidentally hit the wrong button while I was with him. All three doors to the Oval Office flew open simultaneously and agents charged in from all sides—scaring the hell out of both me and the President, the only two people there at the time. At least they didn't draw their guns.

One day some weeks later I was standing in Nell's office when the President succeeded in hitting the right button and got Terry, who entered, and found the President talking to Secretary Kissinger. Kissinger asked Terry to get Helmut Sonnenfelt, one of his aides, on the phone. Terry returned to Nell's office to call Sonnenfelt at the State Department. For some reason he had trouble getting through, and after a brief delay the door to the Oval Office burst open and Kissinger strode out.

"Where is he?" Kissinger demanded.

"We are having a problem reaching him," Terry replied.

"I want him *here,*" Kissinger said, jabbing his finger in thirty directions.

(Text continues on page 153)

THE WHITE HOUSE (Part I)

CHICK HARRITY

"Before Kennerly, the only beards in the White House were on portraits of dead presidents."

Perry Deane Young

ABOVE: *Former Vice-President Agnew on the day after his resignation, 1973.* RIGHT: *Kennerly's first* Time *cover; October 22, 1973.*

TIME®

THE NEW NO. 2

GERALD FORD

INSIDE: Death Struggle In The Desert

LEFT: *President Richard Nixon, in his last public appearance as Chief Executive, waves goodbye before boarding a helicopter on the South Lawn of the White House; August 9, 1974.* ABOVE: *President Gerald R. Ford leaves his Alexandria, Virginia, home for his first full day at the White House.*

A new President with a fresh, relaxed manner: Ford in the White House.

OVERLEAF: *Ford and Secretary of State Kissinger conferring in Oval Office.*

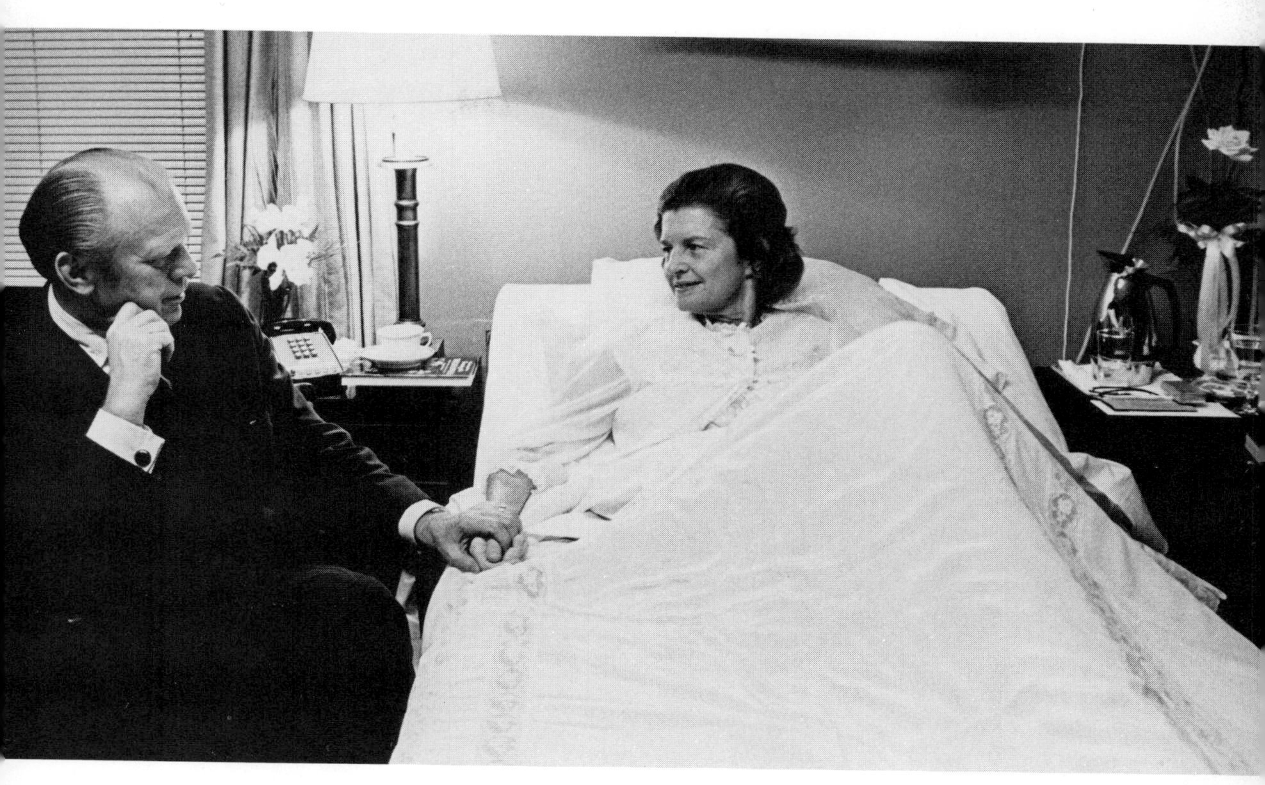

LEFT: *Betty Ford's favorite picture, taken as she looks from the family quarters on the second floor of the White House toward the Oval Office.* ABOVE: *The President and Mrs. Ford at Bethesda Naval Hospital after her mastectomy operation, 1974.*

ABOVE: *General Secretary Leonid Brezhnev confers with President Ford on train to Vladivostok during their first meeting in 1974.* RIGHT: *Brezhnev at the Helsinki Conference, 1976.*

President Ford in Vladivostok.

American delegation takes a break during Vladivostok summit. They discussed strategy outdoors—in −20 degree weather—for fear of being electronically monitored by their hosts inside.

Teng Hsiao-ping, Vice-Premier of the People's Republic of China; Peking, 1975.

Terry interpreted this to mean that the Secretary wanted Sonnenfelt physically present. When he finally did get a hold of Sonnenfelt he told him to get to the White House as fast as possible.

Once again Kissinger came charging out of the Oval Office.

"Where is he?" he again asked, even more impatiently than before.

"He's on his way here," Terry responded.

"What! I don't want him *here*," Kissinger said, pointing to the room in general. "I want him *here*," he said, pointing at the phone. O'Donnell gestured helplessly. Kissinger looked at him with complete disdain and said, "Then get me one of my idiots."

On Sunday, September 8, President Ford faced a single television camera from behind his desk in the Oval Office and read the statement granting a "full, free, and absolute pardon unto Richard Nixon." After signing the pardon, he walked down the hall to the office of Bill Timmons, who was his congressional-liaison man. Hands thrust into his rear pockets, the President paced around Timmons' office, listening to the reactions of various congressmen to his announcement. Timmons read the comments from a clipboard, and they were not favorable. Many of Ford's former colleagues on the Hill were willing to say privately that he had done the right thing, but publicly they were knocking the hell out of him. Ford continued pacing about Timmons' office, rubbing the side of his face reflectively.

Around him, everyone was talking on a telephone—Haig, Timmons, and counselor Jack Marsh. Bob Hartmann, Ford's chief speechwriter, was staring at a picture on the wall. I took a photo of the President at that moment. In back of him, two portraits hung on the wall. One was a photograph of Ford; the other, a picture of Richard Nixon.

That evening I followed Ford upstairs and photographed him sitting in a chair in the First Family's private suite. His glasses were pushed to the top of his head and he had a martini in his right hand. He looked straight ahead, not saying a word. Later that same night I was sitting in a restaurant a few blocks from the White House when word reached me that Jerald terHorst, a former Detroit newsman and Ford's press secretary, had resigned to protest the pardon and the fact he hadn't been informed that it was coming. I excused myself from the table and quickly drove back to the office. I figured this was a moment when the President could use a friend.

I walked through the big wooden doors that lead to the President's private living room. Mrs. Ford, who was wearing a long pink bathrobe, was pouring a cup of tea for the President. He looked really depressed, and I felt my compassion giving way to anger. The President of the United States may seem to be one of the least vulnerable people in the world, protected as he is by guards, aides, and party loyalists, but that's not the case. And while most of us can find a way to blow off steam about something that truly bothers us, he cannot. The terHorst resignation hurt Ford, and that made me angry. It also made me realize how much I had come to care for the Fords. And so I told the President I didn't believe that terHorst had resigned solely for the stated reasons, that I thought the job had simply been too much for him and he had taken the best way out. The President then explained why *he* thought terHorst had resigned. He failed to convince me, but he did calm me down. And in doing so he momentarily forgot how bad he felt.

Roughly a week later terHorst's name cropped up again, this time at the top of a nationally syndicated column. His first piece dealt with how the Presidency had changed Gerald Ford. I felt it drew upon—and misinterpreted—privileged information he had obtained in his position as press secretary. That night, as the President and I were riding together in the elevator, he looked at me and said, "You might be right about terHorst."

The pardon of Richard Nixon blew Gerald Ford's popularity right out of the water. It dropped thirty points virtually overnight. To take his mind off the whole issue I invited the President and Mrs. Ford to a party that a few of the Washington photographers were having. We rode in his limousine to the home of John Full, a UPI photographer. John had a bachelor pad with deep red carpeting, spiral staircases, and lights so low you sometimes wondered if they were on at all. The Fords loved the party, especially the President, who had always liked photographers. "They're the kind of people you can trust," he had said of my colleagues, and he knew most of the regulars around town by their first names.

Two weeks later, Mrs. Ford had to go into the hospital for a major operation, the necessity of which had taken her and everyone else completely by surprise. That night before her surgery I went with the First Family to visit her at Bethesda Naval Hospital. Just before we left the Presidential Suite at the hospital I took a picture of Susan throwing her arms around her mother. The next day the President had to address an economic conference at the Washington Hilton. His voice trembled with emotion as he told his listeners of the successful operation, and for a moment he wasn't the President but just another husband, deeply concerned about his wife.

The President visited Mrs. Ford every day throughout her convalescence in the hospital. He usually took a helicopter to Bethesda for these visits, and one rainy afternoon we almost crashed. On the route from the White House to the hospital is a huge Mormon Tabernacle with gold and white spires that rise 100 feet in the air. Visibility was so poor en route to the hospital that Terry O'Donnell and I couldn't see the spires until we were so close we could almost touch them. The President, who was reading, never noticed our close call—and we never told him about it.

In Mrs. Ford's absence, Susan and I conspired to buy the President a golden retriever puppy to replace one that had died a few months before. This proved easier said than done, for most kennels won't sell you a dog unless they know who wants it and what kind of home it's going to. This one was no different.

"It's a surprise, and I'd like to keep it so," I told the kennel owner on the phone.

"Well, we don't sell our golden retrievers that way," the woman on the other end replied. "I've got to know if the dog is going to have a good home."

"Oh, you can be sure it will," I replied. "In fact, the people are a friendly middle-aged couple who live in a big white house with a fence around it."

"Good," she said. "Do they own or rent?"

"Well, you might say it's public housing," I told her.

"This is a big dog and it is going to eat a lot. Does the father have a steady job?" she wanted to know.

That got me. "He's sure to be in town for a couple of years," I assured her, "but beyond that I can't really tell you."

In the end Susan and I were permitted to purchase the eight-month-old retriever. When we gave her to the President that night, he was overjoyed. Mrs. Ford, on her return, took a dimmer view. She knew from past experience who was going to end up taking the puppy, which they named Liberty, on its walks.

Sheikh Mujibur Rahman of Bangladesh was only one of many heads of state who visited President Ford, but I took particular interest in his state visit because I had been in East Pakistan, now Bangladesh, as that nation came into being in January 1972. I was stationed in Saigon in early '72, but UPI reporter Stew Kellerman, freelancer Matt Franjola, and I decided to spend some of our free time photographing the refugees fleeing East Pakistan into India.

Matt, a tall, husky blond who's always in top shape, had spent ten years in Asia, but even he found everything about the Indian subcontinent totally alien. The drive from the airport to downtown Calcutta is one that will be imbedded in my memory forever. I'd never seen so many people living in such great poverty. Our mouths must have been hanging open as we passed sacred cows aimlessly wandering the streets, deformed beggars asking for money, and thousands of Indians pedaling bicycles.

The hotel we stayed at was a stark contrast with the rest of Calcutta, a holdover from the days of the British Raj with what seemed like miles of dimly lit corridors.

Franjola and I were determined to have a good time in Calcutta. The first thing we did was go out and buy old British army uniforms, complete with hats, for our tour. The second thing we did was visit a house of ill repute.

There's nothing raunchier than a Calcutta whorehouse. The first thing I noticed when we walked in was a group of men looking through tiny openings in one wall. It reminded me in a way of the knothole club at the ball park when I was a kid, except that these guys weren't watching baseball. Sitting around on old, overstuffed chairs were some ladies, and they perfectly matched the furniture. Those who were not old and overstuffed were as skinny as the straightback chairs set against the wall. As I entered they rose in unison and shouted "Ali Baba! Ali Baba!" I later learned it meant "bearded one." We'd had enough. We saluted smartly and departed.

There are times when words and pictures simply will not suffice to describe what your own eyes have seen. This was the case outside Calcutta. Millions of refugees were fleeing from East Pakistan into India to escape the Pakistani army. In a very few hours, we counted more than 20,000 refugees on one road. These people were for the most part Hindus—the Pakistani army was mostly Moslem—and they came with what was left of their lives wrapped in bundles perched on their heads. Vacant stares greeted us; eyes devoid of emotion glanced our way. They'd been shocked and terrified beyond the point where anything could faze them, and the sight of foreigners with cameras aroused no more than flickering interest.

As they passed we talked to a few of them through an interpreter. "Why did you leave?" we asked. "They slaughtered my wife and children, and left them to rot in the sun," whispered a man whose ribs were pushing through his leathery skin. "They burned my village," said another. "They kidnapped my daughter," whimpered a woman who clutched a young child in her arms. They kept coming, in groups of five or six, the luckier ones with carts pulled by donkeys. Two men passed carrying a basket slung between two poles. In the basket was an old woman too infirm to walk.

In trying to describe the emotional intensity of the scene to friends back home, I said "Try to imagine a large, broad thoroughfare like Pennsylvania Avenue with only one lane open to cars. The cars are only able to move at 5 mph because the other three lanes are clogged with people as far as your eye can see. Then imagine these people coming in an unbroken stream for more than a month at that same rate. *That* might give you some idea of what it's like."

Where to put the refugees? It was estimated that between five and seven million refugees had already arrived in India from East Pakistan, placing a terrific economic strain on a country that already had monumental problems of its own. So hundreds of camps were formed. As soon as one filled up, the authorities closed it off and forced weary travelers to go on to the next. (Among these displaced persons were some who had crossed into East Pakistan *from* India when the country was partitioned in 1947.) One such camp lay on the outskirts of Calcutta itself. From a high vantage point one could see a tent city that sheltered some 20,000 people. Blue smoke from hundreds of cooking fires hung in the air, and refugees by the thousands lined up for small portions of rice or for medical help. As we walked past one tent I looked inside and saw a small boy clinging to the leg of his grandfather. The stoic look on the face of the old man seemed tragically contrary to the wide sad expression on the young boy's face. Children were everywhere. Many were covered with open sores, but few children were crying. One small child, head resting on his knee, was trying to sleep as flies buzzed around him, sometimes landing on his festering wounds. Children lay dying of cholera on straw mats. Their parents watched helplessly. The stronger ones picked through garbage piles, looking for food and fighting off huge rats that challenged them for every morsel.

At the airport, other refugees squatted patiently on the tarmac, waiting for the red and white Russian cargo aircraft that would take them to Raiphur, 500 miles away. Most of them had never been in a car, much less a plane. The Soviet aircraft, which had the hammer and sickle painted on their tails, hauled several loads of refugees daily to the outlying camps. I talked to one of the Russian pilots, who was, ironically, killed three days later when his plane full of refugees crashed in the driving monsoon rains. Another tragedy piled upon so many.

The extra burden of these millions of refugees on India's economy was one of the factors contributing to the outbreak of war between Pakistan and India in December 1971. Covering that action wasn't easy. Every day we climbed into a taxi driven by a well-paid, be-turbaned Sikh and sneaked across the border into East Pakistan. The Indian government insisted that we couldn't cover the war without a press pass, and they refused to issue us passes, hence our clandestine trips to the front. We had to make this commute every day to file our pictures and stories.

The advancing Indian army was rolling fast, which meant we had to drive deeper into East Pakistan each day. I shared a car with Dave Burnett, who was working on assignment for *Time*. We sometimes left our driver behind and rode into battle atop a Russian-made Indian tank. The mere sound of these tanks revving up would often bring the Pakistani artillery screaming in on us. When the rounds started dropping close we would slide off the turret and dive into a ditch alongside the road. Burnett once slid right over the top of a huge bolt that was sticking out of the tank, and later complained bitterly that he had almost undergone a change of gender. I didn't hit the bolt, but when a few rounds landed nearby, I dived into a pile of sacred cow chips.

The town of Khulna, 90 miles northeast of Calcutta, was a principal military objective, heavily defended by the Pakistanis. It proved to be the site of the last big battle of the war, and I was with the Indian army when they took it. Along the route Pakistani soldiers lay dead where they had fallen, in or near the trenches. Nearby an Indian tank still smoked after being hit by a recoilless rifle round that had ripped a huge hole underneath the turret. Twelve dead Indian infantrymen were piled behind it. Indian troops hauled away their casualties by lashing them between two poles, the way hunters clear dead quarry.

During the battle I drove to the front with the commander of the Indian Ninth Infantry Division, Major General Dalbar Singh. Pakistani shells were landing all around us when we arrived at his forward command post, only a few hundreds yards from the front lines. A New York freelance photographer who had never covered a war before hitched a ride with me in a jeep heading for where the battle was raging. More artillery greeted our arrival; shrapnel from the exploding shells knocked branches off the trees above us. A heavy machine gun opened up on the attacking Indian troops, and bullets whined over our heads. In the midst of all this a young Indian captain invited us for tea.

"Tea!" I exclaimed. "There's a war on." "Not to worry," he said. "It is tradition that my newly arrived guests should take some tea with their host." We followed him somewhat reluctantly into a small hut. The company was under orders to take the big Pakistani machine gun that hadn't let up since we arrived. Before our unbelieving eyes a soldier walked in with a steaming pot of tea, and the captain invited us to sit at a small table. Plaster was falling from the ceiling. Cracks caused by exploding artillery rounds were appearing in the walls. We expected a shell to crash right through the roof and put an end to our tea party, but none did. The captain never blinked, but it was all I could do to keep from running for the nearest bunker.

At long last the captain rose and said, "Now I must go see to that machine gun." He actually said that. "That's it, I'm getting out of here," I thought, but that proved easier said than done. Because the captain hadn't "seen to that machine gun" yet, it was still pumping rounds our way at a tremendous rate. Time to say adios, I thought. But how to get out? All we could do was press up against a wall and wait for the firing to die down. After a few minutes it did, and we headed back the way we'd come. What we failed to realize was that the road we were on headed toward the front before it curved back toward the rear lines—and the guy firing the machine gun saw us. I happened to have my tape recorder on at the time, and what I recorded was:

"I think we've got it made," I yelled back to my companion. "Just a few more. . . ." *Pop! Pop! Pop!* "Hey, they see us!"

Crash. Next comes the sound of me diving into a depression alongside the road and landing on a dead Indian soldier. My breath is coming in short, fast gulps, and the bullets are cracking overhead. Finally, the firing stops and a jeep comes tearing down the road. We frantically wave it down and cling to the sides as it speeds toward General Singh's command post.

"Whew, we made it," I say as we pull up at the general's command post. My relief is short-lived, however, for although the general's headquarters are in the rear area, they aren't out of Pakistani artillery range.

Once again, we are having tea under fire. General Singh's field office is behind another building, but the first projectile flies right over the top and explodes several yards away. Shrapnel sprays the wall above our heads and kills or wounds several men nearby. Other shells explode harmlessly into the river. The general never spills a drop.

We were with Singh when word arrived that Dacca had surrendered and the war was over. The general ordered an immediate cease-fire and sent word to the Pakistanis, through a captured major, that they should cease and desist.

He waited, we waited, but the shells kept coming and the general got mad. "Have all my guns fire ten rounds each," Singh said, "and see if that doesn't silence the bloody fools." Moments later the roar of Indian artillery resounded across the battlefield, dumping thousands of tons of high explosives on Pakistani positions. When the last echo of the barrage faded away, silence fell over Khulna.

Later that day I went with General Singh to his main command post. A truck loaded with Pakistani prisoners pulled up and the officers were brought before the general for questioning. They appeared dejected but carried themselves with dignity. One officer, a major, quietly smoked a cigarette. The general asked him several questions, and concluded by asking if the men had eaten. When the major said he hadn't, General Singh said, "All right, go do so. I'll not tie you down if you behave like a gentleman. But if you don't, I'll put a bullet in your bloody neck." With that the general turned on his heel and headed to his quarters for a nap. The battle for Khulna—the last of the war—was over, and he knew he'd won.

That night there was a message in the box for me when I returned to my hotel in Calcutta. It was from the information ministry: my press pass was ready. Subsequently, East Pakistan was renamed Bangladesh, and from Calcutta I flew to Dacca, its newly proclaimed capital. When I arrived in Dacca a horrible spectacle was taking place at the central stadium. Horst Faas and Michel Laurent of AP were photographing it. Several Pakistani collaborators were being bayoneted by irate Mukti Bahini, the rebels who had been fighting the Pakistani army. Corpses were on display in the area. The photos they shot that day won Pulitzer prizes for both Faas and Laurent.

Dacca was full of ghastly sights in those days. At a brickyard on the outskirts of town could be found the hastily dug graves of the cream of Dacca's intellectual crop. They had been executed just before the Indian army took over. Dogs pulled at the arms and legs sticking out of the ground, and grieving relatives fought them off as they dug to find their missing loved ones. I started shooting pictures of the scene, but had to stop. It was simply too grisly.

The press, for its part, was awaiting the return of Sheikh Mujibur Rahman, who was being held prisoner by the government of Pakistan. He was the head of the party that would be running the newly formed state of Bangladesh, and he was, in addition, the spiritual leader of the people. In the meantime we were looking for other stories around Dacca. We found one on the outskirts of town. People who had been sympathetic to the old government were interned under deplorable circumstances in camps around Dacca. As usual, children were paying the price of their parents' misdeeds. Whole families were kept in small rooms, food was at a premium, and many of the little ones were starving. Ron Miller of ABC saved at least one child by smuggling him out of the camp in the trunk of his car, but so many others remained behind.

A full month later word reached Dacca that Sheikh Mujibur was coming home. When the big day arrived I was so sick with an intestinal virus that I could hardly walk. More than a million people turned out in the 105 degree heat, which just about matched my fever, to see their hero return. The press was provided with a truck for the motorcade from the airport to Dacca. It was the only way we could photograph the Sheikh as he drove through the pushing, screaming, adoring crowds. By the time the caravan reached the Intercontinental Hotel, where we were staying, I was too ill to go on, and jumped down from the truck. Michel Laurent, my AP competitor, took my cameras and photographed the Sheikh's speech for me—suggesting that my business isn't as cutthroat as many believe. Not so the Sheikh's: some years later he and his family were gunned down in front of their Dacca home during a military coup.

Pictures from the Album

PRESIDENT FORD'S TRIP TO RUSSIA in the fall of 1974 to discuss the SALT treaties also included visits to Japan and Korea.

Japan, our foremost Asian ally, was the first stop. I soon discovered that all foreign trips were surrounded by the tightest security. Every single member of the President's party had to wear a special lapel button to identify himself. My foot hadn't quite touched the ground at Haneda Airport when I was grabbed by several Japanese guards who thought I should be behind the ropes with the rest of the photographers. "Not press, not press," I shouted at them, pointing to my button, but they persisted until a Secret Service agent extricated me from their clutches.

We were put up in the state guest house, a scale model of Versailles called Akasaka Palace. Within hours of my arrival I got a call from a Japanese reporter who wanted to interview me, saying she'd heard about me from the American press. Curious as to just what it was she'd heard, I agreed to meet her outside of the heavily guarded grounds of the palace. The reporter turned out to be a very beautiful young lady, and our interview, which commenced in a small sushi bar, ended in the apartment of Norman Lloyd, a colleague from my Vietnam days who was now living in Tokyo. I later received a copy of her story, which ran along with a photograph of me in my old battered raincoat. The headlines translated to "Colombo of the White House."

The Emperor of Japan officially greeted the President the following morning. The traditional garb for such an occasion is a morning coat and striped pants, which Ford had just donned when I entered his room that morning. "How do I look?" the President asked.

"Your pants are too short," I replied.

"Oh, my God," he said, looking at himself in a full-length mirror. He disappeared into his bedroom, but soon reemerged. "I've discovered the problem," he said. "It isn't the pants."

"What is it?" I asked.

"The suspenders are too short. But if I don't wear them, it's going to be another problem of a more embarrassing nature." So he wore the long-enough pants with the not-long-enough suspenders, and the press gleefully reported that Ford's pants were too short. Nobody noticed that the Emperor's pants were too long.

Wearing fashionable clothes was never a particular concern of Mr. Ford's. During that same trip I took a picture of him meeting with his staff in an ornate room in the Akasaka Palace. He was wearing a checkered bathrobe, striped pajamas, and brown moccasins.

I also remember Mrs. Ford's giving him hell one weekend at Camp David about a favorite old jacket he was wearing. "There's nothing wrong with this jacket," he said defensively.

"Where did you get it?" I asked.

"Malacca, in 1946," he replied. He also had—and probably still has—an old red terry-cloth robe that he wore to and from the White House pool. Mrs. Ford tried several times to throw it away, but he always retrieved it, and when he thought she wasn't watching he'd wear it to the pool.

In Kyoto, Japan's ancient capital, we attended a traditional dinner complete with raw fish and geisha girls. The President did pretty well with the chopsticks, having practiced on the plane, but judging from the amount of food passing from the plate to his mouth, he would certainly have starved to death if he'd been forced to eat every meal that way. Part of the after-dinner entertainment included a Japanese equivalent of our game in which you hold an apple against your neck with your chin and pass it to someone else. Their version involved holding a straw pressed between the upper lip against the nose and passing it to the person next to you. The President looked askance at this procedure, but gave it a try nonetheless and succeeded. All the other staffers followed suit, including Secretary Kissinger, who took off his glasses and scrunched up his face to pin the straw underneath his nose. Most of us had never seen Kissinger without his glasses, and we roared with laughter at his efforts, which made him look like a frog with its face pushed against a window.

Korea was the next stop. President Park Chung-Hee had turned out more than a million people to cheer the visiting President. On the drive into Seoul I ran ahead of the slow motorcade to take photographs of the President, only to have the motorcade pick up speed. It looked like I might get left there in the crowd when a Secret Service man grabbed me by the arm and pulled me into his convertible. It was in Korea that I once again ran into one of the most colorful figures in the Army, Lieutenant General James Hollingsworth, known to the men who served under him in Vietnam by his code name, "Danger Seven Niner." He'd subsequently been given command of one American and twelve Korean divisions, and the Koreans had taken to the crusty, outspoken Texan immediately. (He'd reportedly informed the South Koreans that if the North Koreans ever came across the DMZ he'd "destroy them with violence.")

There were a lot of Hollingsworth stories floating around Vietnam, several of them regarding B-52 missions. A B-52 can drop thirty-five tons of bombs in a single raid, and since they usually fly sorties with three aircraft, it creates one helluva bang. Hollingsworth, in his capacity as an advisor to the ARVN, had gotten a report that a number of North Vietnamese had infiltrated a particular area, and ordered a B-52 strike. After the bombs were dropped, the general received a report that more NVA troops were moving into the area that had just been hit and were holing up in the fresh bomb craters. "Put another one on the same spot," Hollingsworth ordered, thus signing the death warrant for some four hundred V.C.

You might say that Danger Seven Niner was an unadorned personality, something Henry Catto was to discover in my presence. Henry was the Chief of Protocol, and he had just returned from a trip to the Soviet Union. He showed up at a cocktail party in Seoul wearing a hammer and sickle pin, given to him by his Russian hosts, in his lapel. "What kind of a Communist motherfucker are *you*?" Hollingsworth demanded of Catto. As Henry groped for an appropriate response, I said, "General, this is Henry Catto. He is the Chief of Protocol of the United States of America." "I don't give a shit who you are," said Hollingsworth to Catto. "I spend my whole life killing Commies, and now I turn around and here's *one of our guys* wearing their crap." Catto removed the pin.

Vladivostok in the Soviet Union was our final destination. There we were to meet the General Secretary of the Communist Party, Leonid Brezhnev, for what everyone recognized would be the most substantive part of our trip. I was standing in the doorway of the President's plane when I noticed Ambassador Anatoly Dobrynin, the Soviet Union's envoy to the U.S., standing with Foreign Minister Gromyko and Brezhnev. Dobrynin waved, and I waved back. We'd met several times in the States, and I'd always supplied him with photographs of his meetings at the White House. He said something to Brezhnev and Gromyko and then pointed to me. As soon as the stairs had been pushed up to the door, I ran down. What followed was a television rerun of sorts. My feet hadn't been planted on Soviet soil for more than two seconds when once again I was collared, this time by the KGB, who were bigger and tougher than their Japanese counterparts. One of them started to lead me away, then dropped me like a hot cinder. Brezhnev had spoken. I grinned gratefully and waved at the Russian leader, who nodded and smiled.

Ford and Brezhnev held their initial meeting on board the train from the airport to Vladivostok, several miles away. This unique setting made for great pictures. Everyone had assumed that the two leaders would get along well, and they did, perhaps in part because they both came from modest backgrounds.

The SALT talks were held in a conference hall on the grounds of a compound that the Russians described as their equivalent of Camp David. In spirit perhaps, but not in comfort. It was pretty bleak. When I reached the summit hall I was once again nailed by the KGB. Again Brezhnev came to my rescue, and I was free to take pictures. The press always had a tough time with Russian security, and although I wasn't technically one of them, I nonetheless sympathized. (My favorite KGB story is one I heard from a photographer who asked a guard if he could pass through to take a photograph of the summit meeting. "No problem. Impossible," was the hearty response.) I was now fortunate enough to be in the group of those privileged to follow the President closely, and after so many years on the outside it seemed a special luxury.

There had never been photographs taken of previous SALT talks, at least not during the actual meetings, but I took a few at Vladivostok. At certain points during the meetings, both sides took breaks for private conferences. Instead of going to the room provided for them by the Russians, President Ford, Secretary Kissinger, and their entourage assembled outside, to "take the air" under a street lamp. In this case, the air they were taking was 20 degrees below zero, but at least they knew their meetings weren't electronically bugged.

After the conclusion of the talks Brezhnev insisted that Ford see the port of Vladivostok, so the motorcade sped through the town just after sunset. The port had been off limits to foreigners for years, and we were the first Americans to visit there in more than two decades. I'd give anything to be able to describe the place, but as I said, it was after sunset and it was dark. It figures the Russians would show us the city when they knew we wouldn't be able to see it. When we finally winged out of Russia on Air Force One, the mood aboard the plane was buoyant. The only thing better than visiting the Soviet Union, some of us decided, was leaving it.

Things began to deteriorate rapidly in Vietnam in March of 1975. The North Vietnamese had mounted another major offensive, and this time it looked as if the ARVN soldiers weren't going to be able to hold their ground in the northern provinces of South Vietnam. As the crisis broke the President called a meeting with Secretary Kissinger, General Fred Weyand, the Army Chief of Staff, and our ambassador to Vietnam, Graham Martin, who was in the U.S. recovering from a minor operation. I photographed the meeting and then stuck around to listen. Vietnam wasn't out of my system yet.

President Ford asked General Weyand to leave early the next morning for Vietnam. He was to assess the situation and let Ford know if there was anything short of renewed military involvement that we could offer the beleaguered country. After the others had left the office, I asked the President if I could go with Weyand. My personal feelings about the matter were apparent to the President. "Sure," he said. "Besides, I'd be interested to hear your view of what's going on when you get back." With that, I arranged to join Weyand's mission and hung a sign on my office door that read, "Gone to Vietnam, back in two weeks."

Later that evening I went to say good-bye to President and Mrs. Ford. As I was walking out the door I asked the President, "Do you have a few bucks you can lend me? The banks are closed and we're leaving too early for me to get any money."

The President pulled all the bills he had out of his wallet. "Here's forty-seven dollars, Dave. Don't spend it all at once," he said. I thanked him and headed for the door.

"Kennerly . . ." he interrupted. I turned around and he flipped me a quarter, ". . . you might as well clean me out." Then he turned serious: "Be careful," he said, putting an arm around my shoulder.

Our C-141 Air Force cargo plane stopped in Anchorage and Tokyo before reaching Saigon. The trip took more than twenty-four hours, and I was beat when we arrived. Ambassador Martin invited me to stay at his residence with some of the other officials on the trip, among them two top-ranking CIA men and several National Security Council staffers. The one I roomed with was Ken Quinn, who'd spent years in Vietnam with the State Department and was married to a Vietnamese. One of Ken's activities at the time was unofficial—extremely unofficial. He was making preparations to get his Vietnamese relatives and friends out of the country. He and a few other State Department guys had established an elaborate underground network that spirited thousands of South Vietnamese to freedom before the government collapsed.

Saigon was once again a center of action. It seemed that every newsperson who'd covered the war had shown up for the latest action. I had a brief but enthusiastic reunion with all my old buddies at UPI, but the occasion was spoiled by the ominous war clouds that hung on the horizon. My Vietnamese friends were plainly terrified. One of them pleaded with me to take his children with me when I left. "At least *they* will survive," he cried. I was heartbroken, knowing there was no way I could take anyone on the general's plane. I felt utterly helpless, although I later learned that he *had* gotten his family out.

That same day Art Lord of NBC asked if I could arrange an appointment with Ambassador Martin. Lord was in charge of attempting to evacuate all of the network's Vietnamese employees and said it couldn't be done without Martin's approval. The ambassador, however, had refused to speak with him or to any other press people. Glad that I was in a position to help, I set up the appointment and Art made his plea on behalf of his charges. The ambassador pointed out that he had huge problems of his own. Among other things he was personally responsible for the Vietnamese who were or had ever been employed by U.S. agencies and that represented thousands of people. "Besides," he said, "why is it you are wanting to evacuate your Vietnamese when all of your news reports are saying that nothing will happen to the population in the event of a North Vietnamese takeover?" Martin, although clearly extremely bitter about what he considered the hypocrisy of the situation, later relented.

I felt I simply had to get up north, to see what was going on. It was the only way I could make an honest assessment of the situation for the President. After taking a few pictures of Weyand's meeting with President Nguyen Van Thieu—among the last shots of Thieu as President of South Vietnam—I arranged for a plane ride north. Da Nang was in such an uproar that it was impossible to land there. Paul Vogle, a UPI correspondent, had been on a World Airways jet that made it in to Da Nang to pick up refugees. His plane had been stormed by hundreds of frantic people. In their frustration at not being allowed on board, some Vietnamese shot at the aircraft, and one soldier threw a hand grenade that damaged a wing. The plane almost didn't make it, and a man who tried to hang onto the landing gear was crushed between the flaps and the wing when the wheels retracted. Vogle described the ride as a nightmare.

With Da Nang inaccessible, we flew toward Nha Trang on the coast. Refugees had swollen that small coastal town's population to four or five times its normal size and they were still pouring in from the highlands. Montcrieff Spear, the Consul General in Nha Trang, invited me to stay at his home, where I found his wife packing up a few of their belongings and crying. She would be leaving the following day for Saigon, she said. Hope was disappearing as fast as the tears were falling from her eyes. Spear and I flew in an Air American helicopter to Cam Ranh Bay to look at ships filled with refugees coming into that port from Da Nang. We were also looking for Al Francis, the consul general at Da Nang, who was reportedly on one of the ships. We eventually spotted him on the *Pioneer Commander,* towering above the Vietnamese. There were more than 8,000 people on board a sister ship, the *Pioneer Contender,* most of them airborne soldiers who had forced their way on board in Da Nang. Spear dispatched a boat to pick Francis up, and as he did so we took fire from the *Pioneer Contender,* which was filled with escaping South Vietnamese troops. I could see the flashes from the crowded ship as we went by, and so did the pilot, who took evasive action.

There was something surreal about being intentionally shot at by the good guys, and the only reason I could give for their action was that they were frustrated that we Americans had bailed out of Vietnam after more than ten years. Fortunately, we didn't take any hits, and we landed at Cam Ranh ahead of the ships.

State Department officer Walter Martindale was with me at Cam Ranh, and the two of us helped lead some children from the ships onto waiting trucks. I took a photograph of Walter with a barefoot child under each arm as he carried them across the hot pavement. Walter had adopted two Vietnamese children, and he asked me to take them from Nha Trang to Saigon. We got out of Nha Trang only one day before it was abandoned to the fast-advancing NVA troops.

The next day, I flew to Phnom Penh on Air America, the CIA airline. Our pilot circled several times over the airport because it was being shelled by advancing Khmer Rouge soldiers. We corkscrewed down and taxied to a spot in front of the terminal. Magnum photo agency photographer Mark Godfrey and I jumped out before the plane stopped taxiing, but nobody was to be seen. They had all ducked behind sandbags.

We hitched a ride to the Hotel Le Phnom, and there I met my old buddy Matt Franjola. Matt, who was by then running the AP bureau in Cambodia, informed us that "there are only a few days left for this country." He had just filed a story about Sean Flynn, actor Errol's son, who had been missing in Cambodia for several years. Flynn had been captured by the Khmer Rouge on April 6, 1970, as he and Dana Stone, a CBS cameraman, were riding motorbikes down a country road. Since that time dozens of stories about their capture had surfaced, but none shed any new light on the question of whether they were still alive.

Matt had written the latest Sean Flynn story, based on an interview with a Khmer Rouge political commissar who had defected to the government. The official had told Matt that he personally saw Flynn killed by the injection of a lethal drug at a field hospital a year after his capture. The order, the commissar had told Matt, came from a higher command. When Franjola showed the defector a number of pictures of missing journalists, the Khmer Rouge operative immediately picked out Flynn's. As usual, there was no way of verifying the story, but Matt observed that the commissar didn't know who Flynn's famous father was and, as far as Matt knew, he had no reason to lie.

I wanted to see what was happening around Phnom Penh, so Matt and I took off in his jeep. We drove straight to an unfinished gambling casino on the banks of the Mekong River. It was filled with hundreds of refugees from the countryside. As I was walking down one of its dark corridors I spotted a flash of light. Sitting on the dirt floor was a small girl, a tear running down her cheek and a fly meandering across her face. Around her neck was a dogtag, whose glint had caught my eye. Now it was worn as a trinket. Maybe it was her dead father's. Who knows? Her eyes moved me most; they seemed to reflect the horrors of all wars, past and present. They weren't terrified, happy, or sad. They were *vacant*. They were without hope. In that small child's eyes I saw everything I'd ever witnessed in war. It was always the children who really suffered—not the generals or the politicians, but the children.

We then drove to a sports auditorium that had been converted into a hospital to handle the massive influx of wounded soldiers and civilians. Off to one side of the main gymnasium was a small area that had been converted into an emergency operating room for the severely wounded. I walked in to find a man comforting his wife. A huge hole had been ripped in her back by a piece of shrapnel. She died a few minutes later, her husband still clinging to her lifeless body.

I was completely drained and depressed when I returned to the airport and climbed into the back of a small cargo plane to hitch a ride back to Saigon. A smiling Cambodian wearing a helmet and flak jacket waved good-bye to me as he closed the door. As I took his picture I knew it was probably the last I'd ever take in Cambodia.

Back in Saigon I encountered Ken Quinn, whose meetings with certain high-ranking embassy officials had convinced him that "the jig was up." He was certain, after talking to Ambassador Martin, that there was no evacuation plan and that Martin was living in a never-never land. He had therefore called a meeting of four or five like-minded diplomats and they started making evacuation plans of their own. They put together a series of safe houses, where Vietnamese could gather for evacuation, and a communications system to prepare the names of those to go—all without the ambassador's knowledge.

Our flight back to the States was a somber one, and it gave me time to consider everything I'd recently seen in Vietnam and Cambodia. It also gave me a chance to reflect on the things that had been pleasant and memorable: those quiet nights spent with other newsmen, lying on straw mats at Madame Chantelle's opium den in Phnom Penh; the "33" beer and dumplings at the morning restaurants set up outside my Saigon office; being quietly propelled through the crowded streets of Phnom Penh by a pedicab driver. There were so many things I would miss, but above all I was haunted by the face of that little Cambodian girl. I often wonder where she is now. Has she been butchered, along with millions of her countrymen, by the Khmer Rouge, or merely put to work in the fields until she drops over dead? One thing I cannot imagine is that those sad eyes are any happier today.

All that remained for me now was to convince the President that the end was in sight, in the best way I knew—through my photographs. General Weyand and his staff were preparing their report. I was formulating my own. President Ford was in Palm Springs, so that's where Weyand's plane landed. Ford wasn't home when we arrived, but Mrs. Ford was. She was sitting by the swimming pool; when I walked out, she immediately leapt up, threw her arms around me and gave me a kiss. "We got a report that they'd shot at you, David, and we were so worried," she said. I assured her I was all right, but that Vietnam wasn't. We talked for a time and then I excused myself to ship my film on to Washington for processing. I was eager to deliver my photographic report on Vietnam to the President, and as soon as my developed pictures arrived in Palm Springs late the next afternoon, I showed them to him.

"This is what's going on," I said as he slowly studied each photograph. He sadly shook his head, first at the pictures of ships filled with refugees from Da Nang, then at the buses crammed with fleeing villagers in Nha Trang, and finally at the dying civilians in Phnom Penh. "Mr. President," I said, "Vietnam has no more than a month left, and anyone who tells you different is bullshitting." He was devastated.

It may have been the first time in history that an American President had ever been shown the human side of war almost as it was happening. It was one thing to read the weekly body count and the other statistics, and quite another to see those bodies before your eyes. My stark, black-and-white photographs of refugees and civilian casualties soon replaced the color prints of dancers, state visits, and similar events that hung in the corridors of the West Wing. My pictures were everywhere you turned, even in the hallway leading to the staff dining room, and many people reportedly couldn't eat after seeing them. (I only wish my pictures had been hung in the White House when the war began, rather than as it ended.) I began to receive complaints about these grim pictures and decided that the President should decide whether they stayed up or not. "Leave them up," he said emphatically. "Everyone should know what's going on over there."

Matt Franjola was right about Cambodia. It fell exactly when he'd predicted, and he made it out on the last chopper.

The President was in a late-night meeting of the National Security Council in the Cabinet Room at the White House, surrounded by generals, intelligence specialists, politicians, and staff members. Only one man could give the word to pull out of Southeast Asia—the President himself. I photographed him on April 19, his head buried in his hands, moments before he gave the word to evacuate Cambodia and abandon their government. Ten days later, sitting in the same chair, and surrounded by the same people, he gave the order to pull out of Vietnam.

One of the truly unique aspects of the Vietnam withdrawal was that I was able to see both sides of what was going on. I'd been in Vietnam when things started to come unglued, and now I was photographing the meeting at which the entire enterprise collapsed, once and for all. I really envied friends like Dirck Halstead, Matt Franjola, Nik Wheeler and Hugh Van Es, who were in Saigon for the final days. On the other hand I felt it was important to shoot this side of the story.

A few days before the end, former *Life* photographer Dick Swanson, aware that I knew what was really happening in Vietnam, asked me to tell him just how bad it was. I said it looked like a matter of time, and not much time at that. Dick immediately flew to Vietnam and rescued his Vietnamese wife's mother, three brothers, sister, and several nieces and nephews the very day before Saigon fell. In all he brought back twelve relatives.

The President monitored the evacuation closely, and relayed messages to Saigon through Secretary Kissinger. Ambassador Martin was holding out for more choppers, and not until he was told that the last lift was on the way did he abandon his embassy. Kissinger sardonically remarked that Martin "got five hundred of his last hundred evacuees out." A few hours after Martin was evacuated to the Philippines, I walked into Kissinger's office. "I understand Martin's not leaving Manila until he gets all the Philippinos out," I joked.

At the final count the President was responsible for the evacuation of more than 130,000 Vietnamese and might have pulled out more if the NVA hadn't stepped up their attacks on Saigon. He did this despite pressure from some of his top officials, who urged him to forget the Vietnamese and just take out the Americans. "No way," he said, "we'll take as many as we can."

Nevertheless, many people who had performed jobs for the Americans were left behind. This genuinely distressed Ford, and his mood was not helped by a group of people from CBS for whom he agreed to give an interview. In his usual hospitable fashion, he invited them upstairs to his private quarters for a drink. I followed to take a few snaps. Bill Small, vice-president for CBS news, turned to the President. "Well," he said, "at least *we* got *our* people out."

Less than two weeks after the evacuation of Vietnam the President faced another international crisis: a U.S. cargo ship, the *Mayaguez,* was captured by Cambodians. Initially, the administration tried to secure the release of the crew through diplomatic channels, sending messages through the Chinese to the Cambodians. There was no reply, however, and there was some doubt that anyone, including the Chinese, really knew who was running Cambodia at the time. The President knew one thing for certain—he had to get the crew back. The National Security Council was called into emergency session, and contingency plans were presented to the President, ranging from massive B-52 strikes against Cambodia to more localized military operations. Throughout the ensuing debate I shot photographs of the Council in the Cabinet Room. Around the table were the nation's heavies: the President, the Vice-President, the Secretary of State, the Secretary of Defense, the Chairman of the Joint Chiefs of Staff, the director of the Central Intelligence Agency, the Chief of Naval Operations, and the Deputy Secretaries of State and Defense.

I had never before spoken out in a Presidential meeting, but this time I couldn't contain myself. I was almost certainly the only person in the room who had been in Cambodia. The discussion centered on the problem of releasing the captured ship, and each proposed solution assumed the existence of a viable government in Phnom Penh, one that would cave in under military pressure. They were talking about darkening the skies above Cambodia with B-52s flying wing to wing, the very sight of which would bring the Khmer Rouge to their knees. "Has it occurred to anyone," I asked the startled group, "that this whole thing may have been the act of one local commander taking matters into his own hands and seizing the ship?"

The President did not choose to exercise his strongest option, the use of the B-52s. They never took off from Guam. Instead, Navy fighters from a nearby aircraft carrier made an air strike around Kom Pong Som, and the Marines landed on a small island where the seamen were thought to be held. Ford also ordered jet fighters to blow some Cambodian patrol vessels out of the water. It was that act, Captain Miller of the *Mayaguez* later said, that saved him and his crew. I photographed the President jubilantly announcing to his top aides that the crew had been released. You could almost see the weight of the last three days lift from the President's shoulders as he spoke.

Airborne

ONE OF THE RESPONSIBILITIES OF THE PRESIDENT, in his role as a world leader, is to visit other heads of state. He travels on Air Force One, a beautiful blue and silver Boeing 707. Inside, the big jet is plush and functional. The President has his own cabin-office, and he travels with a full staff, including Secret Service, press aides, communications experts, military aides, advance men, secretaries, and his personal physician. The only thing that changes is the scenery.

Air Force One has the best communications setup in the

world, and I occasionally used it for my own purposes. If you were to find yourself on the receiving end of one of my calls, a voice would say, "This is the White House signal operator. I have a call for you from Mr. Kennerly on Air Force One. Please remember that these calls may be monitored, so don't discuss classified information. Mr. Kennerly's code name is 'Hot Shot.' Please use that when talking to him. Go ahead." By this time the party I was calling would be slightly disconcerted, and when my voice crackled on the line the first question was usually, "Where are you, Hot Shot?"

These state visits are superficial, largely ceremonial affairs that transport the Chief Executive and his entourage—including, of course, his chief photographer—through countries so fast that you sometimes wonder if you've really been there. Scheduling is so tight that those who plan the President's itinerary have to build in a few minutes during the day when the President can go to the bathroom. This is called "personal time."

On all previous foreign assignments, I'd had an opportunity to photograph everything that was going on. Not so on a presidential trip, where the man himself was my only subject. On one of these outings there was no way to take in the local atmosphere or the local culture, and certainly no way to get any outside pictures. Unlike the intense experience of war, such trips provided little more than a break in White House routine. They did, however, make for occasional excitement. I prefer to describe the odd, amusing incidents the way they happened: quickly.

SPAIN: On our arrival in Madrid we were met by the aging Generalissimo Franco. He was in failing health, and was attended by two aides. The program called for Franco to make his remarks first, after which the President would speak. The two leaders would then turn toward Air Force One, a signal for the band to pass in review. But when the Generalissimo and the President stepped onto the reviewing stand, Franco forgot what he was supposed to do. In his confusion he stepped to the podium, wheeled around, and faced the airplane. The band leader saw the signal, the drums started banging, and the band began marching. Franco's aides saw immediately what was happening, and while one went up to the Spanish dictator and turned him around, others raced across the tarmac toward the advancing band, their arms wildly waving them back.

When Franco at last made his speech, his voice was so low as to be virtually inaudible. To compensate for this, the Spanish turned the volume of the address system up as high as it would go. What they didn't think to do was to turn it down when President Ford stepped up to deliver his remarks. His first few words knocked everyone's socks off.

The President stayed at the Bourbon Palace in central Madrid, and Terry O'Donnell and Red Cavaney, Ford's head advance man, had everything organized for the first meeting between the President and Franco. It was supposed to occur in a private room just off the lobby area. When we arrived there were two old television cameras set up in the lobby, their wires running everywhere. A score of Spanish generals were also scurrying around, and the effect was chaos. After the two heads of state had seated themselves, Terry noticed two of the Spanish television men pushing their giant camera into the meeting room, almost knocking over the table in front of Ford and Franco. The television crew wasn't supposed to be there, but Terry didn't want to create an embarrassing situation by telling them to leave. Instead, he asked Red and me to pull on the cable attached to the camera, and what transpired was nothing more nor less than a tug of war between us and the cameramen. The camera came slowly back through the door with the Spaniards still trying to hold it back. Another victory for the American team.

AUSTRIA: The President's most spectacular arrival. "Welcome to Salzburg, Mr. President," read the signs at the bottom of the ramp, but Ford had little chance to read them, since he tripped and fell down the stairs. It seems that the day before our arrival the ramp that had been designated for the President's aircraft was taken to the other side of the field. In its place was substituted a ramp that had no antiskid material on the stairs. It was raining when we landed, and a steward handed the President an umbrella as he stepped out of Air Force One. He held it in the air with one hand, and guided Mrs. Ford with the other. Then his foot caught on a stair tread and one of his heels came off. When he pitched forward, Mrs. Ford grabbed the umbrella and moved gracefully aside like a matador passing a bull as the President hurtled by. He wasn't hurt, but he was frightfully embarrassed. Typically, Ford held no grudge against the photographers who took pictures of his fall. "They were just doing their job, and they would have been fired if they'd missed it," he said later.

THE VATICAN: Classified cables had been exchanged by the White House and the Pope's aides concerning my attire for this trip. The Vatican was somewhat concerned about "that wild, bearded photographer the President will have with him." Someone in Rome had apparently read a press clip describing me as frightfully irreverent. I never wore a tie, it said, and preferred blue jeans while working at the White House. The Vatican requested that I wear a dark suit, white shirt and tie when meeting His Holiness, Pope Paul VI. Ford's advance staff assured them that I would be dressed correctly for the occasion.

To get into the Papal Library, where the Pope was waiting, we had to pass under numerous arches and down several long corridors. I walked ahead of the President down these quiet hallways where the only sound was the slap of leather soles stepping on cold marble. Everyone spoke in whispers, if they spoke at all. In order to position myself for a picture of the Pope greeting the President I entered the library first. His Holiness was expecting a President, not a Presidential photographer, even one in a dark suit and tie. His hands were held out in greeting, but he quickly drew them back when he saw me and my cameras.

POLAND: A big motorcade was arranged to greet President Ford on his arrival in Poland in July of 1975. Arrangements are usually made for photo-trucks to carry the photographers on such occasions. In this case, however, the Polish government had arranged for only two jeeps, one for the Polish photographers and one for the Americans. The motorcade got no more than a hundred yards out of the airport when the American jeep stalled. We pulled off to the side of the road and Ford, passing by in his car, gave us a quizzical look. We immediately jumped out of the disabled jeep and started flagging down other cars in the motorcade. Six of us, myself included, piled into a car that looked like a Checker cab but was actually a Russian-made car of some kind.

Everytime the motorcade slowed down we'd make a mad dash toward the front, our objective being the Polish photo-jeep. We were well back in the motorcade at the time, and although I ran as fast as I could toward the President's car, before I could reach it, his car started up again. I was only three or four cars from the front of the motorcade, and I had to do something fast, or once again find myself stranded.

There was a big car near the front with only one lady in the back, so I motioned to her and she waved me inside. I could scarcely talk I was so winded, but I did manage to introduce myself. Her English wasn't good, but she managed to introduce herself: "I'm Mrs. Piotr Jaroszewicz," she said, "and I'd like you to meet my husband the Prime Minister." She pointed to the man sitting next to the driver. "Christ," I thought, "now I'm in for it." I glanced out of the rear window and, sure enough, there was a car full of Polish security agents behind us, and they were madder than hell.

When the motorcade slowed down again, I thanked Mrs. Jaroszewicz for the ride and high-tailed it for the front of the motorcade. This time I made it to the Polish photographers' jeep and they pulled me aboard.

FINLAND: On July 28, 1975, the President and thirty other heads of state attended the Helsinki Conference. It was there that I got one of the best shots ever of one of my favorite subjects, General Secretary Brezhnev. In fact, I liked one so much I later sent it to Moscow for Brezhnev to autograph. The photo showed the

General Secretary, a cigarette in one hand, glancing slyly out of the corner of his eye. General Brent Scowcroft, who had dealt extensively with the Russian leader, told me it captured his personality perfectly. My courier for this errand was Peter Rodman of Secretary Kissinger's staff, and Rodman presented the print to Brezhnev during a break in one of the General Secretary's meetings with the Secretary of State. The Russian leader looked at my photograph for a couple of minutes. He then walked out of the room with the picture and returned shortly, handing Rodman a photo. "I think you'll like this one better," he said. The picture, which he had signed, was a very formal portrait taken several years before. It looked as if it had been hastily removed from a frame in the next room. Brezhnev didn't like my shot, but didn't bother to give it back to Peter.

During the Helsinki Conference I took more pictures of the Soviet leader. His security force was immense: standing rigidly against the wall, within a step or two of where Brezhnev was sitting with other heads of state, were no fewer than fourteen KGB guards, each one of whom looked mean enough to eat hand grenades. Just to the right of these huskies sat a well-dressed man who looked for all the world like a young businessman attending a convention. He was a U.S. Secret Service agent.

ROMANIA: On August 2 and 3 the President took a train ride through the land where Count Dracula is supposed to have lived. The Count wasn't in, but our whistle stop did give Terry O'Donnell an opportunity to drop his favorite line from Mel Brooks's movie *Young Frankenstein:* "Pardon me boys, is this the Transylvania Station?" We visited an old castle that had been built exclusively of wood in the Dark Ages; at any moment I expected some sort of evil presence to step from the shadows. O'Donnell and I understood that the original plans included many secret passageways and bedrooms where the king kept his mistresses. We endeavored to find hidden passages and tried to locate hidden latches under railings. Alas, the only thing we found were a few wads of dried gum.

We also got our hands on a bottle of local brew that had been presented to the President by some officials. Knowing that the Secret Service would never allow Ford to touch it—they never let the President eat or drink any food gifts—we drained the whole jug ourselves. For a while afterward I kept a wary eye on O'Donnell to make sure he wasn't growing fangs.

YUGOSLAVIA: At this point it was the last of a five-country trip, and the President was tired. He'd had one reception too many, and this one almost caused him great embarrassment. He had asked for a few minutes alone to review his notes before meeting President Tito, and was sitting in a chair in the middle of a huge room to which only members of his staff had access. There was a set of giant sliding doors that led to the area where his conference was going to be held, and suddenly these doors opened and President Tito—who was not used to waiting for anyone—entered with the whole Yugoslav delegation and made straight for the President's chair. To his horror, Terry O'Donnell, who was responsible for keeping the President on schedule, noticed that he wasn't getting up to greet Tito. He was sound asleep, the notes for his speech in his hand. Just before Tito reached his chair, an alarm must have sounded in Ford's head; he stood up and stretched out his hand. Terry pulled out his handkerchief and wiped the cold sweat from his forehead.

PEOPLE'S REPUBLIC OF CHINA: I had been thwarted in 1972 in my attempt to photograph Chairman Mao, but I thought perhaps my new status as the President's official photographer would impress the Chinese, and I figured I might have a chance of seeing the legendary Chinese leader.

We landed in Peking and were greeted not by Mao but by Teng Hsiao-ping, China's lilliputian Vice Premier.

During his meeting with Ford, Teng, who is smaller than Napoleon, sat opposite the President in a large, overstuffed chair, his feet barely touching the floor, and chain-smoking. He also wore white socks.

The Chinese were very secretive about when the President would meet with Mao. They scheduled no appointments and traditionally came only at the last minute to collect whomever was to have an audience with the aging Chairman. When Ford's time arrived, I vowed to be in the motorcade that went to Mao's residence and tried everything I could think of to get on the official list. Kissinger also tried on my behalf, but he didn't offer me much hope. As the motorcade began to assemble, we were told that only those who were on the list could get into the cars. I was on no list, but I got into a car anyway. The Chinese promptly threw me out. So much for detente. My final chance to see Mao, much less take his picture, was gone. It was a bitter disappointment. Dick Keiser, the head of the President's Secret Service detail, told me that even *his* men were stopped at the gate of Mao's house, and only the official party was permitted. "For all we know, they could substitute another man for the President," he said, a remark designed to get your sci-fi juices flowing.

In the course of Ford's visit to China, Chick Harrity of AP twisted his ankle. We had been following the President on a tour in which he had to climb a huge set of stairs, and Chick had injured himself during that hike. That night the ankle swelled to twice its normal size, and Chick was in great pain. None of the American doctors traveling with the President were available—they were all attending the formal banquet in the Great Hall of the People—so one of Harrity's colleagues went off to look for a Chinese doctor. Half an hour later he returned with an Oriental dressed in a Mao jacket and cap and carrying a black bag. Through an interpreter the man told Harrity to lie on his stomach, and he began to probe the AP newsman's ankle with his fingers. He then opened his bag and withdrew a number of long acupuncture needles, instructing Harrity's friends to hold his shoulders so he wouldn't move.

The last thing Chick saw before averting his eyes were the huge needles, but at that point his foot hurt so badly that he was willing to try anything. He could feel the small sharp pains up and down his leg, and all he heard was the Oriental's reassuring voice saying that it would only be a couple more minutes. All this time Chick's fellow workers trooped into the room, took one look at what was going on, and hurriedly departed. After fifteen minutes or more, Harrity couldn't stand it anymore and he looked around. There wasn't a single needle in his leg. The "Chinese doctor" tending him was actually an NBC soundman of Japanese extraction. All he'd been doing was pinching Chick's leg. (The colleagues who'd left quickly had done so only to burst into laugher outside the door.) Chick, always game, declared that his foot felt a hundred times better anyway.

Of course, Harrity wasn't the only guy who had one pulled on him. Even Eddie Adams, a Pulitzer Prize-winner and one of the best photographers in the business, was the occasional butt of such pranks. On this particular trip he rushed into the AP darkroom with three rolls of film, insisting "I've got to get these developed right now to make *Time*'s deadline." The lab man said he could handle only one roll and asked Adams to mark the most important roll. Eddie carefully marked that roll, left the other two, and went out. The darkroom man, sensing an opportunity for some fun, developed all three rolls and then substituted a blank roll for the important one.

"Is the film ready?" Eddie asked when he got back.

"I only had time to do the two you wanted," he was told.

"Jesus Christ, can't you get anything straight?" Adams said, holding up his marked roll. "This is the one I need, it has the best pictures of the dinner."

"You better do it yourself, then," the lab man said. "We're tied up now." AP photographer Bob Dougherty waited until Eddie walked into the darkroom, then glanced at his watch to figure out the amount of time it would take for Eddie to remove the exposed film from its protective cassette. Dougherty then opened the door to the darkroom and flicked on the lights. "Anybody in here?" he asked innocently.

"Ahhhhh!" came the agonized scream from Adams, who shoved the exposed film between his legs and bent over double. "Turn off the goddamn light!" he yelled. Adams held the blank film cupped in his hands while they showed him the developed roll.

PHILIPPINES: Manila is a booming town, and the nightlife is spectacular. Happy to be out of prudish China, most of the photographers attached to the President's party went to a real dive called the Eagle's Nest, Manila's answer to Madame Lulu's in Vientiane. That night we reveled, and the next day we paid for it. The President took a boat trip to Corregidor with Philippine President Marcos for ceremonies marking the Japanese attack on Pearl Harbor. Marcos's ship had bands playing and an abundance of food, but I spent most of the voyage in a bunk below.

When we finally reached the island, President Marcos insisted on showing Ford around. There wasn't really time for sightseeing, since the President also had to be at Pearl Harbor that same day for more ceremonies, and Terry O'Donnell kept reminding Ford that we had to leave. Marcos, for his part, kept insisting that Ford take a drive with him, and he won. The two leaders climbed into an old Cadillac and headed up into the mountains. After ten minutes, their car broke down and Terry and I were obliged to surrender our seats to them and switch to an old bus that barely made the hill. Now we really *were* late. Ahead of us lay an eight-hour flight to Honolulu, and we had to make the ceremonies there in time for the scheduled nationwide television coverage. That proved to be our longest day, for by crossing the international dateline we managed to be on Corregidor and at Pearl Harbor at the same time on the same day—December 7, 1975.

Nobody had ever photographed the entire process of Kissinger's "shuttle diplomacy," so when he left in August 1975 on one of his many trips to the Middle East, I went along. A tight-knit group of reporters from various news agencies flew with the Secretary on all these trips, and they ate from the palm of Kissinger's hand. He leaked details to them that nobody else in the press was privy to, and consequently the stories most of them wrote or broadcast reflected what Kissinger wanted to say. Although he didn't actually dictate their reports, in many cases he might as well have.

A Kissinger peace mission was a brutal affair, physically as well as psychologically. On a typical day Kissinger arrived at Tel Aviv airport, was greeted by the Israeli Foreign Minister, and boarded a helicopter for the flight to Jerusalem. Once there, he got into a waiting car and sped to the Israeli Prime Minister's home for a meeting. Afterward, he was driven back to the landing pad, where he boarded the chopper for the flight back to Tel Aviv's Ben-Gurion Airport. He then climbed into Air Force Two for a short flight to a secret Egyptian airbase somewhere near Alexandria. There he got into another chopper for a forty-five minute flight to Egyptian President Anwar Sadat's summer home on the Red Sea in Alexandria. After meeting with Sadat he boarded the chopper, flew to the desert base, climbed on Air Force Two and took off for Tel Aviv. And so it went, day after day.

This process would sometimes go on for weeks, altered only for side trips to Jordan, Syria, and Saudi Arabia to inform those governments of the progress of the talks. In time the marathon was to have adverse effects on Kissinger's staff, his Secret Service escorts, and the press. Many dropped by the wayside, suffering from fatigue or other health problems, but the procedure ground on. On one leg of one such trip I ate something that made me sick and dropped out for twenty-four hours. I was lucky; some developed more serious maladies and had to return to the States. Kissinger himself seemed unaffected by the ailments and bugs that plagued the common run of men, and he kept up the harrowing pace throughout, burning up junior staffers as if they were cheap panatellas.

The discussions themselves were not what I expected. I'd always imagined that the negotiations were carried out by serious, sobersided men dressed formally in dark suits, white shirts, and dark ties who sat across from each other at long, polished wooden tables. Not so. At a meeting held in Prime Minister Itzhak Rabin's office in Jerusalem, for instance, several of Kissinger's aides and some of Rabin's advisors wore short-sleeved shirts and crawled around the floor on their hands and knees while they surveyed a huge map of the border between Egypt and Israel. And in Alexandria top-secret discussions with Foreign Minister Ismail Fahmy and other high-ranking Egyptian officers were held at a beach house where most of the participants wore shorts and flowered shirts. The actual meetings with President Sadat were more what I expected, with one important difference. The long wooden table was set outside, on a lawn overlooking the ocean, and behind it was a windswept tree. I photographed that scene at twilight, and it proved to be the best shot of the trip. During these meetings the second Sinai Disengagement Agreement, which provided for a partial Israeli withdrawal in the Sinai, was reached and formally initialed in Alexandria and Jerusalem. It was a successful shuttle for Kissinger; and, as it turned out, his last.

Personal and Confidential

SOMEBODY TRIED TO KILL THE PRESIDENT IN SACRAMENTO. Her name was Squeaky Fromme, and she was a follower of convicted cult murderer Charles Manson. The President's party, which included me, was walking through a park in downtown Sacramento to a meeting with California Governor Jerry Brown, when Fromme pulled a .45 caliber pistol and pointed it at Ford. Secret Service agent Larry Buendorf immediately spotted Fromme and grabbed for the gun. As he lunged for it, the web of skin between his thumb and index finger caught the hammer of the gun before it could fall. The gun was loaded but, as we later learned, there wasn't a bullet in the chamber, something no one had any way of guessing in the split second it took Buendorf to react. I was a few paces ahead of the President at the time and didn't get a picture of Fromme pointing the gun, but I did photograph the agents hustling her from the area.

Minutes later we walked into Brown's office. The governor wasn't told what had happened, and the President carried on his regular discussion. Not until midpoint in their talk did the subject come up. Sometimes nonchalance can be taken too far.

A couple of weeks later we were in San Francisco, where the President had a speaking engagement. The extra security laid on after the assassination attempt in Sacramento had made everyone rather jumpy, although some of the tension seemed to go out of the group when the President and his staff came down from his hotel room in a large freight elevator. There were some twenty people, fifteen of them Secret Service agents, riding in that car as we headed to the basement. Just as we started to step off the elevator, the door, which came down from above, closed abruptly. It hit the President on the head, but a rubber bumper on the edge of the door saved him from serious injury. The President returned to his room, where Dr. William Lukash, a Navy admiral and Ford's personal physician, put a bag of ice on the bump. I took a couple of photos as the President made light of the incident.

He didn't joke about what happened an hour later. Sara Jane Moore tried to kill him. I had gone down to the street in front of the hotel, where the President's car was parked. A crowd had gathered across the street, and they had been joined by several demonstrators, who were making a lot of noise. A cold chill came over me, the kind that I'd experienced several times in Southeast Asia; the kind of feeling I had the day I told a driver to turn around on a deserted road outside Phnom Penh. I told Ron Pontius, a senior Secret Service agent, of my feelings and asked him not to let the President cross the street to shake hands with the crowd. Pontius agreed with me, although with the demonstration he probably wouldn't have let Ford go anyway.

The President came downstairs, and as he walked out from under the marquee I stood on the other side of his car, taking pictures. He headed straight for the car, pausing only momentarily to wave at the people on the other side of the street. At that moment a shot rang out and Ford winced. Two agents immediately pushed him down behind the car, and I ran around to the other side of the bulletproof limo to take pictures. I could hardly see the President for the agents protecting him. They shoved him into the car and kept him on the floor until they got well out of the area. I barely made it into the control car, which always followed the Secret Service car that tailed the Presidential limousine. We had a wild ride to the airport, where the agents rushed Ford into his compartment on Air Force One. As Mrs. Ford, who was to meet her husband at the airport, was coming in on another plane, we waited there. The President was extremely tense so I stuck my head into his lounge and said, "Other than that, Mr. President, how'd you like San Francisco?" That lightened the atmosphere and seemed to make him feel better. Mrs. Ford arrived shortly thereafter. She had no idea of what happened, and when she walked into the cabin we were all sitting around with the President. "How did it go?" she asked innocently. We all began to laugh. Under the circumstances, we couldn't help ourselves.

The President's reaction to this, the second attempt on his life, was one of anger. He was adamant that these attempts would not keep him locked up in the Executive Mansion. "I won't be held prisoner in the White House by a few kooks running around out there," he insisted, although he did agree to wear a bulletproof vest when making public appearances.

A few weeks later the Presidential party found itself in the same San Francisco hotel, and while we were there one of the Secret Service agents showed me a diagram of the shooting that pinpointed where everyone had been standing at the time the shot was fired. By their computation the bullet had passed within a foot of me and a Secret Service agent.

Word had reached the press that something was going on in my headquarters in the White House basement. On September 8, 1975, *Newsweek* carried an item in the "Periscope" section under the headline "Bye-bye, Birdie?" It read:

> Relations between Gerald Ford and White House photographer David Kennerly, whom the President once called "one of the family," are beginning to fray. The exuberant, free-wheeling manner of the twenty-eight-year-old Kennerly, long an irritant to some senior Ford aides, has apparently begun to annoy the President. Kennerly has been ordered to drop three of his seven-man staff and there have been hints in the White House that the whole operation should be scrubbed.

It was indeed true that some "senior Ford aides" didn't like my close relationship with the President and tried to get me bounced by leaking stories to the press. But after a year on the job I'd learned to expect—and ignore—such charges. And besides, my relations with the President couldn't have been better. It was also true I was told to drop three people from my office. Don Rumsfeld, then Chief of Staff, had ordered the entire White House staff reduced, and because my office was technically an extension of the press office, this created problems. Until then I'd run my operation with no interference from Ron Nessen's press empire, but Rumsfeld's orders were "Cut six people from your staff of 47." Naturally protective of his own staffers, Nessen proposed cutting three from my staff of seven—and three from the remaining forty on his immediate staff. That struck me as grossly unfair, and I detailed my misgivings in a memo to Rumsfeld's office. Among other things I pointed out that such a cut would mean making twelve percent of the total White House staff cuts from one percent of the White House staff. Nessen now suggested that my photo setup wasn't contributing significantly to the overall press operation. I countered with more numbers. How many newspapers and television stations had we provided with photos? I concluded by recommending that my office become a separate entity, with no ties whatsoever to the press office. Rumsfeld, who was in charge of all White House operations, agreed. I did have to make some staff changes, but by juggling a couple of my people to different payrolls I saved all jobs. It was like magic: if you walked into my office and counted heads you'd find seven people, but if you counted them on paper, you'd get five. Presto! Everybody was happy except Nessen, who was given a new quota. He was still under orders to cut seven from his staff, but now that staff numbered only forty.

A couple of weeks later, I was scheduled to do an interview with Barbara Walters on the "Today" show. It was set for a Monday morning and I had gone to New York the night before. While perusing the Washington Sunday papers I came across an item in Maxine Cheshire's column that linked Barbara romantically with a certain U.S. Senator from Massachusetts. On the way to the studio Dave Burnett and I discussed the show. "If she says anything about that *Newsweek* item," I told Dave, "I'm going to bring up that bit in Cheshire's column."

NBC had done a great job on the set. Huge blowups of pictures I'd taken of the President were hanging as a backdrop, and I was facing Barbara eye-to-eye for the interview. After the preliminaries she launched the heavy artillery: "In a recent article *Newsweek* magazine said that you were out of favor with the President, and that your staff was being cut," she said. "What do you have to say about that?" The moment she started to ask me the question, I looked across to Burnett, who was standing just off camera. He covered his eyes with both hands.

"Well, Barbara," I said, looking right at her, "that story falls into the same category as those about you and Senator Brooke. It's all rumor and gossip." That did it. The interview sharply took a turn in my favor after that, and we discussed what I'd hoped to discuss from the beginning: the President, Mrs. Ford, and photography.

Not only were the President and I getting along, he loved making jokes at my expense and sometimes made them publicly. For instance, at the annual dinner of the White House News Photographers' Association, the President made remarks appropriate to that occasion: "At the White House we have a richness of photographic talent," he told the gathering. "There's an old saying that one picture is worth a thousand words. In David Hume Kennerly I get both. I'm sure all of the professional people here are familiar with Dave Kennerly. Dave is known as the Ansel Adams of M Street (naming a legendary American photographer). David is also one of the finest, most talented, most creative, most gifted photographers this nation has ever known. And that's not just my opinion, it's his too."

One of the great things about our relationship was that I could often break the tension for him when he was under stress. Sometimes I'd sit with him in the late evening and talk about matters that didn't relate to what had been going on during the day. I figured if he'd been wrestling with the problems in the Oval Office for twelve to sixteen hours, he didn't need to rehash them at night. His three sons, the eldest of whom was very near my age, were hardly ever there, and he missed them. In many ways I was a son pro tempore in their absence. He trusted me in the same way he trusted them, and he knew I'd never talk about sensitive matters of any sort.

I also dropped by to see Mrs. Ford at least once a day. She referred to the second floor of the White House as "our one-bedroom apartment," and said at times that it was a lonely place. That may be hard to imagine, but the White House is really more a museum than a home. Despite the large staff ready to cater to the First Family's every whim, I got the impression that Mrs. Ford would have much preferred to live in their old home in Alexandria. "I wonder what people would think if I just packed up and moved out?" she sometimes asked me, only half kidding. When I first took the job I already liked the Fords very much, but I had no idea I'd be drawn so close to them. Once they walked through the White House doors on August 9, 1972, their lives changed irrevocably.

Having a job at the White House can be likened to working in a mine field—one wrong step and you get blown to high heavens. It almost happened to me during Ford's 1976 primary campaign battle with Ronald Reagan. Something I had done privately threatened to become public in a way that might possibly have cost the President the nomination. Two months after I'd started the job in the White House, my dentist asked me if I could do a favor for one of his other patients. The patient, a secretary for Congressman Wayne Hays, was Elizabeth Ray. She wanted some pictures for her modeling portfolio. I shot the pictures, some seminude, at my home. This was at least a year before the revelations about Ray and her congressman created a sensation and led to Hays leaving Congress. I'd forgotten all about the session until I picked up a paper and saw her name. My first reaction on seeing the story was, "Hey, I know that girl." It didn't take me long to wish I hadn't. The problem was not that I had taken the pictures, but that I had naively sent the film to the White House lab for development. I had long ago reimbursed the government approximately five dollars for the costs, but that wouldn't have made the slightest difference to those eager to exploit the situation. I could see Reagan supporters gleefully hoisting papers with headlines like "White House Lab Develops Nude Pix." I was a nervous wreck. I sought the advice of Dean Burch, an attorney who was an assistant to the President and a man I liked and trusted. "I'm going to resign before this thing hits," I told him, but Burch advised me not to be hasty. For three days I went through hell, and when it finally appeared the story wasn't going to break, I felt enormous relief.

My political education was coming the hard way. It just wasn't possible for me to be as carefree a character as I had been before joining the White House staff. It didn't seem fair that such a minor thing could ruin my career, and possibly the President's, but that's the reality. That's the White House. It's also one reason why people there stick together.

The President, Mrs. Ford, and I stuck together as well. It often seemed as if I were one of the family, and I naturally wanted to help them out. I especially felt this when I returned from a speaking tour where I had showed slides to professional photographers around the country. On tour I came to the conclusion that the President wasn't being perceived accurately by the American people. "Why doesn't the man in your pictures come across that way in public?" I was constantly asked. A good question, and I knew the answer. I'd always maintained that if every eligible voter in America could see Ford in action, or somehow sit down and talk with him for a few minutes, he could get 100 percent of the vote, come election time. This was of course impossible, and it therefore became the duty of his public relations department—press office, photographers, speech writers, and all the rest—to make sure the *real* Ford translated to the vast majority of the public. It wasn't happening, and as I became more worried I tried to do something about it. I wrote what was, for me, a rare memorandum to the President:

November 18, 1975

PERSONAL AND CONFIDENTIAL
MEMORANDUM FOR THE PRESIDENT

FROM: DAVID KENNERLY

Last week I made four slide presentations in different areas of the country. More than 2,600 professional newspaper photographers, editors and students from practically every State in the union attended. I showed a sampling of pictures I took over the last year, and the response was extremely good. I think it is important to note that the audiences viewed the pictures of you as a true representation of the way you are as a person and of what your job involves. One reaction to the show took me by surprise, however. Audiences consistently said that the public perception of you as the serious, deliberate man handling decisive issues had not been carried across to them—until this show.

These reactions concern me. Because I have spent my professional life on the other side of the lens, recording events and people with my camera, I have a special perspective on the problems of accurate visual communication.

I believe, for one thing, that the public image of you is incomplete because your personality and style have not been fully and accurately reflected through the media.

For one thing, much of the coverage of you at the White House involves insignificant events, and when significant meetings are photographed by the press the coverage does not convey the atmosphere of the meeting itself. There was, for instance, a recent meeting that was used on the networks to illustrate the New York City default story. The pictures, taken before the actual meeting began, showed you and your economic advisors smiling and joking with one another. This certainly does not reflect your real attitude, as my pictures made during the actual meeting show.

Obviously, media cameras can't be present at all times during every meeting. However, this problem could be countered by carefully increasing access during the beginning of some actual working situations. This would allow photographers to capture the flavor of what was happening in the meeting and would be a good first step toward straightening out the public's misconceptions. It would put both you and the press in real situations.

A few nonvisual suggestions: I get the feeling that the American people are much more impressed by, and have more interest in, a working President than a campaigning President, particularly in these days of vast unemployment and a shaky economy. Extensive campaigning may be counterproductive. I therefore think campaign trips should be kept to a minimum. Those trips you do make should be well-planned, with emphasis placed on fresh material for speeches where you will get better press coverage and won't risk overexposure.

In conclusion, what you *don't* want to do is put the media in the position of having to guess who you really are and what you really mean. Your candid forthrightness is what initially gained you the support of the American people. You took over the reins of government at a time when there was no leadership and through your character and skill you provided that leadership. You once told me that you will be elected President because the American people will want you for the man that you are. You said then that you didn't want any false image created to portray you as someone you are not. What is necessary now is to look for situations that give the public an accurate understanding of what you're all about.

The White House, gearing up for the 1976 primary campaign, established a group to run the operation and called it the President Ford Committee. Jerry McGee, a feisty leprechaun who was a vice-president with the New York advertising firm of Ogilvy & Mather, was brought in to write and produce television ads for the primary battles. He was told by the people at PFC that everyone at the White House would cooperate but that there was one guy he should have absolutely nothing to do with—David Kennerly.

Naturally I was the first one he called. "If those jerks thought you were the one to watch out for, then it must be that you can get things done," he said.

Part of Jerry's responsibility was to build a film library of the President in action to be used in producing future ads. The first chance he had to shoot any footage came after the 1975 State of the Union address. Skip Brown, a colorful character who wears aviator glasses and reminds me of Crash Corrigan, was hired to do the camera work. He and his crew filmed the President that night on the second floor of the White House while he watched a taped rerun of his speech on television. They also took some informal footage of Mr. and Mrs. Ford together, then started to pack up. "Stay for a drink," said the President. To be around the President was a thrilling experience under any circumstances, and McGee, Brown, director of filming Danny Fitzgerald, and Don Penny, whose company was producing the film, were overwhelmed at the prospect.

McGee sat on a couch to the President's left. Near him was a phone affixed to a small table. It rang. It rang again. McGee waited for someone to answer it. On the third ring the President gave McGee a nod, suggesting he pick up the phone. It was the White House operator.

"The Speaker of the House would like to talk with the President," she told McGee. He cupped the phone with his hands, and whispered, "It's the Speaker of the House for you, Mr. President." The President took the receiver and talked for a couple of minutes, then handed it back to McGee, who hung it up.

Almost immediately it rang again. With a questioning glance at the President, McGee answered it.

"It's Secretary Kissinger for you, Mr. President," the awed McGee said. Again Ford talked and then handed the phone back to McGee, who hung it up. Again it rang.

"It's the Vice-President for you," McGee said, confidently handing the phone to the Chief Executive.

"Yes, Nelson. Yes, Nelson. Yes, Nelson. Thank you, Nelson. See you tomorrow, Nelson," said the President, and handed the receiver back to McGee. The President now put his hands behind his head, stretched his legs luxuriously out on the coffee table, and with a satisfied little smile said, "It's always good to hear from Number Two."

Our group left the President after that and we went to my place for what turned out to be a rather remarkable meeting. It was in my living room, surrounded by wicker furniture I'd brought back from Bangkok, that the "doo-doos" in the White House came into being. That was the name McGee came up with after our discussion, and although it had a humorous ring to it, the project was dead serious. "We all agree that the President is a wonderful guy," McGee said, "but there's a real problem brewing. The man is getting screwed."

"Who's doing it?" I asked.

"His advertising people at the President Ford Committee," McGee said, "and it's criminal."

"They don't have any overall plan," he went on. "They've got all these people, like Skip here, running around shooting film, spending money, and generally wasting time. There is no point of view and no creative director, and their advertising style reflects that. The reason they didn't want me to call you is because they were afraid of having the whistle blown on their ineptitude," said McGee, "but I can't let it go on any longer."

Penny, Fitzgerald and Brown all agreed that there was a major problem, and that the big loser was likely to be President Ford. "Let's try to do something about it," I said.

"What can a bunch of doo-doos like us accomplish?" McGee asked—and so the doo-doos were born.

This was the chance I'd been waiting for. A few weeks later, having studied for myself what was going wrong with the advertising, I was convinced there was a real problem. I couldn't go to the President with my limited knowledge of the ad business and explain to him what was happening, so I decided to consult with two of the biggest men in the profession. Don Penny, a diminutive fellow who has done everything from winning a Purple Heart and Bronze Star in Korea to winning applause as a stand-up comic in nightclubs, flew with me to New York and introduced me to Charlie Moss, then president of Wells, Rich and Green, and Jim Jordan, then president of BBD&O—they are among the largest companies in the advertising world.

I figured if anyone could tell me how to solve Ford's problem, these two could. I therefore outlined what the PFC's admen were doing, and showed examples of work they had done to each man in a separate meeting. They both agreed the President's ad campaign needed salvaging. One of the commercials was a five-minute film that did little more than reaffirm that Jerry Ford was indeed President. That little bit of information had used up half the advertising budget in the Michigan primary.

Convinced beyond a doubt that the ad setup at PFC was a disaster, I flew back to Washington that night and proceeded straight to the White House to meet with the President. He listened as I repeated what I'd been told by the professionals, adding that all he had to do was give the word and Jim Jordan would come down and talk to him. "Get him here tomorrow night," Ford told me.

Jordan showed up the following evening with his assistant Larry Light, and I took them up to the Yellow Oval Room in the President's residence. When the President arrived, I introduced them; they were soon joined by the former governor of Pennsylvania, William Scranton, Campaign Chairman Rogers Morton, Chief of Staff Dick Cheney, and Don Penny. Morton opened up the meeting by observing how good things looked in the Nebraska primary that day. "The sun is out," he noted, "and the Reagan people will be out in the fields working, which is good for us." (Little did we know then that Morton's picture would appear on the front page of every newspaper in the country the following day, sitting dejectedly in his office surrounded by empty booze bottles. The President had lost Nebraska.) Morton next proposed a fund-raising scheme in which representatives of the PFC would approach the big ad agencies, asking them to get their clients to contribute money. He went on until Jordan interrupted him. "We have advertising to do," he said crisply, "and not much time to do it in."

Jordan, a tall, thin, black-haired man with piercing eyes, sketched the situation: "The way you get people to do what you want is to solve their problems. You are doing that, Mr. President, and the record shows that unemployment is going down, inflation is being drastically cut, and Americans aren't fighting anywhere in the world. Unfortunately, your ads haven't been pointing that out."

"That makes sense to me," Ford responded. "In 1948, as a freshman congressman, I remember driving along the road listening to the radio. They were playing spots for Harry Truman and they hit the same kind of note. I like your idea." Indeed, the President was so pleased by the whole thing that he asked Jordan if he could come up with some examples by the next night. "I'm starting right now," Jordan said as he headed for the door.

Jordan wrote the commercials for radio on the air-shuttle to New York, and the next morning, Fred Collins, a prominent announcer, was hired to record them. That evening Larry Light was on his way to D.C. with the tapes. The big confrontation was to take place in the Map Room, where the President would not only hear Jordan's material but that of the PFC advertising committee as well. What happened that night came to be known among the doo-doos as the "Map Room Massacre."

When the President arrived late that night, the sides were formed. For the doo-doos were Mrs. Ford, Larry Light, Don Penny and, as it turned out, Vice-President Rockefeller, who arrived with Mr. Ford. On the other side, representing the PFC, were Peter Daly, the advertising chairman for the committee; Bruce

(Text continues on page 209)

THE WHITE HOUSE (Part II)

DIRCK HALSTEAD

"Mr. President, it looks like we've had it."

A tearful President Ford dedicates family mural in his hometown of Grand Rapids, Michigan; Election Day, 1976.

LEFT: *A grim Joe Garagiola watches election returns with the President.*
OPPOSITE: *President Ford at 3 A.M. on Election Night.*

BELOW: *The First Family gathers in the Oval Office as Ford prepares to concede election to Jimmy Carter.*

President Ford congratulates President-elect Carter during their first meeting after the election.

The Fords walk back to the White house after looking over office space set aside for former Presidents across the street at Jackson Place.

Wagner, his deputy; Rogers Morton; and their various aides.

Jordan's work was heard first. During the playing of the tapes Rocky kept leaning over to the President and saying they were terrific. "Keep it up, keep it up," I silently urged the Veep. Next it was the PFC's turn, and I had the feeling they knew there was trouble even before they showed their five-minute epic of the Presidency on a videotape machine. After their presentation the President stood up, thanked everybody, and went upstairs to bed. The next morning he fired the PFC admen.

Jordan's commercials were broadcast nationally that same evening. The doo-doos had scored an impressive victory, thanks to people like McGee and Penny. When the primaries ended, a political advertising firm, Bailey, Deardourff & Associates, took over all PFC advertising, and I quietly withdrew from any further involvement. It was now up to them; if mistakes were made at that late stage, it would be too late for change anyway.

Having finished his work for Ford with the primaries, Jerry McGee returned to his job in New York, but he was anxious to get back into political action. Don Penny, who was by now working full-time for the President as a speech consultant, gave McGee a call a few weeks later. "Catch the next shuttle down here," was the message.

"Okay. What's up?" McGee replied.

"Can't tell you, but it's big," Don assured him.

"I'll be there in two and a half hours," Jerry said.

When McGee arrived at the front gate of the White House the guards asked him to wait, assuring him that someone would come down to get him. Five minutes later Penny showed up accompanied by an extremely serious-looking young man in a dark suit. "Who's he?" McGee asked, but Penny simply made a hushing motion with his index finger to his lips. The unsmiling, athletic-looking man said not a word but motioned for them to follow him. McGee glanced apprehensively at Penny. "This is really it," he thought. They walked quickly past the guards and into the main mansion. Their passes would normally have been checked at every corner, but tonight they were waved through every checkpoint. They strode into the President's private elevator, and the clean-cut man with Penny and McGee punched the third floor button. "Jesus," McGee thought, "this meeting is so secret it's not even going to be in the Oval Office."

The door opened on the third floor, and the three hurried down the long corridor, stopping at last in front of a huge brown door.

"In there, please," the young man said. McGee straightened his jacket in preparation for the private audience he'd always dreamed of having with The Man. The huge brown door shut behind him.

"Hiya, big boy," came a soft, sexy voice from the other side of the room, where Susan Ford was reclining on a bed.

At that instant I jumped out from behind another door and took a picture of the stricken McGee. With that Penny and the "agent"—who was actually Mike Duval, a Ford campaign strategist—fell through another entrance, choking with laughter.

After all, McGee had always wanted to meet Susan. We'd obliged.

Covering the Campaign

THE PRESIDENT SQUEAKED BY REAGAN in the New Hampshire primary in February. We had campaigned throughout that sparsely populated State, and during those motorcades the more irreverent members of the staff would say, "Oh, look, there's another voter," every time we sped by a lone man standing by the road. "In this part of the country, that's considered a crowd," someone would invariably add.

After New Hampshire things seemed to be going great for Gerald Ford until North Carolina. That's where Reagan scored his first primary victory over the President, and from that day until the convention itself it was a real battle, one we fought on the ground and in the air in virtually every State. Campaigning is a grueling business, and after a while you begin to forget where you are and what day it is, a natural confusion that occasionally led the President to incorrectly identify the town he was in. This naturally caused guffaws from the crowd, but I doubt if there's a politician alive who hasn't made that mistake on the hustings.

Absurd things happen on the campaign trail, and it was Dick Cheney's job to keep things from getting out of hand. Cheney hated seeing pictures of the President in the kind of silly hats that people were always trying to give him. On one occasion, for instance, the advance staff reported that a certain guy in West Virginia insisted on presenting the President with a coonskin hat. They tried to dissuade him, but he was adamant. And because he was an important politician from the area, the advance men finally gave in. Terry did impose one condition, however; the hat had to be nailed to a board. That problem solved, we promptly ran into another. We stepped off the plane in one city to find two characters, dressed up as Mickey Mouse and Donald Duck, standing along the fence where the President was to greet some dignitaries. "You're finished if the President has his picture taken with those clowns," Cheney told O'Donnell. As he spoke the President headed toward the goofy characters, shaking hands with other people along the way. Terry swiftly interposed himself between the President and the mouse and the duck, and deftly directed Ford to another group of people.

Primaries are traditionally held on Tuesdays, which made that night either especially joyful, if we'd won, or singularly depressing, if we'd lost. The loss of Indiana, in Ford's native Midwest, was especially painful, and that evening it was Nessen and Cheney who came upstairs to the President's private study to inform him of the results. Ford was wearing a white shirt with the sleeves rolled up, and my shots of him receiving the bad news show utter dejection. He stood in the middle of the room with his hands in his pockets as they briefed him. Behind him was a smiling portrait of Mrs. Ford that I'd taken a few months earlier, a stark contrast to the expression on his face. "There's always next week," he sighed at last. The following week was Texas—where the President lost all 96 convention delegates.

Although I'd withdrawn from any further involvement with the advertising, another area really had me alarmed: the President's speeches, which were truly awful. (My opinion on this subject was no secret to anyone, especially Ford.) It wasn't his fault; his speech-writing department was providing him with dull, uninspired material. In all the time I'd known the President, even back in his days as Veep, he and I had engaged in good-natured kidding about his long, sometimes dull speeches. By June of 1976 most of the staff agreed that the President wasn't getting the best possible quality in that area, and that it was hurting him. He needed to completely overhaul his speechwriting department, which was headed by his longtime friend Robert Hartmann. Frustrated and dismayed, I decided to relay my feelings to the President in another memo so very personal that I typed it myself. Some excerpts:

THE WHITE HOUSE
WASHINGTON

June 10, 1976

PERSONAL & CONFIDENTIAL/EYES ONLY

Dear Mr. President,
We've been friends now for over three years, and I can't sit back and watch you go down the tube without saying something. I realize it's easy to be a Monday morning quarterback, to tear apart, to criticize. I just hope you take what I have to say the right way, and know that it comes to you unselfishly from my heart.

At the beginning of your campaign Bo Calloway was brought in to run the show. This was an effort to placate the right wing of the party. It didn't work. He decided Nelson Rockefeller had to go to please the South. That didn't work. . . . Another short-range solution to a long-term problem.

When the Democrats started their campaign, everything was

in disarray. Ten candidates were tearing each other apart, and it looked like the dogfight would swirl right into their convention. The Republicans, on the other hand, faced a mild challenge to the Presidency from Ronald Reagan, of all people. No big deal, everyone said. The challenger would be knocked off long before the convention, and besides, some White House sources said, "The challenge will be good for the party, although it's a shame the convention is going to be so boring."

What the hell happened? The incredible. The unbelievable. Almost overnight a Georgia peanut farmer had united the Democratic party. *Their* convention is going to be a bore, and the dogfight will be in Kansas City.

Now the President is in double jeopardy. A strong challenge from within that threatens to tear up the party, and a solid Democratic front to fight on top of that. The Democrats smell blood. For the first time in eight years they stand a good chance of winning back the Presidency.

Do you realize, Mr. President, that the two of us are among the very few people around this place with actual combat experience? I only bring that up because those of us who have had a few close calls in wartime have a more highly developed instinct for survival. We're in a war now, and my instinct says it's time for a few radical changes to counter Carter. If your old advisors are doing the right things, how come you're so precariously close to losing the nomination? And what's to say, assuming you do get nominated, they will have the right answers?

What I'm going to say next . . . epitomizes the root cause of many of your problems. . . . Your speeches are usually long, boring, and filled with rhetoric that turns people off. I've seen advancemen literally cry when after ten or fifteen minutes after you started speaking the people would start leaving. They worked long, hard hours building those crowds, and in fact begged the speech-writing department to come up with short, lively speeches for certain situations. No deal. A crime, and one you alone will pay the price for if it continues.

Your speech-writing department has driven mediocrity to new heights. If this were my opinion alone, I'd say perhaps I could be wrong. It's not. It's universal . . .

Jimmy Carter. How do you fight him? A man not from Washington. No handle. Nothing to grasp. You need an innovative new strategy. That man hasn't faced up to an issue yet. He's run on his personality, and on an anti-Washington platform. He's pictured as decent, honest, moral, etc. etc. The crucial difference between you and Carter is that he hasn't accomplished anything, and you have.

One answer is new blood. If your Vice-Presidential selection isn't a fresh man, someone of Howard Baker's caliber, it will be a mistake.

Mr. President, you need a bunch of new, hungry, energetic young people to fight Carter. Throw out the rule book; it's no good anymore. Scrap some of the old cronies. If you don't there is only one possible outcome: You will lose, and so will the American people.

With deepest respect,
David Kennerly

The memo was my best shot. And it missed. The President made no changes. Dull speeches, the pardon of Richard Nixon, and the choice of Dole as a running mate cost him the election.

We were deep into the 1976 campaign when the nation's two hundredth birthday rolled around. Never one for extravaganzas, I was less than overwhelmed by the Bicentennial. There were some bright moments, however. The gathering of the Tall Ships in New York harbor was impressive, and from Ford's vantage on board a Navy ship, one couldn't have had a better view.

My favorite part of the whole Bicentennial year was the arrival at the White House of Queen Elizabeth, who came to look over the territory her ancestors had lost two centuries before.

I have to hand it to the person who selected the music that was played that night—they either had a great sense of humor or a frontal lobotomy, for one of the songs was "The Lady is a Tramp." During the ensuing entertainment in the East Room, as guests sitting in gilded wooden chairs listened to the Captain and Tennille sing "Muskrat Love," there was a loud *snap!* An astonished look on Nancy Kissinger's face told the story: her husband had leaned back in his chair, causing it to splinter. A royal titter ran through the assembly, and the show went on.

The main event of the summer was the Republican convention in Kansas City. To win the nomination Ford had to beat back a strong challenge by Reagan.

And then he had to choose a running mate. Late on a Wednesday night the President held meetings with his people to discuss the selection. At approximately 2:00 A.M. on Thursday morning serious talk began about the selection. Gathered around a table in the President's suite were Senator John Tower of Texas, advisor Bryce Harlow, Jack Marsh, Stu Spencer, who was Ford's campaign manager, Senator Robert Griffin of Michigan, Dick Cheney, Mel Laird, and the President. Everyone was tired, but the talk continued. The President was wearing a white shirt that was partially unbuttoned, and his sleeves were rolled up. The others had their suit coats off.

The four names in final contention were those of William Ruckelshaus, Anne Armstrong, and Senators Howard Baker and Robert Dole. One name that wasn't in contention and should have been was that of George Bush. In December of 1975, Bush's name had been withdrawn from consideration as a possible running mate when he was confirmed—by a Democratically controlled Senate committee—as head of the CIA. This was a shrewd move on the Democrats' part, for it eliminated the handsome, articulate Texan from contention. Bush would have been a definite asset to the ticket.

The confab went on until almost 5:00 A.M. Assessments of each candidate were made by the men around the table, with Senator Tower making an especially eloquent pitch on behalf of Anne Armstrong. A little after five o'clock the President got up, stretched, and told the group to come back in four hours for another meeting, and to get some sleep in between. Apparently no decision had been reached; each of the advisors walked out of the room with a slightly different idea of whom the President favored. I went into the next room and told Terry O'Donnell and

Dick Keiser that I was almost certain Ford was going to choose Dole. Why Dole, Terry wondered. "Just the way he was talking about him," I said. "Nothing really concrete, but just the way he said it." The next morning the group met again. The President announced that he had decided on Dole.

Before coming to Kansas City the President had worked on his acceptance speech. He and Penny had gone over it several times, and had even videotaped it at the White House and then reviewed it for ways to make it better. Penny was crucial in improving the President's delivery, jumping up and down like a rabbit when the President muffed a line and making him do it again. Even I would have been afraid to talk to the Old Man like that, but it worked. The essential element Don provided was an ability to recognize the mistakes being made, and, more importantly, to show the President how he could correct them. At times I worried that Penny, who stood only as high as the Chief Executive's shoulder, would be hurled across the room by the former football star, but it never happened. The two got along beautifully.

The President also had a video unit in Kansas City, and he practiced until the day before he was to give his acceptance speech. As a result, when Reagan demonstrators delayed his speech the following night, he was furious. I was in Ford's hotel suite with Cheney and O'Donnell at the time. We watched on television as Chairman John Rhodes tried to bring the convention to order. The Reagan people were going crazy, and the scheduled time for Ford's speech came and went with no end to the demonstration in sight. The President was so angry that I was afraid to take a picture. He started to walk toward his bedroom, then wheeled around and yelled at Cheney. "Get that goddamn Rhodes on the phone, and tell him to do something," he said, and stormed into the bedroom.

Cheney tried to contact his people on the convention floor, but without luck. After a couple of hours things did settle down and they called for the President to come over to the hall. His speech was, by then, almost two hours late, and he missed the prime-time TV audience. To me, that was a crime, for the speech was one of the best Ford ever made.

Strategy for the general election dictated that President Ford avoid the campaign trail until the last two weeks before the election. Up to that time he left the White House only for the televised debates with Carter. Ford liked to campaign, however, and after being caged up for months he set out with a vengeance.

The first campaign stops were in areas that the polls showed as borderline, and places where an appearance could produce the most electoral votes. Every new city produced larger crowds, and the President got more and more carried away. At one point he was standing on top of his limousine, waving to the crowd, when the car started to pull away. The driver inside the car thought Ford was sitting down, and simply took off. One of the agents running alongside the car beat on the window and pointed up. "Stop very, very slowly," he said. The President never lost his balance, and he never stopped waving and talking.

Ford politicked from the back of a train through Michigan, and as the miles passed, so did his voice. He became hoarser with each day, but none of that slowed him up in the slightest. As the end drew near we were all enthusiastic about the chances of winning, and I, personally, was sure of victory. The two-week blitz ended with a huge motorcade in Ford's hometown of Grand Rapids. Thousands of cheering people lined the route as the procession drove through the city Ford had served as a congressman for so many years. With his arm around Mrs. Ford, the President tearfully thanked the people of Michigan. The next morning they voted, and then headed for the airport for the flight to Washington.

That night the President, his family, and a few friends gathered on the second floor of the White House to watch the returns on television. There weren't many joyful moments. Almost from the beginning it looked bad, and although the results were close, there was little hope of victory.

Being a professional photographer means shooting pictures with detachment, but sometimes it's hard. I managed to do it that night, recording the glum expressions on the faces of those around the room. Susan sat on the floor, unable to accept the results. Gayle Ford rested her chin on her husband Mike's shoulder as they watched the returns. Mrs. Ford tried to keep everyone cheered up, but with little success. Joe Garagiola, who had campaigned so hard for Ford, was one of the grimmest. He and the President sat on a couch in the living room, watching the election results on television.

About three o'clock in the morning the President, Senator Jacob Javits, pollster Bob Teeter, and Cheney went into the family dining room for a private conference. I followed. The President listened as Javits declared that it looked as if New York was going for Carter, and with New York went Ford's final hope that the election would turn around. Teeter mentioned something about Hawaii, but all agreed that Carter had won. (The major networks had already declared a Carter victory.) The President, who was so hoarse he could barely talk, stood up, thrust his hands into his pockets, and spoke briefly with the group of his friends in the living room. He then retired. Mrs. Ford stayed up to comfort Susan, who was taking it the hardest.

The next morning at 9:00 A.M. I went to the family quarters to see if the President was up. He was, sitting alone in his bathrobe and slippers in the dining room, reading the paper and watching a small television set. "I guess we've had it," I said glumly.

"Looks that way," he replied in a whisper, smiling at me.

"It was great while it lasted," I said.

"I wouldn't have traded a minute of it," he stated. I half-heartedly took a few photographs, then left. Later that morning Ford called a meeting of his campaign advisors for a postmortem discussion. He then placed a call to Carter and formally conceded the election. Everyone left the Oval Office except Cheney, Marsh, and me. When the call to Carter went through, the President could scarcely talk because his voice was shot. After a few words he told his opponent that Dick Cheney would read the concession statement. Dick had been sitting in a wing chair near the fireplace in the Oval Office, listening on an extension. He started to read the President's words. When he hung up, the President whispered, "That's that. Now let's go see the press."

Mrs. Ford and the children joined the President in the Oval Office. It was decided that the First Lady would read the statement of concession to the press, and as she walked around the Oval Office she went over the words. Susan and Gayle began to cry, and the President put his arms around Susan. Jack looked out the window in back of the desk and Steve stood nearby, dejectedly drinking coffee from a paper cup. Mr. Ford asked me to take a picture of the whole family standing behind his desk. A similar one had been taken the day he assumed the Presidency. This one wasn't as cheery, however, and as they lined up Mrs. Ford reached over and grabbed Jack by the chin, as if to say, "Keep a stiff upper lip."

In the press room the newsmen all stood around Mrs. Ford as she read the statement, and when she finished, the President circled the room, shaking hands with reporters. The President, Terry O'Donnell, and I then walked back to the Oval Office. Terry asked Ford if there was anything he wanted, whereupon the President came out from behind the large wooden desk and put his arm around Terry. "I've never really thanked you for the great job you've done for me over the last two years," he said. "If there's anything I can do for you after we leave here, just let me know." Terry removed his glasses and began wiping his eyes, and for the first time it really hit me. The scene was reminiscent of the day Ford became President, when he asked if my taking a job at the White House would hurt me professionally. Here was a man who had just lost the biggest prize in the world, and he was telling a subordinate that he would do anything he could to help. I turned and walked out of the Oval Office, tears streaming down my face.

On November 22, President-elect Jimmy Carter and Mrs. Carter made their first visit to the White House.

In the Oval Office the President sat in one of the great wing chairs; Carter, in the other. I went to the far side of the room and stood behind Ford's desk for a picture. As I did so, President Ford reached over and shook President-elect Carter's hand. "I never really formally congratulated you," he said. That picture—the desk looming in the front, and the immensity of the Oval Office dwarfing the two men—is what it's really all about.

On January 14, 1977, I wrote my formal letter of resignation:

> Dear Mr. President,
> Effective January 20, 1977, at twelve noon, I hearby resign my position at the White House.
> It's been real! David Hume Kennerly

The letter I got back from him is one of my most valued and memorable possessions. It reads:

> Dear Dave,
> Of all the letters coming to me during these closing days of my Administration, the ones that touch me most are those from members of the White House staff—and yours stood out among the rest!
>
> You say "it's been real," and from working so closely with you, I want to say it's not only been real, but it's been fun. In addition to being the world's best photographer, you have an uncanny ability to put people at ease, to bring out their best. Thanks largely to you and your determined effort to see people as what they are—people—the Ford White House will not go down in history as "stuffy." You photographed history being made, and you helped make it lively as it was happening. Your spirit will prevail in your photographs for years to come and I know that whenever we view them we'll remember the event, and we'll remember the spirit!
>
> You have been a special friend to all our family, and I hope our paths will cross often in the days ahead. Betty and I will be watching your career with enthusiasm and cheers. We send you our wishes for every success and happiness in the years ahead.
>
> Sincerely,
> Jerry Ford

On his last morning at the White House President Ford sat reflectively in his private study in the family quarters. The walls showed the marks where his pictures had hung, and packing paper was strewn across the floor. All that remained in the room was the chair, some memories and Ford himself.

From where he sat he had been informed that the evacuation of Vietnam was complete. And it was there he'd watched the victories and losses during the primaries. There he'd watched the networks report that Carter had snatched the Presidency from him. Perhaps more than all the others, it had been *his* room.

Those moments came flooding back to me as I watched him sitting there. "Well, we better get it over with," he said, standing up.

He and Mrs. Ford rode the family elevator one flight down to the state floor, then walked out onto the North Portico. When Jimmy Carter arrived they adjourned to the Blue Room for coffee. I took a picture of Carter, Ford, Rockefeller, Mondale and their wives. Then I approached Carter and said, "I guess you get the last laugh."

"What do you mean?" he said quizzically.

"A few months ago you visited the Fritcheys, who live across the street from me. John Graham, my next-door neighbor who was also one of their guests, asked me to get a picture of him with you. On your departure John introduced me to you as the present President's photographer. I added, 'And the next one's also.' Obviously, I was wrong. Congratulations," I said, shaking hands with him.

At high noon on January 20, 1977, as Jimmy Carter raised his hand to take the Oath of Office, my White House career ended and I started shooting for *Time* again. I handed my White House cameras over to one of my former employees and picked up my personal gear again. President Ford was no longer my boss, but he was still my assignment. I wish it was as easy to hand over a state of mind as it was those cameras. No one can make the change to private life quickly. The two and a half years I spent at the White House were now a part of me. I felt really terrible for

Mrs. Ford. Tears fell from her eyes as we circled for the last time over the Capitol dome in a helicopter. "That's when it really hit me," she said later. "We put twenty-five years into that place. Leaving it was what hurt the most."

I photographed Ford as he looked wistfully down at the Capitol, where he had spent most of his professional life. And when we flew over the White House I asked if we could make one more pass. "Sure, Dave," was his quiet response. There followed a brief farewell ceremony at the military base, and then the Fords boarded a 707. It was not Air Force One this time, but a back-up jet, the same one that had brought J.F.K.'s body back from Dallas. As Ford settled into the spacious quarters onboard, the day's events began to crowd in. There were no staffers with him: O'Donnell, Cavaney, Nessen, Cheney, Dr. Lukash, the military aide, the secretaries, the communications people—all of those who would normally take the trip with him—were gone. Only Bob Barrett, who quit the Army to be Ford's chief aide, a few newsmen, Liberty, the Secret Service agents forever assigned to the former President, and I were on the plane. The transition was complete.

On My Own

THE NEXT COUPLE OF MONTHS WERE TOUGH FOR ME. What I was going through was nothing more nor less than withdrawal; a withdrawal from power. No matter how much I tried to deny it, the White House years had had a powerful effect on me. For a time I expected the world to beat a path to my door. I sat at home for two or three weeks at a time, not picking up a camera. The phone didn't ring, and as far as I could tell, the path in front of my door was empty.

A phone call from *Time*'s John Durniak finally jarred me back to reality. He assigned me to cover a group of Minnesota businessmen who were being shepherded around Cuba by Kirby Jones, a former press aide to Senator George McGovern. Quite frankly, I needed the work, for the White House was threatening to become an obstacle to my future, just as Vietnam once had. There's an old saying in the newspaper business—"You're only as good as your last picture, and that one's wrapping tomorrow's fish." I was off and running again.

For five days I drove around Havana and the surrounding area taking pictures. What had been one of the wildest of Caribbean pleasure spots was now transformed into a quiet Communist society. If you closed your eyes for a minute, then opened them, it was easy to imagine yourself propelled back in time to 1959. The principal buildings were the same as when Fidel Castro took over, the citizenry was wearing clothes that were at best from the early sixties, and the cars were definitely late fifties vintage. The Cubans, however, are a lively, warm, and happy lot, and I didn't feel at all uncomfortable being in Havana.

The Cuban military involvement in Africa was a big story, and one that at the time was difficult to illustrate. I wanted to find troops in action, possibly preparing to leave for combat duty. I knew I hadn't lost my touch when I succeeded in sneaking a few shots of some troops training with artillery on a beach just outside Havana. As we passed in our bus I poked my lens unobtrusively between the curtains and took a picture of the military exercise. For a few hours I was worried that the authorities might find out and my film would be confiscated, but nobody said a word.

The most outstanding aspect of the Cuba trip was seeing Fidel Castro for the first time. He's a big, bearded, bear of a man who must stand at least six feet two. His very presence creates a furor. The group I was with was composed of politically as well as personally conservative businessmen, and they fell all over themselves trying to shake his hand. Fidel handled them with grace and fine humor, and there wasn't a man in the room who didn't talk about the encounter for hours after he left. I was equally impressed.

Time ran two color pages of my Cuban pictures and once again I felt I was back in the mainstream. Then an assignment to photograph Vice-President Walter Mondale took me back to the White House for a couple of days. The familiar halls were inhabited by aliens now, and I felt uneasy and uncomfortable. My old office, once so warm and inviting, was then occupied by Dr. Peter Bourne, Carter's one-time drug advisor. The round table and Kennedy rocking chair had been replaced with more standard bureaucratic trappings, among them an executive chair and a rectangular desk. The table lamps had been exchanged for overhead fluorescent lighting. The comfortable striped couch along the wall was gone. (One of Bourne's secretaries complained that she'd found a couple of dried-up fish behind a cabinet. I hoped one of them wasn't Zarkov.) So I took my photos and got out, finding, to my great satisfaction, that I didn't miss the place anymore and had no desire to go back. I was cured.

In July and August of 1977 I conducted my own version of a Kissinger shuttle. Egypt, Syria, Jordan, Lebanon, and Israel were on the itinerary, and my assignment was to photograph each country's head of state for *Time.* I flew first to Cairo, where I made contact with President Anwar el-Sadat's staff and arranged to photograph Sadat at his summer home in Alexandria. Getting there involved a four-hour drive from Egypt's capital, so I hired a car and driver. I specified to the rental agency that I wanted a dependable Mercedes and a chauffeur who spoke English. I did not want to break down in the middle of the desert. I was told that the driver would meet me in front of my hotel at 6:00 A.M., and sure enough, he was right on time. He didn't speak a word of English, and he was driving a 1960 Oldsmobile. It was too late to get another vehicle, so we set off.

It was late July, and it seemed that every Egyptian had gone to the seaside resort of Alexandria. I was staying at an old hotel with ceiling fans that turned slowly above several old waiters as they shuffled from one stained tablecloth to another in the dining room. A constant swarm of flies vied for each morsel on my plate, and I was constantly shooing them away. Outside was an esplanade that ran for miles alongside the water and teemed with hundreds of honking cars. Horsedrawn carts piled high with goods wove in and out of the traffic.

Amid this confusion stood President Sadat's quiet, orderly summer home in Mamoura, on the outskirts of Alexandria. The house itself was not opulent, but it was roomy, situated on several well-manicured acres and surrounded by tall bushes and many guards.

The day I arrived Sadat was in the midst of intensive negotiations with Colonel Muammar al-Qaddafi of Libya. The two were not meeting face to face but were using Palestine Liberation Organization's leader Yasir Arafat, as an intermediary. Arafat shuttled back and forth between Tripoli and Alexandria, trying to squelch the ill feelings that had arisen out of a border battle between the two countries a week before. Sadat granted me remarkable access. I was even permitted to sit outside the door while he met with Arafat. Had I been able to understand Arabic I'm sure the lively and sometimes loud exchanges would have been intriguing and possibly disturbing.

Sadat has many residences around Egypt, but his favorite is in his home village of Mit abu Kom, about seventy miles from Cairo. When meeting with residents of the village, he wears the long native dress for men called a gallabiya. As I photographed him, clad in a gallabiya and standing behind this modest home, he looked up at a passing jet and frowned. "These planes never used to come over here," he told me. "Now it gets very noisy." Remembering how Lyndon Johnson once prohibited all planes at National Airport from taking off during ceremonies on the south lawn of the White House, I said, "Well, Mr. President, you could change the air routes." He pursed his lips and, looking back at the disappearing jet, observed, "You know, you're right. Maybe I should do that."

To keep fit, Sadat walks several miles a day. I asked if I could photograph him doing his daily exercises. Those pictures show him in a white straw hat and shorts, striding along with his ever-present walking stick. It's a rare sight to see an Arab leader in short pants, but then Sadat, who moves easily between Western and Middle Eastern cultures, is a rare man. One of his favorite people is Henry Kissinger, and he spent most of one helicopter ride to his home in Ismailia talking about Kissinger. "What do you think of Secretary Vance?" I asked.

"Well," he said, "you can't really compare the two. Vance has a different style and approach. He isn't as witty or as personable." He paused. "But I *like* Vance," he said most emphatically, jabbing a finger at me.

I also took a picture of Sadat standing on the bank of the Suez Canal, watching the ships go by. Each passing vessel toots its horn as it passes Sadat's home, for the captain sees the flag flying above the residence, signifying he was there. "They know I'm here," he said, relishing the attention. Before the 1973 war the Israelis had occupied the very spot on which we stood, and Sadat counted it a tremendous personal accomplishment to have gotten the Canal back.

Hafez-al-Assad, the President of Syria, was not as cooperative as Sadat. Three of the most frustrating weeks I've ever spent were those I logged in Damascus trying to arrange an appointment with Syria's leader. I couldn't even leave the hotel because his press aide had repeatedly informed me that "we will call you as soon as we get word." There's no way of adequately explaining what waiting for a phone to ring can do to you. Every time I'd begin to think "This is ridiculous. I'm leaving this country," an optimistic voice would assure me "tomorrow."

"Bukhara" is the Arabic word for tomorrow, and there's a joke in the diplomatic corps about its definition. A Middle Eastern ambassador and a South American diplomat are discussing the relative merits of their two countries. The Spanish-speaking envoy says, "We have a word in our language which we use to politely put someone off for a day or two. It's 'mañana.'" The Arab statesman says, "In our tongue we also have such a word. It's 'bukhara'—but, it doesn't convey the same sense of urgency."

Assad's press aide did eventually make an appointment for me, but it was in conflict with a date I'd made to photograph President Sadat back in Egypt. Knowing I could count on Sadat, I flew back to Cairo.

Another leader on my list was King Hussein of Jordan. I'd met him at the White House on one of his state visits. He'd sought my advice on some camera gear, and we'd spent a few minutes discussing the relative merits of certain photographic equipment. I arrived in Amman during the celebration of Hussein's twenty-fifth year as monarch. The whole country was in a holiday mood when Yanal Hikmat, Hussein's protocol chief, put me in touch with his boss. For the next few days I photographed the Jordanian king as he attended festivities celebrating his anniversary, including one at which thousands of children in native costumes marched by his reviewing stand. The army was on maneuvers in the desert, and the king paid it a visit. He is, among other things, an excellent athlete, and I took pictures of him climbing over tanks and jumping from armored personnel carriers. His troops love him, and at times appeared to smother the king with their embraces.

King Hussein is also an expert marksman, and I joined him and his guest, the exiled King Constantine of Greece, at a pistol range for a little target practice, which I also photographed. After I'd taken a few pictures King Hussein walked over, offered me his pistol, and asked if I wanted to shoot. "Sure," I said, and gave it a try. All six of my shots went into the bull's-eye, and as the unbelieving monarchs walked over to inspect the holes, Constantine said, "Are you sure your name isn't Dirty Harry?" Hussein added with a smile, "Kennerly, if you could shoot pictures half as well as you do that gun, you'd have it made."

One of the most elusive of all photographic subjects in the world is PLO leader Yasir Arafat. I'd talked to him in Alexandria, where he was meeting with Sadat, and he had given me a tentative okay to come to his headquarters in Beirut to take pictures.

Arafat is a mysterious man. He always appears to have a three-day growth of beard, he wears a pistol in a holster strapped to his waist, and he is generally seen in a red and white headdress and dark glasses. More significantly, the Palestinian leader never sleeps twice in the same place for fear of being assassinated.

To get to Beirut, I decided to hire a car and driver and go by road from Damascus. The road in places is narrow, but it is the main route for truckers hauling produce back and forth between the two capitals. The frames of demolished automobiles and trucks littered both sides of the road the whole way. We were coming up a steep hill when dozens of round objects that looked like green cannonballs came bounding down the middle of the road at us.

"Look out!" I shouted at the driver, who was by that time swerving to avoid the mysterious spheres which were, I soon saw, watermelons. Hundreds of them had spilled from a truck that had overturned, and they were splattered all over the landscape. The thought of getting killed by a flying melon had never entered my head, and all I could think of was how the obituary would read. I made it to Beirut and began my attempts to find the PLO chief. Through *Time*'s bureau manager, Abu Said, I was able to get in touch with some of Arafat's staff, and they in turn promised to drive me to a location where I'd be met by someone who would drive me to another location. The only missing touch was a blindfold. After three or four of these exchanges I was at a loss to pinpoint which city I was in, much less the street.

What transpired over the next few days was right out of *Catch 22:*

"Your appointment with Yasir Arafat will be Thursday afternoon, and we'll pick you up," one of his spokesmen told me. At the appointed hour the PLO representatives did show up, and after going through the musical cars routine again we arrived at a dingy little building. I was led to a small waiting room.

"Is this the place?" I inquired.

"Indeed," they told me.

"When will I get to take my pictures of Arafat?" I asked.

"He's in Tripoli," they responded.

"What?" I said incredulously. "You told me my appointment was at three o'clock today."

"It is," they stated, "and here you are."

"But he's not even in this country," I exclaimed, not really believing the whole conversation.

"Yasir Arafat always keeps his appointments," I was told. I never did see the elusive PLO leader.

Arafat's arch foe, Prime Minister Menahem Begin of Israel, was the next person on my list, and he *was* in.

Getting to Israel is no easy matter. There is no direct air service from any Arab country to the Jewish state, which means that the only way to make the journey is to fly to a country like Cyprus or Greece and then catch a flight from there. I never objected to passing through Athens, however, and whenever I could I took time off for a seafood lunch at one of the fine restaurants in Piraeus. The accountants tended to scratch their heads over my expense accounts, which sometimes showed breakfast in Cairo, lunch in Athens, and dinner in Jerusalem.

The Israelis are conscious of the needs of the press, and as a result they are extremely cooperative. Before arriving in Israel I'd read Begin's book, *The Revolt,* and discovered that Begin's revolutionary commando unit, the Irgun, had blown up part of the King David Hotel in 1947. I was staying at the King David and when I met Begin for the first time I told him I'd slept better knowing he was now in power.

I was able to photograph the prime minister in his office, visiting settlements, and receiving guests at home. Throughout my visit I was impressed by the way he related to other people, especially small children. He definitely could have been anyone's grandfather, and some of the best pictures I took were those of him hugging his own grandchildren.

Sadat and Begin were my most cooperative subjects, and not surprisingly my best pictures were of them. Although I didn't know it at the time, those photos would prove to be the most important of the lot, and would receive dramatic play in *Time* when it was announced in November 1977 that Sadat would go to Israel.

I had been back in New York only two weeks when I found myself on a plane bound eastward again, this time on an assignment to Saudi Arabia for *Time*. As soon as my plane landed in Riyadh I understood perfectly why most wealthy Saudis were in Europe, for as far as the eye could see there was sand, and beyond that, more sand.

I had come not for the vistas, however, but to photograph the royal family, and my first introduction to them was a scene right out of the Arabian Nights. King Khalid was sitting in a huge, deeply carpeted room, and if it hadn't been for the phone by his side I would have sworn I'd stepped back in time a thousand years. Surrounding the king were perhaps two dozen men wearing the traditional robes and kaffias. Many of them were sitting on the floor in front of the king, each with a piece of paper in his hands. This is a custom called the "majis," a session at which the king grants requests from his subjects, requests ranging from gifts of money to land. Khalid accepted the petitioners one by one, and when one enthusiastic old man tried to kiss the king's feet and I tried to take a picture of the scene, the Saudis got angry and forced me to leave. I couldn't convince them that I'd actually missed the shot.

Driving around Saudi Arabia is as hazardous as in the other Arab countries. The only difference is that more expensive wrecks litter the roadside. A Saudi idea of a fun weekend is to drive your car at 100 mph into the desert, and if you make it alive, pitch a tent and have a picnic. One such tent that I passed had a beautiful new Mercedes parked in front of it, and servants were waiting on two Sheiks who were comfortably propped up under a date tree.

Moslem law, which forbids drinking, also has stiff penalties for theft. Each town has an area foreigners refer to as "chop square." It's there, after prayers each Friday, that thieves have their left hand hacked off. Worse crimes are punishable by beheading.

Americans in recent years have flooded to Saudi Arabia to pick off some of the petrodollars being spent on construction and other projects. Even disgraced former vice-presidents are getting in on the action. I walked into the Riyadh Intercontinental one afternoon and spotted Spiro Agnew chatting with a couple of Saudi businessmen. For the most part, Americans don't like living there in the Saudi capital, but they are making so much money it's hard to leave. The oil companies provide comfortable surroundings for their employees, and I photographed them playing golf in the sand alongside a pipeline in Dharan, and skindiving in the Red Sea. It was U.S. Ambassador John West who introduced me to the latter sport, and I was overwhelmed at the beauty of the fish drifting just underneath the surface.

A friend of the ambassador's suggested I try spearing the elusive fish, and I set off in hot pursuit. What I speared, however, was my own foot. It's not easy to do, but I sneezed, recoiled, and drove the sharp rod into my foot. The embarrassment was much worse than the wound, although, as I pointed out later, I was the only one who caught anything.

I'd been back from Riyadh for four days, thinking I wouldn't have to go to the Middle East for a long time, when Sadat announced his trip to Israel. *Time* asked me to cover the historic event. I called an old acquaintance, Hamed Fahmy, the son of Egypt's foreign minister, and asked if he could help me get a seat on Sadat's plane. The overseas telephone linkup between Washington and Cairo was none too good, but even so Fahmy sounded uneasy and was very vague about what he could do. Not a surprise, really; his father resigned the next day to protest Sadat's trip. As Hamed put it later, when I saw him in Cairo, "My trying to get you on the plane would have been about as easy as arranging a trip for Yasir Arafat to the Wailing Wall."

After I got to Cairo, I tried frantically to contact Sadat, even riding the eighty miles to Ismailia the morning he was to leave for Israel, hoping to get a note to him with my request. Sadat's place was totally sealed off by armed guards, and I left the note with one of them. When I returned to my hotel everyone was looking for me. Apparently Sadat *had* received the note, and although there wasn't any room on his plane he'd arranged for me to fly on the plane that was carrying the Egyptian press.

As we crossed into Israeli airspace, the reporters on board began to look out of the window and point excitedly at the lights of Tel Aviv. It was one sight they never expected to see in their lifetime. We arrived ahead of the 707 bearing President Sadat, and when we deplaned we encountered, lined up on a set of risers, more photographers and television cameras than I'd ever seen in my life. "This is going to be a rough one," I thought to myself. When the Egyptian President's jet taxied up and the ramp was rolled to the door, the aircraft was still so far away that I realized I wasn't going to get any decent pictures of that monumental first greeting extended an Arab Head of State on Israeli soil. But then neither would anyone else: there was such a crush at the foot of the ramp when Sadat descended to greet Begin that everyone was blocked out.

The date was November 26, 1977. Sadat was going to stay in Israel for two days and I had the funny feeling I was never going to get another picture of him. Everything was so tightly controlled that only select "pools" of photographers were going to be able to cover the events. Because I'd come with the Egyptians at the last minute, they didn't have any press accreditation for me; and due to the fact that I'd arrived in Jerusalem at the same time Sadat did, the Israelis didn't have any for me either. This meant I had to cover the biggest story of the last score of years, taking place under what the Israelis said was the "tightest security ever," with no piece of paper identifying me as press. To complicate things still further, I hadn't bothered to renew my Washington, D.C., press ID after leaving the White House. No matter. The closest I got to Sadat and Begin the following day was watching their motorcade move down the street.

On previous trips to Jerusalem I'd spent a lot of time in a pub called the Goliath Bar across the street from the King David Hotel. (They billed themselves as being "Just a stone's throw from the King David.") It was from one of their bar stools that I decided to watch history sweep by me, for the King David was where Sadat was staying.

Late the next afternoon, through the good offices of Alon Reininger, a fellow photographer and friend of the Begin family who was also shooting for *Time*, and Moshe Milner, the official Israeli photographer, I was able to secure a place on the pool covering the farewell dinner at the King David. Being in the bus with the pool would get me past the first barricade, and near the hotel, but without a press pass there would be no way to get through the main entrance. While sitting in the Goliath the day before I'd noticed that their paper coasters were the same yellow color as the official press pass, and just for the hell of it I stuck one in my pocket. And that's what I waved in the face of the guard at the door of the hotel. He let me by: Goliath had beaten David.

My photos of the dinner were some of the best of the trip, and having gotten into the hotel, I decided I wasn't going to leave. That's why I was standing in the lobby when Walter Cronkite came rushing by. He had an interview with the two leaders after the dinner and I'd found out about it. "Mind if I shoot a few snaps during your interview, Walter?" I asked. "Not at all," he said. "Come on." I followed him up the stairs to a room where the CBS camera was set up and once again I found myself watching Cronkite in action, which is always a memorable experience. During the course of their conversation Begin mentioned that he and Sadat were going to conduct further talks in the Egyptian President's suite, and after the interview I asked Sadat if I could come down and take a few shots of that meeting as well. "For sure," he replied.

Those photos weren't great, but they were the only exclusives of the whole trip, and taking them gave me the chance to ask Sadat a crucial question: "Could I fly back with you to Cairo?"

"Only if you promise to pay your own way, Kennerly," Sadat joshed.

Figuring that nobody would believe me if I went out of the room and told one of his staff, "Oh, by the way, President Sadat has invited me to fly with him to Cairo tomorrow," I tried something else.

Gesturing at one of Sadat's aides I asked, "Would you like Mamoud here to make the arrangements?" I put my arm around Mamoud.

"Yes. Make sure that he gets on the plane, Mamoud," the President ordered. I walked out of Sadat's suite still unconvinced that it could possibly work.

The next morning I arrived at the outer perimeter of the hotel, about a hundred yards from the building itself, at the prearranged time. The guards, who were supposed to be informed of my arrival, wouldn't let me in, so I asked them to deliver a message to Sadat's party. I even tried calling Mamoud from the Goliath. It was now about thirty minutes before Sadat was due to leave, and nobody had showed up for me. Twenty minutes before, and still nobody. I could see people starting to get into cars. At ten minutes to go I thought I'd had it. Five minutes before departure an out-of-breath Egyptian security guard came running up to ask why I wasn't in my car. "Ask Israeli security," I said. Without further ado he escorted me through the lines and to the car. Riding with me in the motorcade from Jerusalem to the airport to Tel Aviv was Sadat's interpreter. It was he who had provided the running English translation during Sadat's speech, capturing every inflection and pause perfectly, and I complimented him on a beautiful job.

When we arrived at the airport and leaped out of the cars, my lack of identification was again a problem. The cops wouldn't let me through, but Sadat's interpreter grabbed me, and, speaking rapidly to the confused guards, pulled me to the ramp of the plane.

On the ramp were more security guards, and they didn't have my name on the list. The interpreter spoke to them, turned to me, and waved me on board. When Sadat climbed the steps of his plane he turned and waved at the assembled crowd. Begin, who was at the foot of the ramp, saluted him. I stood right behind Sadat; with my camera held over my head for a better angle, I took a picture that showed him in the foreground and the Ben Gurion Airport sign behind. It also showed several hundred photographers lined up in the stands. Had they been selling David Kennerly voodoo dolls in the airport that day they would have gone like hotcakes.

Shortly after we took off from Tel Aviv, two Israeli Kfir jet fighters appeared off each wing to escort us out of Israeli airspace. I immediately ran into Sadat's cabin, which is very similar to that of the American President's on Air Force One, and tried to get a shot of him looking at the fighters. But every time I got ready to shoot, the Israeli aircraft dipped just below the wing tip. Sadat eventually tired of my saying, "Wait a minute, wait, wait . . . There! . . . Missed it. . . . One more minute. . . ." and he started to give me the what I now recognized as his "You better hurry" look. I finally got my shot, and although it wasn't the greatest picture it did capture the moment.

As Sadat's plane rolled to a stop in Cairo, an NBC correspondent on the ground described the historic moment: "Sadat's jet has just taxied up. The ground crew is rolling the ramp to the plane. The door is now being opened from the inside. We see movement. Yes, someone is in the door. It's, it's . . . it's David Kennerly?" The NBC newsman, who had once covered the White House, told me later he simply couldn't believe his eyes. "I thought we were back in Washington for a moment," he said.

Sadat was greeted by a million cheering people, and although the Egyptian president can turn out a big crowd anytime he likes, this particular reception moved him deeply. He wasn't sure the population was genuinely behind his "sacred mission," and the massive turnout proved his initiative had popular support.

Then it was back to the States, this time, I felt certain, for a long while. Wrong again. *Time* had secretly selected Sadat as its Man of the Year and asked me to return to Cairo to do the story. I was by now well-acquainted with TWA's flight to Rome, Athens, and Cairo. Normally, doing a Man of the Year photographic layout is no problem, for the subject is usually more than willing to cooperate. Sadat was perfectly willing to go along with the idea, but the first Israeli-Egyptian meeting was underway in Cairo at the same time and the place was swarming with press, all wanting interviews and pictures of Egypt's leader.

I wasn't interested in the day-to-day coverage. I wanted a biggie: Sadat at the Pyramids, alone. After two scouting trips to the site I found the perfect locations, one in front of the Pyramids, the other near the Sphinx.

Sadat liked my proposal, and said in his booming voice, "Why not?" He didn't say when. Some time later the Egyptian president informed me, "Tomorrow I will go to the Pyramids."

That evening I went with Sadat's security people to show them exactly where I wanted to do the two shots so there wouldn't be any foul-ups. Early the next morning I arrived at Sadat's small house overlooking the massive stone monuments. Dave Burnett was with me to lend a hand. To our dismay we encountered a crew from ABC television and correspondent Frank Reynolds. I said to Reynolds, "Look, I don't care what you do as long as you don't shoot the same picture of Sadat that I'm going to take. I've been arranging this setup for ten days and I don't want anyone to see it on TV before the magazine comes out." My problem was soon solved, not by Reynolds but by one of Sadat's security people, who asked Reynolds and his crew to leave. This made Reynolds angry, and UPI carried a story that afternoon to the effect that I had somehow evicted Reynolds and his crew from the scene. It said that ABC producer Arnold Collins had pleaded with me for a short interview with Sadat, but that I'd turned him down. Collins had not even been there, as a matter of fact, and the story was blown way out of proportion.

Sadat flew to my location by helicopter, passing over Mena House, where the joint Egyptian-Israeli talks were being held. Several hundred press people at Mena House thought he was going to make an appearance at the peace talks. When they heard him coming, little did they suspect that he was coming to have me take his picture. Sadat stepped from his chopper, and we took the first shot. It was on the very spot where he posed with President Nixon in 1974. Sadat stood in profile, the Pyramids in the background: a modern-day Pharaoh against a backdrop of his nation's heritage. It was smashing.

The next picture location was half a mile away, and Sadat climbed into a small car for the ride over. My careful plans started to disintegrate at this point. I was barely able to jump into the last car of the motorcade as Sadat and some hundred security men drove off. And despite my careful instructions to Sadat's men, the motorcade drove right past the location I'd chosen and stopped at the bottom of the hill in front of the Sphinx.

"You're not going to like this, Mr. President," I said when I ran up, "but the picture I want to take has to be farther up the hill." He shot me one of his looks, but he walked back to where I wanted to shoot. Parked exactly where I wanted him to stand was a car, and it took me several harried minutes to find the driver and have it moved. By this time a large crowd was gathering to see Sadat, and the situation was rapidly turning into a circus. A film crew from NBC showed up. (They had seen his helicopter over the conference center and dashed over.) Sadat, meanwhile, was saying to me, "Make haste, make haste." So after shooting a few frames I said "to hell with this" under my breath and thanked the president.

The crowd by now had turned into a cheering mob, and Sadat's security men were holding them back. He smiled, waved, got into his car, and drove off. As the car containing Egypt's leader receded into the distance, I noticed him wiping his brow. Burnett and I just looked at each other in silence.

Only one picture was missing from my layout: President and Mrs. Sadat together. Their schedules were never the same, and it was tough lining up the shooting. Finally, the day before the film had to be shipped to New York, Mrs. Sadat intervened on my behalf. By this time the president was really tired. "Don't you have enough?" he asked. "Oh, all right," he said with resignation, and the two of them looked out of a window toward the Nile. As I was taking the last couple of shots, Sadat, who was staring sternly ahead, said, "Kennerly, when this is over I think I shall have to throw you in jail." It was the perfect time to wrap up the story. I thanked both of them and left.

The next time I saw Sadat was almost a year later and it was from behind a fence. He was stepping off a helicopter at Camp David and greeting President Carter with outstretched arms. A few minutes later Prime Minister Begin arrived, and the three leaders began an unprecedented summit meeting at the presidential retreat in Maryland.

For two and a half years during the Ford Administration I'd had the run of Camp David. Now I was on the outside with little hope of getting in, since the press was barred from the conclave. Three weeks before the summit, I had written a letter to Gerald Rafshoon, President Carter's media man, and he had been genuinely enthusiastic about the idea of my shooting the inside story for *Time*. But Carter had personally vetoed the project, which meant that the only coverage of the actual meetings would come from official photographers, with prints being handed out by the White House. It was an frustrating situation for me, for I knew only too well what was going on behind the perimeter fence. On my many trips to Camp David with the Fords, I had stayed in the very cabin Sadat was using. In those days I had been the official photographer, and no meetings were closed to me. Now I was merely part of a press pool—and even *they* were excluded.

For the next two weeks I camped out at the Rambler Motel in Thurmont, Maryland, with the other newsmen who were not covering the summit conference. Every day I'd drive the mile to the Thurmont Legion Hall, where a press center had been set up. Every day I'd ask one of the junior staffers from the White House press office if there was any word on my request. And every day I'd be told no. Nobody got an exclusive out of Camp David, but the ceremony in the East Room with the three leaders at the end of their conference was impressive. The most memorable moment came when Begin hugged Sadat. That photo alone almost made the wait worthwhile.

The Shooter's Life

I WAS SENT TO NORTHERN IRELAND ON assignment for the *Time* in June of 1978, the tenth anniversary of the renewal of violence there. I hadn't been in Belfast three hours when the radio reported that two policemen had been ambushed near Besbrook, fifty miles south of Belfast. I headed in that direction.

When I arrived investigators were still looking for clues. A yellow chalk outline marked where a body had fallen, and a spot of blood at the scene indicated where Hugh McConnell, a young constable with the Royal Ulster Constabulary (RUC), had fallen. McConnell and another policeman had been ambushed by Provisional Irish Republican Army (IRA) gunmen as the policemen drove up a lonely road outside Besbrook. The killers had waited in a thicket for them, and as the police car drove by they opened up with automatic weapons. At least thirty rounds hit the automobile, which swerved into a fence. Officer McConnell was dragged from the bullet-riddled car by the IRA gunmen, who finished him off with a bullet through the head. His badly wounded companion was carried off by the ambushers, and it was later announced that the IRA had executed him. His body was never found.

I looked around the site of the ambush, noting that the IRA gunmen had apparently been in no hurry: the thicket in which they had hidden contained not only shell casings but empty sandwich wrappers. The dead officer was thirty-two years old and the father of two small children. He and his wife, Elizabeth Ann, had both grown up in Besbrook and had married in the local church. It was in the graveyard of that church, in the shadow of the police station where he had worked for four years, that Hugh McConnell was buried.

Only a combination of moving pictures and sound could have done complete justice to Hugh McConnell's funeral. The casket, draped with the Union Jack, was carried from McConnell's small home by an honor guard dressed in dark-green uniforms. His young widow stood by as the wooden box was carried toward the waiting hearse, and every few seconds she emitted an anguished cry. "No!" she would scream, "no!" A uniformed man and woman tried to comfort her, but she wept openly as the casket was put into the black vehicle.

A police band walked in front of the slow-moving hearse, playing a dirge. The procession wound its way down through the green countryside, past a herd of cows and into the small village of Besbrook. All the stores were closed and the inhabitants, most of whom knew the officer personally, lined the streets. There must have been two thousand people in the funeral procession at this point; it stretched for a quarter-mile behind the flower-draped hearse. Some of them were wiping tears from their eyes. Except for the slap of feet hitting the pavement and the low music, not a sound could be heard. Waiting at the entrance to the church were three ministers dressed in white. The widow, who had arrived before the hearse, was also standing in the courtyard. As the casket was brought in she reached toward it, sobbed, and then turned and went inside.

A few days later I returned to Besbrook to talk to Mrs. McConnell and to photograph her and her two children. "Did you think anything like this could ever happen?" I asked her.

"Hugh and I never discussed the possibility," she said softly, her voice trembling. "I thought for the first year he was on the force that the IRA might come into the house and take me prisoner, then kill Hugh when he came home. But after a couple of years I quit worrying. It could never happen in Besbrook."

Death and the British army were everywhere in Northern Ireland. The green-clad soldiers, carrying automatic rifles and wearing bulletproof bests, moved in squads about the countryside, and they were omnipresent in the bigger cities of Belfast and Londonderry. I accompanied four soldiers on patrol in Belfast while they stopped cars, checked for identification, and sometimes frisked the occupants for weapons. "This is where one of my mates had a close call last night," said Sergeant Johnny Pain, my escort. "They were riding patrol, just like we are now, and a sniper took a shot. The bullet tore right through his shirtsleeve but didn't touch him." As our jeep crawled slowly through the streets I had the same feeling I used to get on

(*Text continues on page 257*)

THE WORLD

DAVID BURNETT

"Kennerly, when this is over I think I shall have to throw you in jail."

Anwar el-Sadat

A gun-carrying British soldier is ignored by passers-by; Belfast, Northern Ireland, 197

ABOVE: *On the road to a Mid-East peace settlement, Henry Kissinger confers with Egyptian president Anwar el-Sadat and his delegation; Alexandria, Egypt, 1975.*

OVERLEAF: *Kissinger in this room in the King David Hotel overlooking the Old City of Jerusalem, 1975.*

Sadat photographed against the backdrop of the Great Pyramids of Giza, 1977.

Sadat at his home in Alexandria, Egypt, 1975.

President Sadat, President Carter, and Prime Minister Begin during ceremony at Camp David, Maryland, 1978.

OVERLEAF: *Bodies of Reverend Jim Jones's followers; Jonestown, Guyana, 1978.*

DECEMBER 4,

TIME

Cult of Death

deserted roads in Cambodia and Vietnam—a tightness in the shoulders and neck that comes when you feel certain that someone out there is looking down the barrel of a gun at you. As we drove down one narrow street several dogs gave chase to our jeep, barking wildly. "Those are Catholic dogs," a soldier remarked. "Do they bark at civilian cars as well?" I asked. "No, just us," he sighed. Some say it's the smell of fear that excites the dogs.

In order to present balanced coverage of what was happening in Northern Ireland, I endeavored to photograph the burial of three IRA men who had been killed by the British army as the men were trying to blow up a post office, an experience that proved as terrifying for me as any I'd ever had in combat. The Catholic services were being held in a part of Belfast where Protestants didn't venture. I hired a Catholic taxidriver to take me there, and when we pulled up at the church I asked if it would be all right for me to photograph the funeral. Nobody wanted to tell me anything, and some wouldn't talk to me at all.

A few minutes later a very tough-looking man in his late forties came over. "Step this way," he said in a manner that suggested that his offer was in fact an order. "This way" was a very dark and narrow alley. He asked for my identification, and I showed him my U.S. passport and my Washington, D.C., press card. He kept looking from the photos on the ID's to my face and back. I was ready to show him my driver's license, credit cards, and laundry tickets when he handed the papers back to me. "You'll have to go," he said. I attempted to convince him that I needed the pictures in order to fairly present both sides of the story, but he wasn't listening. Neither were the five men who had silently slipped in back of me. They just stood there, hands stuffed into the pockets of heavy coats, collars turned up, cigarettes dangling from their lips, eyes partially hidden by hats pulled tightly over their ears. I knew it was indeed time to go.

After returning to my car I asked the driver to take me to the nearby Sinn Fein headquarters. The Sinn Fein is the only public organization connected with the IRA, and through them I hoped to get a press card to cover the funeral. I was still a bit shaken by the experience in the alley, so the driver tried to cheer me up. "Don't worry, lad," he said with a twinkle in his eye, "they surely would have given you a fair trial before they killed you." We arrived at a run-down building with a green front, which was the Sinn Fein headquarters, and I entered and walked up some creaky steps. It was so dim I could hardly see. In a small room I found a slight, red-headed man, showed him my ID's, and told him why I needed to photograph the funeral. After lengthy questioning he decided that I was legitimate and issued me a press card. It read: "Press Card—Belfast Republican Press Centre. BRITS OUT."

We made it back to the church just as the three coffins—draped not with the Union Jack but with the orange, green, and white flag of the Irish Republic—were being carried up the street. "Don't take any pictures of faces," I was told by a swarthy-looking man. Marching alongside the coffins were several young men wearing black jackets, black berets, and dark glasses, for this was a "military" funeral for IRA soldiers. Unlike the big police band that played at Constable McConnell's funeral, only two women, clad in black and playing bagpipes, marched ahead of the dead Provos.

Just before the column reached the graveyard, all three coffins were set down on the street. Four of the black-bereted men raised .38-caliber pistols and fired three volleys. I had been warned I couldn't photograph the salute—"Something might happen to your cameras . . . or worse." I decided not to try.

No one is spared the violence in Northern Ireland, and Protestants and Catholics suffer alike. In Belfast I talked to a Protestant named Joan Orr. She sat in the small living room of her home and told me about her two boys, who had walked out one evening to visit friends in the Catholic section. (One of them had a Catholic girlfriend.) At some point along the route they were picked up, taken outside of town, and beaten to death.

Joan Orr's boys left their house for the last time at 8:20 P.M. on July 4, 1972. Not long after that Mr. Orr died of cancer. Looking at me with sad, brown eyes, Joan Orr said, "At eight-twenty in the evening this July fourth I'll walk that route, hoping and praying to find a clue as to who did it or why. I'll do that every year for as long as I live."

On Springfield Road, not too far from Mrs. Orr's house, lives the family of Anthony Meli. Their home is on the Catholic side of the street. Across the way is the Protestant section, and there is very little, if any, interaction between the two sides. Mr. Meli owns a fish and chips place a few blocks from his home, and while Meli's thirteen-year-old son, Tony, was visiting the shop one day he picked up a small transistor radio he found there and turned it on. It exploded, blowing off one of his arms and blinding him in one eye. Tony now has a hook instead of an arm.

"Why don't you leave?" I asked the Melis. "Where would we go?" Mr. Meli responded. "My business is here, and so are my friends." His wife, Rose, added, "The street still feels like home." I asked Tony's brothers and sisters if they knew any Protestant kids. They didn't, but it turned out that Tony did. "I do," said Tony shyly, half hiding his hook behind his mother as he spoke. "Where did you meet them?" I asked. "In the rehabilitation center," he replied.

Later I took pictures of Tony and his brothers and sisters outside their home. From the other side of the street a group of Protestant children yelled for me to take their picture as well. After a few minutes some of them tentatively crossed Springfield Road and approached us. Few of them were more than eight or nine. "Take my picture with them," Tony insisted. Mr. Meli took in the scene and shook his head and said in amazement, "That's the first time those kids have ever come over to this side."

My best assignments have tended to come toward the end of the calendar year—the Sadat cover for *Time* in 1977, for example—and 1978 was no different. Arnold Drapkin, the new picture editor of *Time*, called in late November to ask if I'd be interested in doing a major story on the vast increase in dope smuggling between Colombia and the United States. "Great!" I told him. Two days later I was in Miami, in the company of Don Neff, *Time*'s New York bureau chief, photographing a group of Colombian sailors who'd been arrested at sea by U.S. narcotics agents who'd confiscated their cargo—twenty tons of marijuana. The seamen were at present chained to the deck of a U.S. Coast Guard cutter. With photographs of the incarcerated sailors and the tons of contraband, I was off to a good start.

We planned to depart for Bogotá on Sunday, November 19, so I intended to spend that Sunday morning having a leisurely breakfast, a swim in the pool, and a relaxed perusal of the newspaper. The *Miami Herald*'s headline changed all of that. CONGRESSMAN SHOT IN GUYANA, it screamed in bold black letters. I made straight for the pool, located Don, and told him what little I then knew about Guyana. "I'll check what New York is doing about the story," he said. "Why don't you go call the airlines." A few minutes later Don returned to announce that *Time*/New York had not yet dispatched a correspondent, and only one photographer, Matthew Nathons, was trying to get there from Costa Rica. "Take off," he said.

There were no commercial flights to Guyana until the following day, so we hired a Lear jet. At this stage we knew only that a U.S. congressman and several newsmen had been shot. One of them, Don Harris of NBC, had covered President Ford's campaign with me.

We arrived in Georgetown, the capital of Guyana, late Sunday night. We had no notion of what to expect, but then I don't think anyone was prepared for the news that poured forth from a remote jungle clearing in the wilds of the little-known South American country over the next week. Washington *Post* photographer Frank Johnston, an old friend of mine, had already arrived in Georgetown and was sound asleep in his hotel room when we arrived. I beat on his door. When a bleary-eyed Johnston opened it, I told him I just happened to be in the neighborhood and thought I'd drop by. Once he had recovered from the initial shock of seeing a familiar face in such an unfamiliar place, Johnston filled me in on what had happened.

A *Post* reporter named Charles Krause had been at Port Kaituma, an airstrip that was the site of the assassination. Krause had gone there with California Congressman Ryan to investigate reports that followers of the Reverend Jim Jones, most of them Californians and several constituents of Ryan's, were being held in nearby Jonestown against their will.

The shooting occurred after Ryan, several of Jones's disenchanted followers, and the newsmen were boarding the two light planes that had brought them to Port Kaituma for the visit to Jones's settlement. Aboard the single-engine Cessna, Larry Layton, who was one of Jones's closest followers and who was posing as a defector, pulled a gun and started shooting. He managed to wound a female aide of Ryan's before the gun was wrestled from him. At the same time a tractor pulling a trailer filled with armed men rolled onto the dirt airstrip, and they opened up on Ryan's unarmed group as they prepared to board the twin-engined Otter. In the ensuing fusillade, Ryan, photographer Greg Robinson of the *San Francisco Examiner,* Don Harris, NBC cameraman Bob Brown, and Jonestown defector Patty Parks were cut down. Eight others, including Krause, were wounded before the murderers withdrew into the jungle.

This was the story Frank Johnston told me in his hotel room that Sunday night. What neither he nor anyone else knew at this time was that Jones, having ordered the slaughter of Ryan's party, would set an even more bizarre plot in motion—one that would culminate in the apparent mass suicide of more than nine hundred of his followers. Jones, we later learned, assembled the members of his cult around an open pavilion in the center of the Jonesville compound and there ordered them to commit "revolutionary suicide" by drinking a vicious purple brew laced with cyanide. The children, some 280 in all, were the first to go—the lethal liquid was squirted directly into their mouths with syringes. Others may not have gone quite so willingly: a tape machine that was left on during the initial phases of the grisly event records screams of protest. Those who defied the crazed leader were subdued and apparently poisoned against their will.

The next morning, Monday, November 20, the Guyanese government held a press conference at which it was reported that there had been a large number of suicides at Jonestown—possibly as many as four hundred. The authorities didn't have full details. Communications between Georgetown and Jones's camp, some hundred and fifty miles away, seemed negligible, possibly even nonexistent. It was nevertheless clear by then that something awful had happened. At the press conference, it was decided that due to the lack of adequate transportation in Guyana, only a small pool of press people could go to Jonestown. Frank Johnston and Charles Krause were selected. Neff and I were not, but we were determined to get in on our own. To complicate matters, a national emergency had been declared and no unauthorized aircraft were being permitted to fly over the Jonestown area. CBS, NBC, and ABC all had chartered planes standing by, but these aircraft had been chartered outside the country; the government had specifically forbidden non-Guyanese pilots to fly into Port Kaituma. Neff and I began a frantic search for an aircraft that met the government's requirements . . . and found the only one in the country that did—the small Cessna that had been involved in the shooting. There were two bullet holes in its side and dried blood all over the inside, but it could fly. The pilot, the same one who had been present at the shooting, was Guyanese. The owners of the plane said we could lease it if the government gave us permission to land at Port Kaituma.

The next step was to camp out in the information minister's office, trying to get her to call the director of civil aviation for official permission. Neff and I spent most of Monday imploring her, and late in the day she relented and called the aviation chief. All we now needed was a letter of permission addressed by the information minister to the director, the only man who could give permission for an airplane to take off and, we understood, a real stickler for protocol.

To our dismay the information minister departed without writing the needed letter. We thought we'd missed our chance. But during the course of the day we'd become rather friendly with an extremely efficient secretary who worked for the information minister. Neff, in desperation, asked her to write a letter of authorization for us. Knowing that we had verbal permission from her boss, she agreed to do it—the letter she produced satisfied the aviation director.

At daybreak on Tuesday, November 22, we were winging our way to Port Kaituma. We had invited an NBC crew to join us. They had been unable to get in on their own and Don and I felt that because their people had been shot up, they deserved a chance to cover the story.

Nothing I'd seen in my entire life, including wars, plane crashes, and natural disasters prepared me for the horror that was Jonestown. As our plane dipped low over the jungle clearing we could see scores of small, tin-roofed buildings grouped around a much larger structure.

Encircling the pavilion at some distance were scattered pieces of what appeared to be brightly colored cloth. As we closed in the cloth became dolls, strewn casually about. Closer in, the dolls appeared for what they really were—bodies, hundreds and hundreds of them. We circled twice, taking pictures, then headed back to Port Kaituma to land.

The twin-engine Otter was still on the airstrip, one of its tires shot flat. While we waited for a Guyanese army chopper to take us the six miles to Jonestown, Matthew Nathons and I explored the scene of the assassination. The bodies of the congressional group had been removed two days before, but brain matter of our fallen colleagues remained on the airfield. Nathons, a medical doctor from San Francisco who takes pictures in his spare time, helped me bury the remains by digging holes with a metal plate we found. "Do you think we should say something?" Nathons asked as we finished the job. "I think it's all been said already," I replied.

The government helicopter finally arrived, and we boarded for the flight to the death site. What we witnessed from the air prepared us in part for what we encountered when we entered Jonestown to cover the story close up.

We fashioned face masks from a towel I'd brought from our Georgetown hotel, then dashed cologne on it for good measure. The bodies we'd seen from the air had been out in the tropical sun for two and a half days, and the stench would be overpowering. "I think I'm going to get sick," a television cameraman remarked. "If you think that before we get there, you've got a real problem," I told him.

Again we circled the area, then landed a few hundred yards from the main group of bodies. I walked apprehensively down the path towards the large building, took a deep breath, and prayed I'd be able to go through with taking the pictures. The only other time I'd ever felt remotely that upset was in Dacca—and this was a hundred times more disturbing.

I came upon the first body, a man hunched on his knees, his face in the ground. He was all alone behind a small structure. The main group was on the other side. Had it been a scene of obvious violence it might not have seemed so surreal, but it was so tranquil. It looked as if most of them had simply lain down and gone to sleep. Most of them appeared to be family groups, face down with their arms around each other. The little feet of children stuck out from beneath those of adults.

I moved about mechanically, taking the pictures. While stepping over a dead dog, I noticed a big brown vat. Inside was the purple death potion that Jones's followers had consumed. I photographed that scene, container in the foreground and bodies strewn behind it—and *Time* chose that picture for its cover.

Dozens of crossbows were stacked nearby. We speculated that there must have been guards standing by, ready to shoot those who refused to participate in the ghastly rites. The field around the meeting place was covered with bodies. At the time we were told there were four hundred; later we learned the total was more than nine hundred. I didn't stop to count. Inside the pavilion were rows of pews. At the front was a chair, set up like a throne, from which Jim Jones had ruled Jonestown. It was surrounded by bodies. Jones himself lay just outside, a bullet hole in his head. His abdomen had been slit open and then crudely stitched closed by the doctor who performed the government-ordered autopsy on the cult leader.

As I walked among the dead under the big tin roof, I started getting the eerie feeling that one of those lifeless people was going to grasp me around the ankle—and I high-tailed it outside to join my colleague. Nathons, for all his medical training, declared he could take no more, and neither could I. We headed back to the chopper.

Neff and I shipped my film to New York on a chartered NBC jet. We departed the next day for Barbados, where Neff could use the better communications facilities to file his story—and we could put some distance between us and the horror of Guyana.

The wars I have covered, for all their violence and gore, have never given me nightmares. Somewhere in my subconscious is a safety-valve that spares me that. Not so with Jonestown. A week after my departure I woke up in the middle of the night in a cold sweat. I'd dreamed that I had walked into a room and encountered the bloated—but living—body of Jim Jones, seated on this throne. I turned to escape but found my path blocked by one of Jones's followers, flesh dripping from his bones. I twisted into wakefulness just as a rotting hand reached for my throat.

After Jonestown, everything seemed anticlimatic, but Neff and I still had an assignment to complete in Colombia. So we headed south again, this time to Caracas. Because we were unable to obtain reservations on an airliner from Caracas to Bogotá, we hired a small twin-engine plane to fly us over the mountains to the Colombian capital. We ran into a severe storm—a downdraft that dropped us almost 1,500 feet in a matter of seconds. The jolt was so severe it ripped one of the seats right out of the floorboards. Everything flew through the air, including the contents of our pockets. When we landed in Bogotá, the badly shaken pilot studied the plane and said, "It wouldn't have taken another drop like that."

After such a ride—and after Guyana—Neff and I wanted to be especially careful. We had heard that Bogotá was the rip-off center of the world, that hoodlums on the street would just as soon murder you for your valuables as pick your pockets. This proved to be no slander: on our second day in the big city someone tried to steal my watch, while it was on my wrist, as we drove through downtown Bogotá. Neff and I were sitting in the back seat of a car; my arm was resting on the door frame. Suddenly someone grabbed my hand, and I instinctively reached across with my other. A man was holding my watch in both his hands and trying to jerk it off my wrist. Neff, acting the karate master, kicked the guy in the chest with his foot and drove him off. "Welcome to Colombia," our smiling driver said.

After a few days in Bogotá, during which we secured permission to go out into the field with the army to photograph its war on drugs, Don and I flew to the northern port city of Barranquilla. With us was Tim Ross, an Englishman who speaks Spanish fluently and is *Time*'s stringer in Colombia and Ecuador.

Barranquilla is a center of the smuggling operations and also one of the dreariest and most depressing places I've ever visited. In his book *Snowblind* author Robert Sabbag describes it well: "The second largest city in Colombia, it's a combination port city and industrial sewer. Barranquilla displays all the drawbacks of South American coastal life and none of its advantages. An embarrassment to most Colombians, it is a city choked and teeming with disease—a south-of-the-border Dickensian cesspool, decidedly urban, but in no way cosmopolitan. . . . Americans never hear about it until they get there."

We were only using Barranquilla as a base of operations, but even so our hotel lived up to Sabbag's description: the first night we had no lights; the second, no water. We didn't stick around to see what would happen on the third.

Our mission was to photograph fields of marijuana; one didn't have to go far to find them. There are many acres under cultivation in Guajira Province alone, mainly around the Sierra Nevada mountains. The Guajira is a region that civilization has overlooked—or perhaps one where civilizing influences have never been welcomed. It is also the site of a vast, and vastly lucrative, smuggling operation. As a consequence the region is largely inhabited by what can generally be classified as very dangerous people. Because its inhabitants have no desire to communicate with their countrymen to the south—their customers are foreigners who land and take off from remote jungle airstrips, coming with cash and departing with marijuana by the ton—the Guajira peninsula remains almost inaccessible by land. To cover the story we would have to fly in.

As we droned through the mountain passes, looking for the illegal fields of weed, my thoughts drifted back over my career, and I found myself thinking again how lucky I am. From the age of fifteen I've known what I wanted to do—and I have turned out to be good at it. There's no question in my mind that everyone has a talent for something, but sometimes it's tough to figure out what it is. Fortunately I found out early what it was, and have been able to pursue that talent ever since. There's nothing on this earth I'd rather do than take pictures, but there are drawbacks to the shooter's life. Its immediacy is what makes it so endlessly fascinating, but it is also what makes it frequently frustrating. You go directly to the very heart of history, record the moment, and move on. And in so doing you seldom see a story, a war, a life played to its conclusion. You tail an American Vice-President daily for weeks on end, then he resigns under threat of indictment and you never take his picture again. You dog the heels of his successor—even moving with him into the council rooms and private quarters of the White House, and then he is turned out of office and you are cut loose.

What you end up with are episodes of intense involvement, but little in the way of sustained interaction. You see a few stories through to their conclusion, but you never know how the people involved have fared. What has become of Tony Meli, for instance? And where is the little girl I photographed in the corridor of a refugee center as the Khmer Rouge advanced on Phnom Penh?

The curse of the shooter is that he is always an observer, never a participant. And the longer I am in this business the more strongly I feel the need to see one or two stories through to the end. To find Tony Meli and see how he's faring. To track down that Cambodian waif, wherever she is, and somehow participate in, rather than merely record, her future. . . .

My reverie was shattered by the sound of gunfire from the ground. "Hey, those smugglers are shooting at us," yelled the pilot, putting the plane into a sharp turn. "Time to go back to work," I thought, raising a camera to my eye.

AUTHOR'S NOTE

My thanks to my mother, Joanne Hume Kennerly, who has devoted much of her life to giving me love and attention; to my father, O. A. ("Tunney") Kennerly, who instilled in me a sense of what is right in this crazy world—and to both of them for encouraging my independence; to the Fords, my second family; to Verna Carothers Bennett, my old friend and first grade teacher who, along with my mother, taught me the importance of the English language; to Darrell Greenlee, my high school photography instructor, and Wally Pond, my journalism teacher, who together propelled me in the right direction for my career; to David Falconer, the *Oregonian* photographer I looked up to and tried to emulate; to Bill Blizzard of the *Lake Oswego Review*, who gave me my first job; to Robert Pledge, who helped select the pictures for this book; to Ivan ("Ciccio") Dallatana, who made most of the prints; to Peter Ross Range, who provided some excellent editorial guidance; to Edwin Bayrd, the editor, who smoothed out the rough spots; to Mary Ann Joulwan for this book's design; to Sandra Eisert, the picture editor's picture editor; to Felix Shagin, who greatly encouraged my writing; and especially to Grazyna Bergman, whose assistance and advice over innumerable hours made this first literary effort come together.

Also a debt of gratitude to my late uncle, Byron ("Jack") Kennerly, whose exploits as a pilot with the Eagle Squadron during World War II inspired my deep-rooted sense of adventure and whose spiritual guidance I always treasured.

Finally, and most particularly, a special thank-you to Paula Ahalt, whose understanding of people—one specifically—made it possible for me to complete this venture. For her there aren't enough ways for me to express my gratitude.

David Hume Kennerly

New York City
March, 1979

Index

Humphrey
press
JULY 27-29-1968
DAVID KENNERLY
UPI
VICE PRESIDENT OF THE UNITED STATES
PRESS PASS
KENNERLY
President
Visit to
Japan, Korea,
United States Senate
Swearing-in Ceremony
FOR THE
Vice President of the United States
Thursday, December 19, 1974
Sergeant at Arms
U.S. Senate
ADMIT BEARER
SENATE GALLERY
THẺ BÁO CHÍ
PRESS CARD
168
BC
DAVID K
CO QUAN
Phủ Tổng
大卫·凯纳利
姓 名: David H.Kennerly
国 籍: 美国
性 别: 男 年 龄: 25
住 址:
代表机构:
电报挂号: Uniphoto
HONGKONG
登记日期: 1972年9月24日
有效期限: 自1972年9月24日起
至1972年9月30日止
使 用
此证只限本人使用;
让; 不得作为旅行护照
他证明之用; 如有遗
立即告外交部新闻
PRESS
PUEBLO
COMMAND
INFORMATION
BUREAU
PASS NO.
UNITED S
PORTLAND, OR
DAVID KENNERLY
STAFF PHOTOGRAPHER
DAVID KENNERLY
TIME
888 SIXTEENTH STREET, N.W.
WASHINGTON, D. C. 20006
293-4300
Fire Lines
DAVID HUME KENNERLY
NAME
UNITED PRESS INT'L.
EMPLOYER
SEX Male
AGE 22
DAVID HUME KENNERLY
U.P.I.
NAME
This is to Certify that the above-named person whose photograph appears hereon, is a duly accredited representative of the press.
SHERIFF
UNITED NATIONS
1 MAY 1970
(Expiration date)
#2818
Mr. KENNERLY, David Hume
of UNITED PRESS INTERNATIONAL
is accredited to the United Nations
at Headquarters, New York
FILM-PHOTO
1969
ASSISTANT SECRETARY-GENERAL
MAR.
8
8:30 P.M.
1971
RINGSIDE WORKING PRESS
PRESIDENTIAL T
DEPARTED